Taming the System

Taming
the System

The Control of Discretion
in Criminal Justice
1950–1990

SAMUEL WALKER

New York   Oxford
OXFORD UNIVERSITY PRESS
1993

Oxford University Press

Oxford   New York   Toronto
Delhi   Bombay   Calcutta   Madras   Karachi
Kuala Lumpur   Singapore   Hong Kong   Tokyo
Nairobi   Dar es Salaam   Cape Town
Melbourne   Auckland   Madrid

and associated companies in
Berlin   Ibadan

Library of Congress Cataloging-in-Publication Data
Walker, Samuel, 1942–
Taming the system : the control of discretion in criminal justice,
1950–1990 / Samuel Walker.
p. cm.   Includes bibliographical references and index.
ISBN 0-19-507820-9
1. Criminal justice, Administration of—United States—Decision making.
2. Judicial discretion—United States.
3. Police discretion—United States.
I. Title.   KF9223.W254   1993
345.73'05—dc20   [347.3055]
92-20014

1 3 5 7 9   8 6 4 2

Printed in the United States of America
on acid-free paper

PREFACE

The administration of criminal justice in the United States consists of a series of discretionary decisions by officials. This point is now a truism among experts on criminal justice. Much of the research, public policy debates, and reform over the past thirty years has been devoted to attempts to control that discretion. This book is a history of that effort.

The primary purpose of this book is to analyze the origins, nature, and impact of various efforts to control discretion. Four particular decision points are selected for detailed examination: police discretion, bail setting, plea bargaining, and sentencing. Many other decision points in the criminal justice system are not examined. These four decision points were selected to illustrate general phenomena related to the control of discretion.

This book is designed as an "interim report." A little more than twenty years ago, Kenneth Culp Davis wrote the first comprehensive discussion of discretion in criminal justice, subtitling it *A Preliminary Inquiry*. This book is a follow-up to that book. Much has happened since the publication of Davis's book. He wrote at the early stages of what can now be seen as a national movement. Many reforms have been proposed, and many have been implemented. This book is an interim report on "what works."

Much has been written on the individual subjects examined here. There are large bodies of literature on police discretion, bail, plea bargaining, and sentencing. Yet there has been no comprehensive assessment of the discretion control effort—either within those four areas or for the administration of criminal justice as a whole.

Much of the literature cited here falls within the category of "evaluation research," evaluating the impact of a particular reform or change.

The field of evaluation research is notoriously short-ranged in its focus. A three-year follow-up is considered standard. This book takes a much longer historical view. First, it views the discretion control movement as a unified phenomenon, now thirty years old. Second, it argues that the effort to control discretion is the dominant theme in criminal justice history over that period. Third, it raises questions (and suggests some answers) about the long-term effect of various changes. These are the kinds of changes that are generally not covered in evaluation research and may not even be amenable to that style of research.

This book concludes on a cautiously optimistic note. The record indicates that there has been some success in controlling discretion in the criminal justice system. Moreover, the controls that have worked have reduced disparities based on race or social class. Given the widespread belief that "nothing works," that well-intentioned reforms of the criminal justice system always fail, this is a somewhat surprising conclusion. But some things do work. Discretion can be controlled. While the criminal justice system has not been completely tamed, some important progress has been made. This is a significant achievement and is worthy of close examination.

Omaha   S.W.
July 1992

ACKNOWLEDGMENTS

The Ford Foundation provided a fellowship that supported the research reported in this book. The fellowship was specifically awarded for research on the history of the American Bar Foundation Survey of the Administration of Criminal Justice. The history of the survey is summarized in Chapter 1 and examined in greater length in an article published elsewhere. Research on the survey stimulated my thinking about the general question of discretion and led me to write this book. I am indebted to the Ford Foundation for its generous support and its policy of letting scholars do their work free of time-consuming bureaucratic oversight.

Frank Remington and Herman Goldstein of the University of Wisconsin Law School also deserve much of the credit for helping me write this book. They were instrumental in recommending me for the Ford Foundation fellowship. More generally, as key figures in the American Bar Foundation Survey they have played important roles in the broader effort to control discretion in criminal justice. I thank both Frank and Herman for their interest in and support of my research.

David Rothman of Columbia University and Susan Herman of Brooklyn Law School read the manuscript and made a number of suggestions that greatly strengthened the final version. Cassie Spohn, a colleague at the University of Nebraska at Omaha, read several of the chapters and made extremely helpful suggestions. On a number of points, the book is much stronger as a result of her comments. Dennis Kenney, another colleague, read the chapter on police discretion and made several helpful comments. At Oxford University Press, Nancy Lane was once again a marvelous editor. This is the third book we have done together over the past fifteen years. It has been an extremely rewarding relationship. My heartfelt thanks to Nancy.

CONTENTS

Taming the System

1

Discretion and Its Discontents

Two Black Men: Symbols of Crime and Justice

Edward Garner and Willie Horton are symbols of the bitter politics of crime and justice in contemporary America. The controversies surrounding their lives reflect the deep divisions in American society about the apparent failures of the criminal justice system. For some, the system has failed to promote justice by discriminating against the poor, racial minorities, and other powerless people. For others, it has failed to control crime, leaving the law-abiding majority vulnerable to dangerous criminals.

Edward Garner was only fifteen years old when he was shot and killed by members of the Memphis, Tennessee, police force on October 3, 1974.[1] Officers Elton Hymon and Leslie Wright spotted Garner climbing a chain-link fence. Suspecting him of burglary, they shouted "Police, halt." When he did not stop, they shot him in the back of the head, killing him. Garner was 5 feet 4 inches tall, weighed between 100 and 110 pounds, and had in his possession a stolen purse with $10 in it.

A suit on Garner's behalf eventually reached the Supreme Court, and in 1985 the Court declared unconstitutional the "fleeing felon" rule under which the Memphis police had shot Garner. *Tennessee v. Garner* was one in a long line of Court decisions placing procedural restraints that are designed to control the discretion of police officers and other officials.

Willie Horton's name was engraved in American political history during the 1988 presidential election campaign. A television ad supporting Republican candidate George Bush charged that Horton, a convicted felon, had raped a young woman while he was on a weekend furlough from prison through a Massachusetts work-release program. Bush branded his opponent a liberal who favored social programs that allowed dangerous criminals to prey on the public. Some observers believe that the "Willie Horton" issue was the decisive one in the election.

At the most visceral level, the "Willie Horton" issue pandered to the racial fears of white America: Horton was a black man and his victim a white woman. On a different level, the issue expressed the belief, held by many Americans, that the justice system is soft on crime and fails to punish dangerous criminals. To prevent these offenders from getting off too easily, conservatives argue, official discretion should be curbed.

The Problem of Discretion

The Garner and Horton controversies dramatize the subject of this book: the problem of discretion in the criminal justice system. Discretion pervades the administration of justice. What we call the criminal justice "system" is nothing more than the sum total of a series of discretionary decisions by innumerable officials. Decisions about whether to arrest, to prosecute, or to imprison annually affect the liberty of millions of Americans.[2]

The problem is not discretion itself, but its misuse. It is now generally accepted that discretion is not only a pervasive feature of the administration of justice but one with certain positive aspects. Kenneth C. Davis argues that police officer discretion not to arrest represents the triumph of common sense over the excesses and "unwisdom" of legislators.[3] The Supreme Court recently declared discretion "fundamental" to the criminal justice system. According to the Court, it offers "substantial benefits" to a criminal defendant: a jury can acquit, a prosecutor can decline to prosecute, a prosecutor can seek the death penalty, and so on.[4] The Court offered this view in the highly controversial case of *McCleskey v. Kemp* (1987) when it refused to overturn McCleskey's death sentence on the basis of statistical evidence of racial discrimination in the application of the death penalty. The *McCleskey* decision focuses attention on the basic issues explored in this book: the proper scope of discretion, the kind of evidence that indicates misuse, and the proper remedies for the misuse of discretion.

The great divide in American politics with respect to criminal justice is between those who think the problem is an absence of justice and those who believe it is ineffective crime control. Generally, liberals believe that the police engage in systematic discrimination in making arrests and using deadly force, that the poor are denied release on bail, that plea bargains force defendants to give up their Fifth Amendment rights, that black and poor offenders are imprisoned more than white and middle-class offenders, and that blacks receive the death penalty far more frequently than whites who are guilty of comparable crimes. Conservatives, meanwhile, believe that the police cannot control crime because their hands are tied by too many restraints, that judges release dangerous criminals on bail, that plea bargains result in systematic leniency, that judges place dangerous prisoners on probation, and that parole boards release prisoners too early.

These competing perspectives on criminal justice were defined twenty-five years ago by Herbert Packer in a classic essay, "Two Models of the Criminal Process."[5] What Packer called the "due process" model is, in the terms of this book, the attempt to enhance individual rights through procedural restraints on official discretion. His "crime control" model emphasized a freer exercise of discretion in order to enhance the ability of criminal justice officials to apprehend, convict, and punish wrongdoers.

Much has happened since the publication of Packer's classic essay. The criminal justice system has experienced enormous changes as a result of reforms, court decisions, and changing public pressures. At the same time, there has been a research revolution that has enormously expanded our knowledge about the administration of criminal justice.[6] It is fair to say that the bulk of the accepted body of knowledge about criminal justice has appeared since 1968. While Packer's concept of the two models is still an extremely helpful way of thinking about criminal justice in the abstract, we now know far more about discretion in practice. The major struggles in criminal justice during this period involved the control of discretion. This book is a history of the movement to control discretion and an analysis of the results of those control efforts.

A Brief History of the "Discovery" of Discretion

Before you can address a problem, you have to know that it exists. Discretion was not always seen as a problem in criminal justice. Prior to the late 1950s, the leading experts in the field barely acknowledged its existence, much less saw it as a central problem. The relatively recent discovery of discretion is an important part of the story that follows. We are currently somewhere in the middle of a historic process regarding the control of discretion. It is still too early to say where it will lead. Examining the discovery of discretion sheds some light on why discretion was ignored for so long and on the halting and tentative efforts to control it.

The American Bar Foundation Survey

Discretion in criminal justice was "discovered" by a remarkable research project, the American Bar Foundation Survey of the Administration of Criminal Justice. Beginning in early 1956, the ABF survey conducted the first systematic field observations of criminal justice officials at work. Although the published findings of the survey were late in appearing, they spread quietly among experts in the field and eventually established the paradigm that dominates teaching, research, and professional thinking today.[7]

The "discovery" occurred in the spring and fall of 1956. In a September 24, 1956, memo to members of the survey's field research team, research director Frank Remington observed that "to a large extent, the administration of criminal justice can be characterized as a series of important decisions from the time a crime is committed until the offender is finally released from supervision."[8] A truism today, this observation was an exciting new insight that emerged during the first weeks of field research.

The survey did not set out to discover discretion. At best, it began with a strong but ill-defined sense that the most important elements of the administration of criminal justice were not known. The history of the survey is a remarkable story of a large and expensive gamble on an open-ended research project that began with no clearly defined hypothesis but that eventually overthrew the existing paradigm of criminal justice and replaced it with another.

The survey originated in 1953 at the suggestion of Supreme Court Justice Robert H. Jackson. In a speech to the American Bar Association, he expressed alarm over the "breakdown, delay and ineffectiveness of American law enforcement."[9] He went on to urge the bar to undertake systematic research on the the day-to-day administration of justice. Jackson's call led directly to the creation of the American Bar Foundation as the institutional locus of research for the survey and other projects.[10]

The immediate cause of the ABA's interest in criminal justice research was the growing national concern about organized crime. Senator Estes Kefauver conducted highly publicized hearings on the issue in 1950 and asked the ABA to assist by studying certain legal issues. The ABA responded enthusiastically, creating the Commission on Organized Crime. The commission's recommendations led directly to Jackson's speech and the idea of a comprehensive survey of criminal justice.[11]

Justice Jackson's proposal for a study of criminal justice was quickly supported by the Ford Foundation, which granted $50,000 for the development of a detailed research plan. The resulting *Plan for a Survey* by Arthur Sherry described a "pilot project" involving direct observation of criminal justice agencies in three states: Kansas, Wisconsin, and Michigan.[12] This would test the research methods to be used in a full-scale national survey. Ford accepted the *Plan* and awarded the first two of many grants that eventually totaled $520,000 (the equivalent of $3 million in 1992 dollars).[13] Frank Remington was hired as director of research. He recruited a staff and the field research began on February 6, 1956.

Rejecting the Old Paradigm

The crucial element of Sherry's *Plan* was its explicit rejection of the prevailing paradigm of criminal justice. This paradigm was embodied in the more than forty crime commission reports that had been published since the early 1920s.[14] For present purposes, the most important aspect of that paradigm was its lack of awareness of discretionary decision making. The intriguing question, of course, is how forty crime commissions, which involved the best minds of their day—Felix Frankfurter and Roscoe Pound, among others—could fail to see such a crucial feature of the administration of justice. The answer is that phenomena which are self-evident to one generation are not necessarily evident to others. This highlights the role of paradigms in scientific research. Paradigms describe observed phenomena, define problems, and guide research.[15] Phenomena that fall outside the prevailing paradigm either are not noticed at all or are dismissed as unimportant and not worthy of investigation. So it was with discretion for the early crime commissions.

The earlier crime commission studies reflected the assumptions of pre–World War I Progressive reform. Generally, Progressivism sought to remold social and economic institutions into effective instruments for coping with the needs of a modern urban-industrial society.[16] The major problems with public institutions, the Progressives believed, were corrupt political influence, unqualified personnel, and inadequate resources. Underlying this analysis was an ill-disguised political agenda. The Progressives' idea of expert leadership meant people from their own social and professional class, rather than people connected with the blue-collar political machines.

The impact of the Progressives' reform assumptions is most evident in the way the crime commissions explained the systematic attrition of cases and mitigation of punishment.[17] They found that large numbers of arrests were dismissed; that most of the resulting cases were settled by guilty pleas; that many of those pleas were to lesser offenses; that many of those found guilty were not imprisoned; that most prisoners were released early on parole. The crime commissions did not examine the decision-making process, however. Instead, they began with the assumption that the attrition of cases was a sign of failure and then concluded that failure could only be the result of political influence, bad people, and inadequate resources. It followed that good people (educated, trained, politically independent) would do the right thing.

It is important to note what the crime commissions did *not* see. They had no appreciation for the variety of factors that enter into the handling of criminal cases: the impact of work loads; concern about bureaucratic self-interest; concern about maintaining good relations with other institutions; use of the criminal law for purposes that had nothing to do with punishing lawbreaking. In short, they had no understanding of the sociology of criminal justice.[18] The crime commissions' blindness to these considerations was dictated by ideology and reinforced by methodology. None of the crime commissions undertook any direct observation of officials at work, relying instead on official data about arrests, convictions, and so on. They began with the assumption that every arrest was valid; therefore, every decision that failed to result in full prosecution and punishment was a symptom of weakness or failure.

The first weeks of the ABF survey's field research opened a new window on the administration of criminal justice. Members of the field research team were staggered by their observation of rampant lawlessness, racism, and casual unprofessional conduct. On his first night with the Milwaukee police, John Warner spent the entire evening drinking in bars.[19] In Detroit's vice-ridden Thirteenth Ward, the police routinely broke into buildings and made "sweep" arrests of gamblers, drunks, prostitutes, and homosexuals.[20] During an interrogation, one suspect was administered a fake polygraph, whose parts included a kitchen colander.[21] Defense attorneys routinely billed prostitutes for obtaining their release on writs of habeas corpus, knowing that release would be forthcoming in any event.[22] Prosecutors detained suspects by lying about delays in fingerprint checks.[23] Officials not only flouted the law but often were ignorant of it. When one Wisconsin police chief was asked about the exclusionary rule, then in effect in the state, he replied, "Oh, we never exclude anyone from the courtroom."[24]

But as Herman Goldstein, one of the original team members, recalls today, what struck team members most vividly was not the lawlessness but the pervasiveness of decision making.[25] Within a matter of weeks, research director Remington and special consultant Lloyd Ohlin reoriented the research effort. They advised the field research team that the topics in the original research plan should no longer "be taken as a day to day guide for research."[26] Instead of the purely formal aspects of agencies (their official legal jurisdiction, number of personnel, formal lines of authority, etc.), they should emphasize such things as "the actual practices of arrest, search and seizure."[27] By focusing on actual decision making, the survey began to fashion a new paradigm for criminal justice.

Defining the New Paradigm

The new paradigm did not immediately spring full-blown upon the world after the survey team completed its field research. The survey was subject to many difficulties and at one point appeared to be near collapse. Overwhelmed by the data at hand and denied further funds from the Ford Foundation, the staff dropped the planned national survey and converted the "pilot project" into the final product. The principal publications based on the data were delayed many years. Several of those items eventually became recognized classics in their respective fields: Joseph Goldstein's pioneering article on police discretion; Wayne LaFave's book, *Arrest*; Donald Newman's book on plea bargaining, *Conviction*; and Sanford Kadish's articles on correctional decision making.[28] While these individual items exerted an enormous influence, the survey itself faded into undeserved obscurity.

The new paradigm of criminal justice consisted of several interrelated propositions, of which discretionary decision making was one key element.

The first proposition involved the complex role of the criminal law. The survey's field research team found that the criminal law was frequently used for purposes unrelated to the punishment of criminals, particularly for handling myriad social problems involving alcohol abuse, mental illness, family problems, indebtedness, and so on.[29] Public pressure about maintaining order often conflicted with the restraints imposed by the law. Police, prosecutors, and judges resolved these often conflicting pressures through an informal and largely hidden decision-making process.

The complex and often ambiguous role of the criminal law laid the foundation for discretionary decision making. Police officers, for example, used their own judgment about when to arrest and for what purpose.[30] Prosecution was either continued or dropped for a variety of reasons.[31] What stunned the survey's field research team was the fact that the routine business of criminal justice involved the making of critical decisions without either formal controls or reference to legal norms.

The survey's third principal finding was the existence of a criminal justice "system." The various agencies did not stand alone, as the old crime commissions had assumed. Decisions in each one influenced, and were influenced by, those in other agencies. The concept of a criminal justice system was eventually popularized by the President's Crime Commission in 1967,[32] but credit for the original insight properly belongs to the ABF survey.

Discretion as a National Problem

The survey's findings began to circulate at a propitious moment in American history. In the early 1960s, issues of crime and justice became the focal point of a national crisis. Several forces were at work in this process. The civil rights movement focused attention on race discrimination, particularly with respect to the police. A series of controversial Supreme Court decisions threw the national spotlight on long-hidden police practices related to searches, seizures, and in-custody interrogations. Finally, a dramatic increase in the crime rate, together with urban riots and campus disorders, generated a powerful public demand for tough crime-control measures. The issue of "law and order" appeared in a presidential election for the first time in 1964.[33]

The response to this crisis was an unprecedented reexamination of the criminal justice system. The ABA set out to write a comprehensive set of standards in 1963.[34] The American Law Institute began drafting the *Model Code of Pre-Arraignment Procedure* the same year.[35] President Lyndon Johnson created the President's Commission on Law Enforcement and Administration of Justice in 1965. The commission's 1967 report, *The Challenge of Crime in a Free Society*, was the most comprehensive study of the American criminal justice system. Congress responded the the national crisis the following year by creating the Law Enforcement Assistance Administration (LEAA), which eventually pumped over $700 million a year into the criminal justice system.

With respect to discretion, the most important developments were the Supreme Court decisions on the police and other aspects of criminal justice. The controversies surrounding the exclusionary rule and the *Miranda* warning are familiar to most people. From the standpoint of this book, those decisions and the others that constituted the Court's "due process revolution" should be seen as challenges to discretionary decision making. The *Mapp* decision established the exclusionary rule as a limit on discretionary searches; the famous *Miranda* warning is a detailed set of rules governing arrest procedures.[36]

The enormous furor over these decisions set in motion a national debate over the best methods of controlling police behavior. While many liberals and civil libertarians placed all their hopes in the Supreme Court as the watchdog of the criminal justice system, some supporters of the decisions in question acknowledged that the Supreme Court was a weak instrument for regulating the police and other agencies. Other methods, they argued, would be far more effective.[37]

The national debate over the best method of regulating the criminal justice system that emerged in the 1960s forms the context of the chapters that follow. The fact of discretionary decision making quickly became part of the new paradigm or conventional wisdom. The debate then turned to questions about the dynamics of that decision making, whether the outcomes represented discrimination or excessive leniency, and the best methods of controlling discretion.

Perspectives on Change

This book is an inquiry into a thirty-year effort to control discretion in the criminal justice system. To that end, it approaches the subject from several different perspectives.

At the simplest level, it is a history of American criminal justice since the late 1950s. It argues that the dominant theme of that period is the attempt to control discretionary decision making.[38] This theme lends coherence to the many different changes that have swept over the criminal justice system during the period: the civil rights movement, the landmark decisions of the Supreme Court and the resulting political controversies, and the many specific reform movements related to bail, plea bargaining, sentencing, prisoners' rights, and others.

At another level, this book is an exercise in social science evaluation research. It reviews the literature on a number of reforms and attempts to answer the question, What works? Specifically, it focuses on four critical decision points in the criminal justice system: police discretion, bail setting, plea bargaining, and sentencing. It examines the various reforms that have been proposed, the major ones implemented, and the impact of those reforms. In the end, it attempts to draw some general conclusions about the possibilities for the control of discretion. Is any meaningful control possible? If so, are some approaches more effective than others? Are some decision points more amenable to control than others? If so, which ones and why?

The four decision points examined here hardly represent an exhaustive treatment of discretionary decision making. Indeed, it would be difficult to produce a comprehensive list of all the decision points in the system. The four decision points examined here are intended to illustrate general phenomena, and the conclusions reached are seen as having general applicability.

There is much to be gained through a comparative analysis of discretion control. Although the attempt to control discretion pervades criminal justice, there has not been, to date, any comparative analysis.[39]

Much has been written about the "fragmentation" of the criminal justice system. That fragmentation is intellectual as well as institutional. The leaders of criminal justice institutions, and their respective professional associations, are extremely isolated. Police chiefs, judges, and wardens are generally overwhelmed by the crisis of the moment and have little time for communication with people in other fields, much less for reflection upon their common problems. Academics, meanwhile, are notorious specialists. Experts on police use of deadly force, for example, are often not knowledgeable about plea bargaining or sentencing. This book is an attempt to bridge that gap.

Third, this book is an essay on the sociology of law or, more precisely, the historical sociology of law. In a very general sense, it is an inquiry into the question of how law affects human behavior. More specifically, it inquires into how law affects the behavior of criminal justice officials. The social science question about what works reappears as a question about compliance with formal rules. Do officials comply with rules? Do formal rules achieve their stated goals?

Whether or not officials comply with rules is an extremely important question with respect to social policy. Put simply, is it possible to achieve any coherent goal? Given our commitment to equality and fairness, is it possible to eliminate discrimination through law or other formal social controls? If the reduction of serious crime is the primary goal, can it be achieved through changes in criminal justice decision making?

The trend toward controlling the actions of public officials through formal rules should be seen in the context of alternative mechanisms of control. The most important rejected alternative is the classic model of professionalism, which seeks to control discretion through the training, socialization, and peer control of officials.[40] The fact that the trend of events has been in the direction of legal control, at the expense of classic professionalism, does not necessarily mean that it is the most effective or the most desirable path. But it is the path we have taken and it deserves careful scrutiny on its own terms and in the context of rejected alternatives.

Viewed from this perspective, the effort to control discretion in criminal justice is not unique. Every institution in American society has been affected by the same forces that have reshaped criminal justice: charges of racial discrimination, the intervention of the federal courts, a pervasive public feeling that institutions are failing in their primary task. The problems in the public schools, in health care, and in other areas, have, to a great extent, been defined in terms of the abuse of discretion.[41]

This book views the efforts to control discretion as driven by strong and often shifting political forces. Discretion as a phenomenon in the administration of justice was discovered through disinterested social science research, in the classic mold. But efforts to control discretion have been driven by political events. To cite only one example, bail reform emerged in the early 1960s because a network of reformers were convinced that prevailing bail practices discriminated against the poor.

What is called the political environment also turns out to be an extremely complex phenomenon. This book suggests that we should be extremely skeptical of broad characterizations of the political tone of a period. Labels such as the "liberal" 1960s and the "conservative" 1980s can be very misleading. Some of the most significant advances in the control of police discretion—on use of deadly force and police handling of domestic violence—occurred in an allegedly conservative period. The fact that efforts to enhance protection of racial minorities and women could enjoy considerable success in a supposedly hostile political climate suggests that we should look beyond popular stereotypes.

The political perspective of this book sets it apart from the most thorough study of decision making in criminal justice published to date. Michael R. Gottfredson and Don M. Gottfredson's *Decision Making in Criminal Justice* reviews the literature on the outcomes of discretionary decisions. Yet the subtitle of the book, *Toward the Rational Exercise of Discretion*, reveals its technocratic and apolitical orientation. The "rational" exercise of discretion, in their terms, means that decisions are consistent with agreed-upon goals. But, as they concede, "in the criminal justice system now, however, clear agreement on objectives is not easily found."[42] That observation is a major understatement. There has never been consensus over the goals of the justice system. Issues of law, order, and justice are fundamentally political questions, and always have been.[43] The pressures that impinge on criminal justice agencies and affect decision making reflect profound divisions within contemporary society.

Controlling Discretion? Four Reservations

Virtually all experts on criminal justice recognize the pervasiveness of discretion, but not everyone believes that it can be controlled. And among those who do believe that some controls are possible, there is great disagreement over which approach is most effective and exactly how much control can realistically be expected. Out the outset, therefore, it is appropriate to address the reservations expressed by the skeptics who question the possibility of effective discretion control.

The first reservation is the cynical view that "nothing works." There is a significant body of criminal justice literature arguing that reforms do not achieve their ends, that they "backfire," thus producing only adverse unintended consequences.[44] A more moderate version of this view is that reforms fail because they are frustrated by the sheer intractability of the criminal process.[45] There is a good deal of evidence to support the cynical view, but there is also evidence to support a more optimistic conclusion. As the chapters that follow indicate, some reforms do work. One of major purposes of this book is to identify not only what works but the conditions of success.

A second reservation is that rules designed to control discretion degenerate into empty formalism. According to this view, Supreme Court rulings, police departments' written procedures, and similar rules have no practical effect on day-to-day operations. Officials may go through the motions of compliance—police officers reading the *Miranda* warning, obtaining a waiver, and then proceeding to extract a confession, for example—but this has little real impact on the quality of justice.[46] A study of search warrants found most to be boilerplate. Virtually identical language appeared in numerous applications for warrants.[47] The basic question is whether reformers delude themselves into believing that "passing a law" (read: creating a rule) solves the problem.

This is the most serious objection of all because it suggests that rulemaking makes matters worse. Some of the initial research on the exclusionary rule, for example, suggested that it encouraged police lying: officers claimed that they obtained the evidence not through a search but when the suspect dropped it on the ground (hence the so-called dropsy phenomenon).[48] Other research, however, suggests that police officers comply with restrictive rules, including the exclusionary rule. In the chapters that follow there is much discussion of the question of whether rules produce compliance or rule-breaking.

The fourth reservation raises a more complex question: Do rules designed to control discretion only serve to move it around? Do limits on plea bargaining, for example, only shift the discretion "upstream"

to the police and/or "downstream" to the judge? There is some evidence
to support this proposition. But this evidence is not the entire story and
there is some counterevidence to suggest that, despite some shift in
discretion, gains do result.

In the chapters that follow, these reservations are addressed. The
conclusion here is a moderately optimistic one. The control of discretion
is possible. But the examples cited clearly indicate that it is possible
only as long as expectations are modest and the reforms carefully tailored
and implemented. There is much wisdom in the conclusions reached
by a recent review of sentencing reform: meaningful change is "not
hopeless, merely difficult."[49]

Modest Expectations: From Abolition to Regulation

The attempt to control discretion tends to follow a similar trajectory in
every area of criminal justice. The discovery of discretion is accompanied by cries of outrage and calls for its abolition. The first detailed
article on police discretion, for example, concluded that it was illegal
and should not be permitted.[50] Several years later the National Advisory
Commission on Criminal Justice Standards and Goals called for the
abolition of plea bargaining within five years.[51] Ultimately, outrage
gives way to chastened acceptance. Further research and discussion
indicate that discretion is an inescapable reality, and the focus of reform
shifts to efforts to regulate it.

The national debate over controlling discretion was framed by two
books, published in 1969 and 1971, which offered the first comprehensive discussions of the discretion problem. The second of these two,
Struggle for Justice, a report on criminal justice by the American Friends
Service Committee, devoted a chapter to discretion and called for its
abolition. The report generally focused on the socially and politically
repressive aspects of the criminal justice system and stated unequivo-
cally that "discretion is at the core of the problem." "The elimination
of discretion," it continued, "would make the lives of the bulk of the
clients of the criminal justice system more tolerable."[52]

In at least one respect, *Struggle for Justice* was extremely influential.
It was one of the pivotal documents in the sentencing reform movement
that arose in the mid-1970s.[53] With respect to discretion generally,
however, the report was far less influential. In fact, a careful reading
reveals that there was far less to its call for "abolition" than first

appeared. *Struggle for Justice* conceded that police discretion could not be completely eliminated and, with respect to bail, it only called for the elimination of the money bail system.[54] On several key points, then, even the seemingly radical Quaker report envisioned simply the regulation of discretion.

The control of discretion was the central thrust of Kenneth C. Davis's highly influential *Discretionary Justice: A Preliminary Inquiry*. For all practical purposes, it established the framework for the consensus of opinion that has subsequently emerged.[55] The essential elements of that consensus are (1) that discretion is inescapable, (2) that the real problem is uncontrolled discretion, (3) that, properly controlled, discretion has certain positive features, and (4) that the best way to control discretion is through the technique of administrative rulemaking.

Davis approached the subject of discretion in criminal justice by simply borrowing well-established concepts and techniques from the field of administrative law, of which he was one of the foremost experts.[56] This highlighted the extent to which the field of criminal justice had neglected the subject of discretion, compared with other areas of the law. Second, Davis was an unabashed—and almost uncritical—enthusiast for administrative rulemaking. He announced that "the procedure of administrative rulemaking is . . . one of the greatest inventions of modern government." "Much experience," he added, "proves that it usually works beautifully."[57]

The administrative rulemaking approach attempts to strike a proper balance between the ideal and the real. The ideal in Anglo-American law is that officials conform to the rule of law, that their decisions are not arbitrary, capricious, or whimsical. The realist view of the "law-in-action" is that discretion is an inescapable fact of life and that the rule of law model represents an impossibly "mechanical" form of jurisprudence. The challenge is to strike the proper balance and determine the scope of appropriate departures from legal rules.[58]

The conclusions reached in this book are consistent with Davis's basic approach, although a bit more skeptical about the general applicability of administrative rulemaking. While there is evidence of important progress in controlling discretion, it is also clear that administrative rulemaking has its limits. Defining the exact nature of those limits is one of the main purposes of the four chapters that follow.

Davis subtitled his book *A Preliminary Inquiry*. This was an apt description, because it was the first comprehensive examination of the problem. Since then, many ideas have been proposed and many discarded. Some reforms have been attempted. A few have been institutionalized, others abandoned. Some of these reforms have been independently evaluated. The passage of time alone adds valuable perspective. It must be hoped that wisdom accumulates. We are in a far better position to draw some general conclusions about the control of discretion than was Davis in 1969. If his was a preliminary inquiry, this book should be seen as an interim report on what works.

A Few Words About "Rules"

One of the limits of Davis's approach is that, because of his area of expertise, he focused very narrowly on administrative rulemaking. This is a very promising approach, but it is only one of several methods of controlling discretion. This book generally refers to "rules" and it is appropriate to make it clear just what is meant by a rule.

A rule is *any formal directive designed to limit or control the discretion of a criminal justice official.*[59] The generic term rule is useful because, in practice, many of the rules are known by other names.

The broadest and most fundamental rules are the various provisions of the Bill of Rights in the U.S. Constitution and the equivalent provisions in state constitutions. The Fourth, Fifth, Sixth, and Eighth Amendments are a set of rules on what criminal justice officials must do and must not do. These protections are interpreted by the courts and the resulting body of case law comprises an additional set of rules. Probably the most celebrated court-developed rule in the history of criminal justice was issued in the *Miranda v. Arizona* decision. There are also the rules of criminal procedure, specified by state and federal law. Finally, operating agencies develop their own internal policies instructing their employees on how to act. These are the administrative rules so favored by Kenneth C. Davis. Police department policies on the use of deadly force are the best example of this approach, but many prosecutorial offices have developed rules governing plea-bargaining decisions as well.

Thinking about rules generically serves several purposes. First, it provides a comprehensive picture of all of the controls affecting the behavior of criminal justice officials. Second, it highlights the point that there is a complex "mix" of rules emanating from different sources. Finally, it helps to shift our thinking away from the Supreme Court as the principal source of rules. This point has important empirical and political implications and deserves further comment.

Many Americans, but especially civil libertarians, liberals, and constitutional scholars of all persuasions, are transfixed by the Supreme Court. To a great extent, we are still living in the shadow of the Warren Court (1953–1968), which played such a dramatic role in expanding the scope of individual rights in this country. From our perspective, the Supreme Court is only one potential source of rules designed to protect individual rights. As Chapter 2 argues at some length, the two most important advances in protecting the rights of victimized groups—police rules on deadly force and domestic violence—developed without benefit of a decision by the Court (the 1985 *Tennessee v. Garner* decision did not go as far as the existing rules of most police departments).

The latter point has enormous political implications in the current legal environment. The present Supreme Court appears aggressively oriented toward crime control, almost always ruling in favor of criminal justice officials, expanding their discretionary authority at the expense of protecting individual rights. The development of rules from other sources in recent years suggests that the effort to control discretion can and should be shifted away from the Supreme Court.

A comprehensive picture of the ''mix'' of rules also provides valuable insight into the dynamics of how rules develop. The view here is that the various sources of rules interact with one another in a complex manner, with changes in one area stimulating or forcing changes in other areas. The impact of the Court's rulings in *Mapp* and *Miranda*, for example, has been felt far beyond the precise holdings of those decisions. They stimulated a broad reform movement within policing that encompasses improvements in recruitment standards, training, and supervision—including measures designed to control discretion.[60]

Prisoners' rights litigation stimulated the development of an elaborate network of rules within prisons—rules on the nature and length of disciplinary actions, the right of prisoners to appeal those actions, and so on.[61] In the case of both the police and prisons, litigation prompted the development of professional accreditation movements. Many of these reforms now have their own momentum, continuing to develop without further prodding from the courts.

The control of discretion does not have a simple linear history. It is not a matter of going from no rule, to a simple rule, to a more detailed rule. Instead, it is a complex process of interaction between different rules from different sources. The politics of the control of discretion is often a matter of the struggle to control one or more rulemaking authorities. The Warren Court issued many historic rulings controlling discretion for the purpose of advancing principles of due process and equal protection. Conservative Republicans, however, won every presidential election but one between 1968 and 1992 and completely reshaped the Supreme Court. The present Supreme Court has revised Warren Court precedents more extensively in the area of criminal justice than any other area of constitutional law. Yet, as this book argues, the movement toward discretion control, including some notable gains in protecting individual rights, has continued through the 1970s and 1980s. In other words, rights advocates shifted their focus and pursued other sources of rules. This development provides a model for future developments and offers some hope to those alarmed by the current posture of the Supreme Court.

Consideration of the "mix" of rules introduces another way in which this inquiry departs from Davis's pioneering work. He begins by framing the issue in terms of a choice between law and discretion. He observes that "where law ends, discretion begins."[62] This represents a false dichotomy. We do not face a choice between a rule, in the sense of a formal directive, and unlimited discretion. As Davis explains, the major contribution of rules is to confine the exercise of discretion. That is to say, they leave a certain amount of discretion in place. The detailed rules on police use of deadly force that have developed still require officers to exercise considerable discretion or judgment in specific situations. They rule out shootings in some situations and eliminate those discretionary choices. Discretion remains, but in a greatly narrowed range of situations. The choice, then, is not between rule and discretion but between different kinds of rules and different degrees of permissible discretion. There are four relevant questions regarding a particular rule: What should it cover? How detailed should it be? How narrowly should it attempt to confine discretion? And, finally, how will officials be held accountable for complying with the rule?

2

Police Discretion

The Problem of Police Discretion

The videotaped beating of Rodney King by Los Angeles police officers on March 3, 1991—an event that electrified the country—dramatized the problem of police discretion. The officers involved acted out their worst impulses, obviously believing they would never be caught or punished. The fact that a sergeant was present and that the officers later discussed the incident over the police radio is the most damning evidence of their sense of immunity.[1]

The incident summed up everything that the most severe critics of the police have always believed. First, it highlighted the fact that most police work is a "low-visibility" phenomenon, occurring in a setting where officers are not monitored by any external authority. When a citizen does complain it is difficult to sustain that complaint with independent evidence. Second, the investigation following the incident clearly found that the internal system of police discipline had failed. The Christopher Commission identified forty-four officers who were guilty of multiple abuses of citizens yet had never been punished for persistent misconduct. Third, the incident illustrated the point that low-income black men are the most common victims of police misconduct.

In short, not only is routine police work free of effective external scrutiny, but the internal mechanisms of accountability appear to have failed. And it is worth noting that the Los Angeles police department (LAPD) has long enjoyed the reputation of being the most "professional'' of all American police departments. In the world of policing, professionalism has come to mean high standards of recruitment, training and supervision of officers. If the LAPD represents the height of professionalism, one wonders what happens in less professional departments.

Actually, there is good reason to believe that the situation is not as bleak as these observations might lead us to believe. The beating of Rodney King had the unfortunate effect of creating the impression that no progress has been made in the control of police behavior over the past thirty years. In fact, considerable progress has been made in terms of personnel standards, training, and supervision. There have also been significant improvements in the control of police discretion, notably in the use of deadly force. It is also possible to argue that the LAPD is an exception and that a culture of violence that flourished there does not necessarily reflect other police departments.

A Brief History of the Politics of Police Discretion

The history of the effort to control police discretion has been dominated by two factors. First, the entire subject of discretion has been discussed in the context of police misconduct. Second, the effort to curb that misconduct has been have been viewed largely in terms of the Supreme Court. As Chapter 1 indicated, the Court stepped into a void left by the failure of other governmental agencies to act. It is fair to say that the Court has been the driving force for change in policing for thirty years.[2]

The dominance of the Supreme Court has had several unfortunate effects on discussions of police discretion. First, it has focused attention on the Court and drawn attention away from other means of controlling police discretion. Second, the discussions of the role of the Court have been heavily skewed in the direction of a preoccupation with the exclusionary rule. This has the effect of focusing attention on search and seizure, to the near-exclusion of a host of other important discretionary decisions. Thus for many people, the question of the extent to which the Court has modified (some would say gutted) the 1961 *Mapp* decision, and might overturn it completely in the near future, is the beginning and the end of their thinking about controlling police discretion and police misconduct.

The discussion that follows takes a very different approach. First, it redirects our thinking to the broad range of discretionary decision points. Second, it operates on the assumption that the Supreme Court is not presently the primary instrument for either controlling police discretion or reducing police misconduct. The preferred approach is the technique known as administrative rulemaking, the process by which law enforcement agencies attempt to control officer discretion through their own internal rules.

The analysis that follows, like the book as a whole, is selective. It does not attempt to discuss in detail all of the various police decision points. Instead, it examines in detail recent developments surrounding a few important decisions. The purpose is to identify rules that have developed to govern police discretion, to examine whether those rules work, and finally to draw some general conclusions about the possibilities for controlling other police discretionary decisions.

Decision Points

Police discretion is not a single decision point or event. Police officers routinely exercise discretion in a broad range of decisions affecting the life and liberty of citizens.[3] Because these decisions are made by different officers in different assignments, policing represents a form of "horizontal" discretion. To control police discretion, then, it is necessary to disaggregate the various decisions and focus on each one separately.

The excercise of discretion at each point, moreover, is not a simple either–or choice. In most cases, the officer chooses one of several possible alternatives. Thus controlling discretion is usually not a matter of simply forbidding something; it is more often a matter of encouraging officers to choose one option over another. A few examples illustrate the range and complexity of police discretionary decision points.

The arrest decision, far from being a simple either–or matter, is extremely complex.[4] First, it is only one alternative among a number of possible responses to a difficult situation. Second, when an arrest is made, the officer has considerable discretion over the exact charge. The robbery suspect can be arrested and charged with larceny, the rape suspect with assault, and so on. The officer's decision is heavily influenced by the victim's preferences and this, in turn, can be influenced by the officer's behavior. In subtle or not so subtle ways, the officer can encourage or discourage an arrest.[5]

Driving a patrol car involves a number of important decisions. Responding to a routine call for service, an officer may decide how quickly to get the scene. Officers have been found to deliberately delay getting to the scene. The high-speed pursuit of fleeing suspects, which can pose serious risks to the officer and innocent bystanders, is a matter that has recently received an enormous amount of attention. In just a few years there appeared a new set of rules designed to control the decision to pursue.[6]

Once at the scene of a call for service, officers can actively take charge of the situation or do little and leave quickly. They can be relatively courteous or discourteous. They can make an effort to mediate the dispute or to refer the parties to a social service agency, or they can do nothing at all. All these are alternatives to arrest.[7]

If a crime has occurred, or is alleged, the officer has complete discretion over whether to fill out a crime report.[8] "Unfounding" a crime has enormous implications. It has the direct effect of lowering the official crime rate. Rejecting the citizen's claim that a crime occurred is justified in many instances; people do not understand the criminal law. But in others it is not justified, and unfounding denies people the full protection of the law. If a crime occurred and there is no immediate arrest, a series of decisions must be made about how seriously to investigate. Most cases get little if any detective work. Most of the work involves the shuffling of papers.[9]

Decisions about whether to "found" a crime, to investigate, and to investigate vigorously can be influenced by police officer bias. Gary LaFree found that rape investigators tended to discount rape allegations where there was evidence that the complainant did not conform to conventional moral behavior—as indicated by drinking, style of clothing, apparent sexual lifestyle, and so on.[10]

The investigation of suspected crimes involves a series of decisions about searches, seizures, and interrogations. These include the decision to stop and question someone on the street, whether or not to frisk the suspect, short of arrest, and what kind of questions to ask.[11] Field interrogations provoke great resentment among young black men. Warrantless searches are especially problematic, particularly in the case of narcotics and weapons possession cases. Finally, there are a number of highly intrusive investigative techniques: the use of informants, undercover investigations, wiretaps, and so on.[12] Illegitimate investigations, such as spying on lawful political activity, is a special problem in policing.[13]

In the event of an arrest, the arresting officer makes a decision about what charges to file. As will be discussed in detail in Chapter 4, the prosecutor's critical decision about the nature of the charge is, in the first instance, shaped by the charge filed by the officer. "Overcharging" (filing charges higher than are warranted) influences subsequent plea negotiations; "undercharging," meanwhile, means that the suspect will necessarily avoid the most serious possible punishment.[14]

Even the apparently straightforward decision to use deadly force is more complicated than a simple shoot–don't shoot matter. In practice the decision to shoot is preceded by three distinct "phases" in a broader encounter between police officer and citizen. Scharf and Binder describe these three phases as "anticipation," "entry and initial contact," and "information exchange." Within each phase the police officer and others make critical decisions (interpreting information and body language, seeking more information, etc.) that increase or decrease the risk of a shooting.[15] Efforts to control police use of deadly force increasingly focus on these initial phases of potentially violent encounters.[16]

These examples hardly exhaust the list of decision points. Before proceeding, several points deserve mention. It should be obvious that all decisions are not equally important. Some—deadly force and arrest— are far more serious in their consequences than others. Also, some decisions are subject to more rules than others. One point of this inquiry is to determine why this is so. Are some decisions inherently more controllable? Or are some simply more visible and consequently politically sensitive? Or is it that, given the very unsystematic fashion in which rules have generally developed, we just have not addressed all the important decision points?

Controlling Police Discretion

The Use of Deadly Force

The control of deadly force is arguably the great success story in the long effort to control police discretion. It is the one decision point where we have persuasive evidence documenting a positive impact of new rules without any unintended and undesirable consequences. The number of people shot and killed by the police was reduced by at least 30 percent between the early 1970s and the late 1980s. At the same time, the disparity between black and white citizens shot and killed was cut in half, from roughly six blacks for every white to three to one.[17] This is a substantial accomplishment, which advances fundamental principles of due process and equal protection and has saved many lives.

Thirty years ago the police officer's decision to shoot was completely uncontrolled.[18] Officers acted in a vacuum in terms of law and policy. With respect to legal doctrine, the common law fleeing-felon standard allowed a police officer, for purpose of arrest, to shoot to kill any suspected felon. Given this broad mandate, it is hardly surprising that there were so many patently outrageous incidents where officers shot and killed unarmed fifteen-year-olds like Edward Garner.

What the law permitted, police departments tolerated or even encouraged. In the police academy, recruits received many hours of training in marksmanship but not one word on when to shoot. Once on the street, they were guided by policies that were often framed in terms even more vague than the fleeing-felon rule. A 1964 survey found that the policies in ten of forty-five departments merely advised officers to use "good judgment" in shootings, while three had no written policies at all.[19]

Nor did officers have to worry about the consequences of shooting and killing someone under questionable circumstances. Paul Jacobs found that in the mid–1960s the Los Angeles police department conducted a mandatory investigation whenever an officer damaged a patrol car but had no similar requirement for shootings until 1965—and then only in response to intense pressure from civil rights groups. At the time the LAPD was widely regarded as the paragon of police "professionalism": with the best training, the highest recruitment standards, and the tightest supervision of any department in the country. Jacobs also found that of the sixty-four instances in which a citizen was shot to death by an officer sixty-two were ruled justifiable homicide, despite the fact that twenty-five of the people were unarmed, twenty-seven were shot in the back or side, and four had committed no crime at all.[20]

Police shootings have always been a civil rights issue. Many of the riots of the period were sparked by shootings. In 1964, for example, an off-duty New York City cop shot and killed a fifteen-year-old black youth.[21] Research indicated that the disparity in persons shot and killed by the police was as high as eight blacks for every one white. These data lent support to the allegation that the police had two trigger fingers, one for whites and another for blacks.[22]

The first authoritative call for limits on shootings was the American Law Institute's Model Penal Code in 1962.[23] It recommended that deadly force be used only for purposes of arrest in the case of felonies where the officer believed that ''there is substantial risk that the person to be arrested will cause death or serious bodily harm if his apprehension is delayed.'' This proposal had some modest impact on public policy as a number of states revised their criminal codes, adopting all or most of the Model Penal Code. Yet even by the time of the 1985 *Garner* decision, twenty-three states still retained some form of the fleeing-felon rule.

There is some reason to question the efficacy of state statutes in controlling police use of deadly force. A study of shootings by Philadelphia police found that they increased after the legislature adopted a more restrictive statute in 1973. Several commentators pointed out that state statutes are a relatively weak instrument for controlling police behavior because they are extremely remote from the decision point.[24] The most effective controls, according to this view, are those developed and enforced by the operating agencies in question. This argument is one of the central points advanced by advocates of administrative rule-making as a remedy for police discretion. Because of its importance and potential for general applicability, it is worth stating directly: rules that are developed and enforced by the agency are more likely to be effective than those imposed by some external agency.[25]

Rulemaking and Police Shootings

The turning point in the history of deadly force policy was the highly restrictive policy adopted by the New York City police department (NYPD) in 1972. It was significant for several reasons. First, by virtue of its size and location in the media capital of the country, the NYPD commands national attention. Second, quite apart from his position as New York City police commissioner at the time, Patrick V. Murphy was an influential figure in the law enforcement profession. Third, the impact of the new shooting policy was rigorously evaluated in what eventually became one of the most influential pieces of research in the history of policing.[26]

The 1972 NYPD deadly force policy set the standard for what eventually became a national consensus on the issue. By 1978 Lawrence W. Sherman could detect a "distinct national trend" toward restrictive policies, finding that several big-city departments had policies that were more restrictive than the applicable state statute. His prediction that a 1972 FBI policy limiting shootings to situations where the officer believed he or another person was "in danger of death or grievous bodily harm" might serve as a national model proved to be very accurate.[27] In 1980 the International Association of Chiefs of Police (IACP) embraced the defense of life standard. Finally, in 1983 the Commission on Law Enforcement Accreditation (representing the IACP, the National Sheriffs Association, the Police Executive Research Forum, and the National Organization of Black Law Enforcement Executives) adopted a similar standard.[28] In short, a consensus on the defense of life standard had developed by the early 1980s.[29]

This consensus was not reached through dispassionate deliberation by any means. Each change in a police department shooting policy was the result of conflict. The common scenario involved a highly questionable shooting, community protests, and often a lawsuit. In some cases, a lower court decision forced a change in policy. In other cases a police chief revised the department's shooting policy only after several controversial shooting incidents. The Supreme Court eventually ratified the new consensus in 1985 by declaring the fleeing-felon rule unconstitutional. Significantly, however, the Court did not require the kind of detailed controls that already existed in most departmental policies.[30]

Deadly Force Policies in Operation

The key elements of the new standard were both substantive and procedural. Since there is now considerable uniformity among local departmental policies, we refer to a generic standard. For purposes of illustration, the Omaha Police Department policy, which is typical of prevailing policies, is reproduced in Figure 2.1. Substantively, it restricts the use of deadly force to the defense of the life of the officer or another person. It also specifically prohibits firing warning shots, calling for assistance shots, and shooting at or from moving vehicles. In Kenneth C. Davis's terms, these restrictions *confine* the officer's discretion.[31]

Procedurally, the policy includes an important accountability mechanism, requiring the officer to file a written report after *any* firearms

POLICE DIVISION – RULES OF CONDUCT
OMAHA POLICE DIVISION
OMAHA, NEBRASKA

CHAPTER 1 – SECTION 23
FIREARMS: (SPECIFICATIONS – INSPECTION – PRACTICE – PROPER USE)

An officer of the Omaha Police Division may use his firearm in the performance of duty for any of the following reasons:

(a) To defend himself from death or serious injury.

(b) To defend another person from death or serious injury.

(c) To effect the arrest or capture, or prevent the escape or rescue, of a person whom the officer knows or has reasonable grounds to believe has committed a felony, when the crime for which the arrest is made involves conduct including use or threatened use of deadly force or when there is a substantial risk that the person to be arrested will cause death or serious bodily harm if his apprehension is delayed when:

    (1) Such force may only be exercised when all reasonable alternatives have been exhausted and must be based only on facts or what reasonably appear to be the facts known to the officer at the moment he shoots. It is not practical to enumerate specific felonies and state with certainty that the escape of the perpetrator must be prevented at all costs or that there are other felonious crimes where the perpetrator must be allowed to escape rather than shoot him. Such decisions are based upon sound judgment, not arbitrary check lists.

    (2) An officer shall not shoot at a fleeing felon whom he has reasonable grounds to believe is a juvenile. However, when the escape of such a suspect can reasonably be expected to pose a serious threat to the life of another person, then, under these circumstances, an officer may shoot to prevent the escape of such person.

    (3) A locally stolen vehicle that is not connected with any other felonious crime should not be considered a violation which would permit the "use of deadly force". Deadly force should not be used in effecting the arrest or capture of perpetrators of this crime.

    (4) The "use of deadly force" is prohibited in the apprehension of parties suspected of felony traffic violations.

(continued on page 30)

FIGURE 2.1. Omaha Police Department rules of conduct.

(5) The firing of weapons at a moving vehicle or from a moving vehicle shall be discouraged and shall only be done under extreme, close-range circumstances when all other means of stopping the vehicle containing a felon who is a danger to the officer or others, now or later, have been attempted and have failed.

(d) To kill a dangerous animal, or to kill an animal so badly injured that humanity requires its removal from further suffering.

(e) To give an alarm or call for assistance when no other means is available.

The playful drawing of a weapon or unnecessary exhibition of same is forbidden.

Caution must be exercised to insure that no innocent bystander is injured as a result of firing. Warning shots will not be used by a police officer in effecting any type of arrest. No firearms shall be used in the apprehension of or preventing the escape of a misdemeanant (whether suspected or convicted).

FIGURE 2.1. (*continued*)

discharge. These reports are then subject to automatic review by higher ranking officers. Similar report and review requirements are now standard in big-city deadly force policies. In Davis's terms, this process *checks* discretion. For reasons that are discussed in more detail later, this accountability mechanism is the key element in the success of the deadly force policies.[32]

Impact of Policies on Shooting Patterns

Fyfe's study found that the restrictive New York City policy reduced shootings by 29.9 percent.[33] The reduction was greatest in the "prevent or terminate crime" category (85%), with a smaller decline (24%) in the "defense of life" category. In short, the new policy succeeded in reducing the kind of shootings it was intended to reduce. Significantly, there were no unintended adverse consequences. The crime rate did not go up and there were no increases in either assaults on officers or officers killed in the line of duty. Thus fears that restricting shootings would allow criminals to escape and put police officers at risk were unfounded.

Fyfe's research was based on the official officer reports on shooting incidents. The obvious question is whether the officers completed the required reports truthfully. This goes to the heart of the matter of controlling discretion. Put simply, do officials obey rules? Rules that are easily evaded will have no effect. In the case of shootings, the simplest

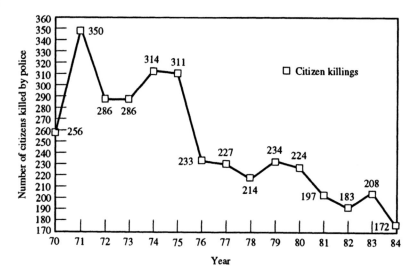

FIGURE 2.2. Citizens killed by police in fifty cities of over 250,000 population (1970–1984). (Lawrence W. Sherman and Ellen G. Cohn, *Citizens Killed by Big-City Police, 1970–1984* [Washington, D.C.: Crime Control Institute, 1986])

way to evade the rules is to record an improper shot was an "accident." Fyfe found that reported accidental shootings did increase by 71 percent after the new policy went into effect. But even then they represented only 9 percent of all discharges, suggesting that there was no pattern of massive evasion and lying.[34]

National data on trends in shootings provide further evidence that restrictive policies have reduced police shootings. Sherman and Cohn found that the number of persons shot and killed in the fifty largest police departments declined by about 30 percent between 1970 and 1984, from an average of about 300 a year to about 200 (Fig. 2.2).[35] In a study for the IACP, Kenneth Matulia found similar reductions between 1970 and 1983 in the fifty-seven largest cities. Interestingly, there was an ambiguous pattern for the country as a whole.[36] The difference is probably due to the fact that restrictive shooting policies were more prevalent among the largest cities.

In an equally important finding, Sherman and Cohn found that the racial disparity among people shot and killed was cut in half, from about six to one to about three to one. The reason for this is obvious. The greatest racial disparities in persons shot and killed have always involved unarmed persons. Fyfe's data on police shootings in Memphis found that fourteen of the thirty-four people shot and killed between 1969 and 1976 were unarmed and not assaulting the police officer. Thirteen of these fourteen were black. This represented half of all the blacks shot and killed.[37] Thus it is possible to argue that an unrestrictive shooting policy allows officers to act out their racial stereotypes: that the black man lurking in the shadows is inherently dangerous, whereas the white suspect is not. Restrictive shooting policies, although nominally addressed to race-neutral situations, curb the effect of racial stereotypes, with rather dramatic results.

It is worth noting that as the number of persons shot and killed declined, the number of police officers killed in the line of duty also fell by half, from 131 in 1972 to 65 in 1990.[38] Among the factors that probably account for this decline are the increased use of bulletproof vests and the 24.9 percent decline in the robbery rate between 1974 and 1989 (reducing the number of events most likely to result in armed confrontations between criminals and police).[39] But it is also likely that restrictions on police shootings produced fewer shots in return. In short, restrictive shooting policies led to a general deescalation of violence and enhanced police officer safety.[40]

Conclusions

These data support the conclusion that administrative rules have successfully limited police shooting discretion, with positive results in terms of social policy. Fewer people are being shot and killed, racial disparities in shootings have been reduced, and police officers are in no greater danger because of these restrictions. Officers appear to comply with the rules. This is an accomplishment of major significance and one that provides a model for other discretion control efforts.

It is important, however, to temper this generally favorable conclusion with some cautionary thoughts. Continued compliance with formal policies depends on the enforcement of meaningful discipline by the department. The investigation of the Los Angeles police department following the 1991 beating of Rodney King, for example, provided compelling evidence that the department systematically failed to discipline officers guilty of excessive use of physical force.[41] There are anecdotal accounts of other departments winking at their deadly force policies.[42] The ongoing effect of deadly force policies needs to be carefully monitored in the years ahead. Two alternatives are possible. An optimistic scenario has the formal policies bringing about a permanent change in police practices, with potentially positive effects on the police subculture. A less optimistic scenario has the impact of policies slowly eroding, with shootings increasing in response to lax enforcement and community pressures to get tough with crime. At this point, it is simply too early to make a definitive judgment on which scenario will prove correct.

The model offered includes not just the substance of the policies but the process by which they were developed. The rules did not appear by magic or, for that matter, through the good will of police chiefs. Police shootings have been a bitterly controversial civil rights issue and the new rules were developed in response to a combination of local political protests and litigation in the lower courts. The Supreme Court merely ratified (and even then only inadequately) a national consensus that had already developed. What the Court delivered in *Tennessee v. Garner* was too little and too late. This suggests that the present conservative orientation of the Supreme Court, and its disinterest in protecting individual rights, is no necessary barrier to the control of police discretion. With this in mind, we now turn to a second important development over the past twenty years.

Police Response to Domestic Violence

Paralleling the growth of the new deadly force policies has been a movement to control police officer handling of domestic violence incidents. There are important similarities between the two movements. Both involve alleged police discrimination against a powerless group. Both have come to rely on the same reform strategy: controlling officer discretion through written policies. The attempt to control police handling of domestic violence is important for another reason. It represents the only attempt to control the arrest decision, arguably the most important decision in the entire criminal process.

From Arrest Avoidance to Arrest Preferred

The evolution of domestic violence policy dramatizes the impact of political events on criminal justice reform. Between the mid-1960s and the late 1970s the "best thinking" on the police and domestic disturbances underwent a 180-degree shift. In the mid-1960s reformers recommended arrest avoidance. Except in cases of serious criminal violence, police officers were to attempt to solve disputes through mediation, counseling, or referral to social service agencies. Departments were to provide training for these activities.[43] Morton Bard's Family Crisis Intervention (FCI) experiment, which trained police officers in dispute-resolution techniques, was one of the most highly publicized innovations in policing during that period.[44]

Arrest avoidance reflected the related philosophies of rehabilitation and deinstitutionalization, which dominated criminal justice policy in the 1960s. The goal of criminal justice policy was to rehabilitate offenders, and this could be best accomplished outside of criminal justice institutions. Probation was preferable to imprisonment; diversion preferable to prosecution.[45] In the case of domestic problems, counseling or mediation were preferable to arrest. Philosophical considerations aside, police officers traditionally practiced arrest avoidance. Officers systematically underenforced the law with respect to all offenses.[46] An arrest is "work"; it is often difficult and dangerous work that increases the chances of an attack on or complaint against the officer. Arrests for minor crimes, including most domestic assaults, are not valued and rewarded by police departments (the proverbial "big bust" of the armed robber, rapist, or drug dealer is rewarded).

Research on arrest discretion also found that the nature of the relationship between disputing parties had a significant influence over police officer decisions. The more intimate the relationship, the less likely an arrest. Thus officers were less likely to arrest in the case of assaults between married couples or lovers than in the case of strangers. Officers defined the problem as a "private" matter. In the worst manifestation of this attitude, officers adopted the sexist view that violence by husbands against their wives was not a crime.[47]

The idea of arrest avoidance died a sudden death in the 1970s. The women's movement identified spouse abuse as a major problem and focused on the failure of the police to arrest male assailants. Lawsuits challenged arrest avoidance on the grounds that it denied women equal protection of the law by leaving them vulnerable to future violence.[48]

The two most important suits, in Oakland and New York City, resulted in consent decrees that included new police department policies. The new Oakland policy (Fig. 2.3) explicitly stated that the department "will not employ an arrest avoidance policy." While officers "shall

---

OFFICE OF CHIEF OF POLICE
OAKLAND POLICE DEPARTMENT
SPECIAL ORDER NO. 3853

November 1, 1979

Domestic Violence

1. It is the policy of the Oakland Police Department to treat complaints of domestic violence as alleged criminal conduct. For the purposes of this order, "domestic violence" refers to offensive or harmful physical conduct of one spouse or cohabitant, or former spouse or cohabitant, towards the other.
2. The Police Department will not employ an arrest avoidance policy in response to incidents of alleged domestic violence. Although officers shall exercise discretion and shall utilize less punitive options when appropriate (*e.g.*, citation, dispute mediation, referral, citizen's arrest), arrest shall be presumed to be the most appropriate response in domestic violence cases which involve an alleged felony, physical violence committed in the presence of an officer, repeated incidents, or violation of a restraining order.
3. Departmental policy and procedures regarding domestic violence cases are set forth in detail in Training Bulletin III-J, DOMESTIC VIOLENCE AND DOMESTIC DISPUTES.

FIGURE 2.3. Summary policy statement on domestic violence by the Oakland police. (Nancy Loving, *Responding to Spouse Abuse and Wife Beating* [Washington, D.C.: Police Executive Research Forum, 1980], p. 163)

exercise discretion," arrest was declared "the most appropriate response" in cases involving an alleged felony, violence in the presence of the officer, repeat violence, or violation of a protective order. The New York City policy mandated arrest in felonious assaults and specifically stated that the fact that the two parties were married should not be cause for refusing to arrest.[49]

The Impact of Mandatory Arrest

The rising frequency of mandatory arrest focused the attention of researchers on the questions of whether arrest deterred violence. A Police Foundation experiment in Minneapolis found that arrest was more successful in deterring violence over the following six months than either mediation or separating the two parties.[50] Although there were a number of questions about the design of the Minneapolis experiment, it achieved instant notoriety and gave powerful support to the movement for mandatory arrest policies. Between 1984 and 1986 the percentage of departments with mandatory "arrest preferred" policies for minor domestic assault increased from 10 percent to 46 percent. Moreover, 30 percent of all the departments reported that the Minneapolis experiment had influenced their policy.[51] Sherman was criticized for advertising the Minneapolis findings and promoting policy changes on the basis of insufficient empirical evidence (one study).[52] And, in fact, subsequent studies of mandatory arrest have found that it did not deter violence more than alternative dispositions. One even found that arrest increased the violence in the case of unemployed men.[53] These later findings did not noticeably affect the frequency of mandatory arrest, however.

Beginning in the mid-1970s there were also many changes in state statutes on domestic violence. Many states revised their criminal codes to redefine domestic violence, increase the penalties, require more detailed reports of police and/or prosecutors, mandate arrest, or increase police arrest powers in misdemeanor assaults or for violations of protection orders. Prosecutors changed their own policies, almost always in the direction of a more punitive approach.[54]

In important respects, the dynamics of the changes in domestic violence policy were similar to the changes in deadly force policy. In both cases there was a well-organized political constituency pressing for change. Police shootings was an African-American civil rights issue; domestic violence was a feminist issue. It might be noted that although domestic violence was a feminist issue, the idea of mandatory arrest was consistent with the conservative crime control mood of the late 1970s and 1980s. Thus it was swimming with rather than against the political tide.[55]

Mandatory Arrest as Routine Policy

The public's enormous interest in mandatory arrest has focused almost exclusively on the question of whether it deters violence. Only recently have questions been raised about other issues, including possible undesirable consequences.[56] Almost no attention has been focused on the question that concerns us: whether, under routine conditions, police officers will carry out a mandatory arrest policy. Compliance was not an issue in the Minneapolis experiment because the design of the experiment controlled officer discretion. To ensure random assignment of cases, officers were given color-coded incident report forms and instructed to handle each incident in the manner indicated by the top form.[57] This effectively eliminated the officer's use of discretion.[58]

The critical question is whether, under routine, nonexperimental conditions, officers will comply with a mandatory arrest or arrest preferred policy. The evidence on the deadly force policies is extremely relevant here. Despite basic similarities, there are significant differences between the deadly force and domestic policies. In addition, domestic violence and shooting incidents are inherently different, with important implications for the control of discretion.

The first problem is that the new domestic violence policies have no reporting and review requirements (see Fig. 2.3). In the absence of a compliance mechanism, there is good reason to expect that officers would resort to the traditional arrest avoidance practice. A mandatory arrest policy, however strongly worded, may become nothing more than an empty promise, with no effect on actual police practice.

Profound differences between shooting incidents and domestic disturbances also have important implications for control efforts. First, shooting incidents are invested with enormous moral significance: it is a decision to kill someone. This commands the attention of police officers. Written policies and formal training reinforce the moral significance of shooting someone. Second, shootings are relatively rare events. From an administrative standpoint, it is much easier to isolate, focus attention on, and control a rare (and highly serious) event than a common occurrence. Third, shootings are public events. The loud gunshot, the presence of at least one person at the other end, and an unknown number of potential witnesses raise the potential "visibility" of the event. This is a powerful incentive for the officer to complete the required report. Police departments are notorious for being "punishment-centered bureaucracies" which punish officers for breaking a minor rule, such as the failure to fill out a report, while ignoring abuse of citizens.

Domestic disturbances, by contrast, are numerous, ambiguous, and private. Although they account for only about 1 to 10 percent of all police calls (depending on which study you prefer), the cumulative total over the course of a year gives them a routine quality.[59] Nor do they have the same moral significance as shootings. Domestic disturbances occur in private places where there are no potential witnesses who can give an independent account of the incident. Except for the most serious incidents requiring medical attention, domestic assaults do not leave much physical evidence. The shooting incident leaves a fired weapon, a bullet that might be recovered, damage by the bullet—and that is true even if no one is wounded or killed.

Finally, domestic disturbances are extremely ambiguous events. Discussions of the subject have been confused by imprecise terminology. The terms ''domestic disturbance'' and ''domestic violence'' are often used interchangeably.[60] In reality, there are extremely important differences. ''Disturbances'' is a very broad category that includes arguments involving nothing more than loud noise. Only a few police calls to disturbances involve criminal assault. Most of these assaults, moreover, are misdemeanors, with a low level of violence. Relatively few are felonious assaults. The distinction between misdemeanor and felony assault is extremely important in terms of police arrest powers. Generally, officers may arrest in misdemeanors only when the crime occurs in their presence. Some states have recently revised their laws to expand arrest power to include domestic misdemeanor assaults not committed in the presence of officers.

These distinctions over the degree of seriousness have important ramifications for the attempt to control police discretion. Research has indicated that the arrest decision is heavily influenced by the seriousness of the offense. Arrest is far more likely in the case of felonious assault, especially where there is injury, or where a weapon has been used.[61] In other words, the police generally make arrests in the most serious assaults. The new mandatory arrest policies really address a specific category of domestic incidents: the less serious felonious assaults. The point is that in the context of routine police work this is a very small percentage of all domestic incidents.

Another problem is that the new policies do not eliminate the exercise of discretion. The officer has to apply the policy to the facts: Was there in fact an assault? Was it a felonious assault? How serious is that injury? These questions go to the heart of matter in the effort to control discretion: no matter how precisely worded a policy might be, at some point, an official has to apply that policy to the facts and make a decision. Ultimately, there is no escaping discretion.

The fact that nearly all domestic violence incidents occur in private further complicates control efforts. Who is to know that the officer labeled it a misdemeanor assault, despite evidence to the contrary, warned the two parties, and left? Even if the department did have a reporting requirement, it would be extremely difficult for subsequent investigators to determine that the officer misapplied the policy. These incidents are far more numerous than shootings, do not include potential witnesses, and leave no physical evidence.

These cautionary thoughts are intended to raise questions about the efficacy of the new domestic violence policies. The burst of enthusiasm for mandatory arrest in recent years slighted all of these considerations. There are two schools of thought regarding the larger impact of domestic violence, shootings, and other decisions. The cynical view argues that the policies are purely symbolic and are designed primarily as sops to placate the groups advocating them. There is some question about whether new policies are effectively communicated to rank and file officers. Most students of the police have encountered situations where officers are simply unaware of official policy.[62] An alternative view argues that changing police practices is a task akin to turning an ocean liner. It cannot be done suddenly but must be done slowly and in a wide arc. In the case of policing, this means changing the norms of the police officer subculture over a long period of time.[63]

The problem of controlling arrest discretion is an even broader one, however. As indicated previously, domestic violence is the only arrest decision that has been subject to any kind of controls. With this in mind, we now turn to the problem of the general arrest decision.

Arrest Discretion, Generally

Although the use of deadly force is obviously the most critical decision, arrests have a far more pervasive effect on peoples' lives. There are over 13 million arrests a year,[64] and this represents only a portion of all the people who are deprived of their liberty.

Official arrest statistics record only those incidents where the officer completes an arrest report—another important discretionary decision. A Police Foundation survey found great variations among police departments as to *when* officers complete those reports.[65] Most do not fill out arrest reports until the suspect is formally booked at the station house. Yet day in and day out innumerable people are stopped and detained on the street. In both legal and psychological terms, they are under arrest: they are not free to go about their business. Most are quickly released with no official record made. Some suspects are taken to the station house, held, and in some instances questioned briefly before being released. In most departments, no arrest report is made. Yet the deprivation of liberty, the humiliation, the air of suspicion attached to an arrest is the same. As Wayne LaFave put it, "The mere fact that the detention is not called an arrest by police is no basis for distinguishing it from practices which police do refer to as arrests."[66] In short, the actual number of arrests every year could be as high as 26 million people; we really don't know the exact figure.

Nor is the burden of arrest distributed evenly. The police arrest young black men out of all proportion to their presence in the population. A study of arrests in California estimated that 24 percent of all the members of one age cohort were arrested between the ages of eighteen and twenty-nine. By category, the rates were 35 percent for all males, 11 percent for all females, 66 percent for black men, and 34 percent for white men.[67] In other words, two-thirds of all black men in California can expect to be arrested before they reach age thirty. And this does not even count juvenile arrests. Moreover, at least half and perhaps more of the *recorded* arrests do not result in prosecution. Many arrests are dismissed by the police. About half of those that are presented to the prosecutor are subsequently dismissed. The prevalence of arrests among black men, even without prosecution, inevitably creates a sense of oppression.[68]

These data dramatize the impact of routine arrest. Yet this critical decision remains essentially ungoverned.[69] It is important to note that police procedure manuals and police academy training have always focused on technique: how to approach the suspect, how to notify him that he is under arrest, how to frisk for possible weapons, when and how to use handcuffs, and so on.[70] Many of these procedures are designed primarily to protect the officer's safety—as opposed to guaranteeing the rights of the suspect. The emphasis on mechanics and the neglect of substantive decisions are identical to the state of police practices regarding deadly force thirty years ago.

The probable cause standard is the primary instrument for controlling arrest discretion. In practice, however, it is an extremely weak instrument. As a sanction it is essentially reactive and punitive, coming into play only when the arrest reaches a higher level of "visibility," or scrutiny by other officials. At booking, a sergeant may dismiss the case because of weak evidence. In California, 11 percent of all arrests are rejected by the police; another 15 percent are rejected by prosecutors.[71] At the initial appearance before a magistrate, the defense attorney can object to a lack of probable cause. As the case proceeds, it becomes increasingly visible and the standard becomes progressively higher.

As already noted, however, at least half of all arrests never reach even a minimal level of visibility. The probable cause standard does not check the harassment arrest. Nor does it have any impact on failure to arrest. The decision not to arrest is virtually as unreviewable by the judiciary as is the jury's decision to acquit.[72] As the domestic violence issue illustrates, systematic failure to arrest may result in discriminatory outcomes: young black men may be arrested where young white men, for whom there is equally probable cause, are not.

In sum, then, the critical arrest decision represents a major gap in the entire area of discretion control. The most important in–out decision in the entire criminal process—one that affects over 20 million people a year—remains essentially ungoverned.

There is no compelling reason why this should be the case. The domestic violence policies provide a model for possible reform. Departments could draft similar policies designed to guide officers' discretion. In the case of minors in possession of alcohol—where officers frequently confiscate the alcohol and send the kids on their way with a warning—a policy could explicitly state whether arrest is preferred, prescribe criteria (the amount or type of alcohol involved, etc.), outline procedures for notification of parents, and so on. Whether such policies would work is an open question at this point. Nonetheless, there is no reason not to begin to think about means of controlling the critical arrest decision.

Controlling High-Speed Pursuits

The attempt to control high-speed police pursuits is a relatively new development, emerging in the 1980s and gaining ground rapidly by the end of the decade.[73] The emerging policies closely resemble those developed to control deadly force. The decision to pursue is governed by a written policy that guides the officer's discretion, specifying criteria to be considered and leaving open the officer's decision on a narrow range of possible situations. Officers are required to account for their actions in a written report.

Concern about high-speed pursuits had a somewhat different origin than was the case for either deadly force or domestic violence. Pursuits are more random events and do not produce a clearly defined group of victims. A particular family might be roused to action when a family member is injured or killed in a pursuit, but this outrage does not resonate with a broader group that could mobilize politically. Concern about pursuits is largely a matter of municipal liability, with police chiefs or other city officials worried about costly damage suits.

Pursuits resemble shootings in that both involve a discretionary decision that poses substantial risk to human life. The decision, in both cases, was traditionally left entirely to the discretion of the officer. Empirical research on pursuits has found that they pose dangers to both police officers and citizens. In many instances, these risks are unnecessary because the fleeing person is suspected of having committed only a minor crime. Alpert's study of pursuits in Dade County, Florida, found that 33 percent (310 of 952) ended in an accident. Slightly more than half of those accidents (160 of the 310) resulted in an injury. Thirty involved injury to a police officer, 13 involved injury to a bystander, and 7 resulted in the death of the fleeing person. Whereas injuries and deaths as a percentage of all pursuits are not great, the cumulative total is fairly significant for a two-year period (mid-1985 through 1987) in one metropolitan area.[74] In Chicago, meanwhile, a third of all pursuits ended in accidents, with about a quarter of all accidents resulting in injury.[75]

Pursuit Policies

The new policies designed to control pursuits parallel the deadly force policies by asking police officers to weigh the seriousness of the crime against the risk to the community. The guidelines developed by the Ohio Governor's Law Enforcement Liaison Committee (Fig. 2.4) are illustrative of recent policies.

The Ohio guidelines seek to accomplish two things. First, they ask officers to *think*: to think about what they are doing, to weigh the risks, and to make an intelligent choice. Second, they *communicate a set of values*. They make it clear that arrests are not always the highest priority. In some situations the safety of other citizens or the officer's own personal safety has a higher priority. The deadly force policies communicate values in the same fashion. They tell the officer that an arrest is not always the highest priority. Human life is more important. Better, in some situations, to let the suspect flee than to risk a life.[76]

The new pursuit policies confine discretion, in Davis's terms, by specifying a number of forbidden actions. Most of these are the actions

Before pursuing, an officer should ask these questions:

1. Does the seriousness of the crime warrant a chase at excessive speeds?
2. What is the possibility of apprehension?
3. Will the pursuit take place on residential streets, a business district, a freeway, or narrow country type roads?
4. What are the traffic conditions?
5. What are the weather conditions?

FIGURE 2.4. Ohio Governor's Law Enforcement Liaison Committee guidelines. (Geoffrey P. Alpert and Roger G. Dunham, *Police Pursuit Driving* [New York: Greenwood Press, 1990], pp. 131–138)

favored by Hollywood crime movies: ramming cars, "caravanning" (several police cars pursuing in close order), blockades, and so on. Police chiefs face the problem of making sure their young officers do not regard the latest Mel Gibson movie as a training film. The policies also impose an elaborate set of administrative controls to check discretion. Officers are instructed to terminate pursuits if dangerous conditions appear. Sergeants and dispatchers are given explicit authority to order a pursuit terminated if they feel conditions warrant it.

Finally, like the deadly force policies, virtually all of the new pursuit policies require a written report by the officer, with the report being subject to automatic review by high-ranking officers. In Davis's terms, this checks discretion.

The development of police pursuit policies has been somewhat haphazard—as is the case with most police policies. Some states, however, have taken a relatively comprehensive approach. In 1981, for example, Nebraska passed a law requiring all police departments to adopt pursuit policies. The law did not specify the content of that policy, only that there be one.[77] This approach follows the general model of administrative rulemaking, where statute compels rulemaking but leaves the specifics to the agencies in question.[78]

The Impact of Pursuit Policies

Pursuit policies are relatively new and the research on the nature of pursuits is very recent. To date, there are no evaluations of the impact of restrictive policies on pursuits and we have only impressionistic evidence that they reduce pursuits, deaths, and injuries.

There are good reasons to believe that policies may succeed in achieving their intended results. Pursuits resemble shootings in important respects. First, they are public events. The officer must assume that other people in the department and the community will be aware of the event. This encourages compliance with departmental policy. Moreover, pursuits are not split-second events. Unlike shooting incidents, the officer does not have to make an immediate decision on the basis of incomplete information. There is time to consider all of the factors indicated in the written policy (the suspected offense, road conditions, presence of bystanders, etc.). The lapse of time also allows other police officials (the sergeant, the dispatcher) to have a voice in the matter.

Finally, the consequences of not pursuing are substantially less serious than not shooting a suspect. In the respective worst case scenarios, not shooting might mean death for the officer, whereas not pursing would mean only the escape of a suspect (but with increased safety for the officer).

Searches, Seizures, and Interrogations

Because of the long controversy over Supreme Court decisions, the areas of search and seizure and interrogation are probably the most well-known instances of rule-governed police behavior. Virtually everyone has heard about the exclusionary rule and the "*Miranda* warning." Unfortunately, few people have a good understanding of the full impact of the decisions in question. The enormous political controversy surrounding these decisions over the last thirty years has been framed in very limited terms. With the passing of time, the ground has shifted. There are new developments and important new data, both of which are relevant to the control of police discretion.

From our perspective we should view the *Mapp* and *Miranda* decisions as court-developed rules limiting police discretion. In the case of *Mapp* the Court created no new rule but rather a means of enforcing an old rule, the Fourth Amendment protection against unreasonable searches and seizures.[79] That enforcement mechanism is the exclusion of illegally gained evidence and possible loss of the entire criminal case. *Miranda*, on the other hand, created a new and very detailed set of rules designed to enforce the general command of the Fifth and Sixth Amendments.[80] It used the same enforcement mechanism, the exclusion of the evidence (in this case testimony) obtained in violation of the rule.

The controversies surrounding *Mapp, Miranda,* and other Court decisions concerning the police involve a number of different legal and political issues. Should the Supreme Court take an activist role or exercise judicial restraint? Should it insist on national standards, based on the Bill of Rights, or defer to the judgment of state legislatures and state courts? What priority should it give to individual rights as opposed to other considerations (e.g., public safety)?

Our concern here is not with the jurisprudential issues but with the practical effect of the decisions as rules governing police discretion. The Court explicitly fashioned the exclusionary rule as a deterrent to police misconduct and characterized the *Miranda* rules in similar terms. After more than twenty-five years, it is safe to say that neither conservative nightmares nor liberal dreams have been realized. The decisions have not crippled law enforcement, as conservatives feared,[81] nor have they ended police misconduct, as liberals had hoped. Nonetheless, the decisions have had subtle long-term effects that are relevant to the question of discretion control.

Politics and Police Discretion

CONSERVATIVE NIGHTMARES. Abundant research has demonstrated that neither the exclusionary rule nor the *Miranda* warning limits the crime-fighting capacity of the police. Attempts by the Reagan administration Justice Department to prove otherwise failed spectacularly.[82]

The evidence is overwhelming that the exclusionary rule has no impact whatsoever on police handling of the "high-fear" crimes of murder, rape, robbery, and burglary. Due process problems as a whole accounted for only 5 percent of the dismissals at the initial screening in Washington, D.C.[83] A larger study of dismissals in California found the rule affected only eight-tenths of 1 percent of all felony cases, and the rule accounted for only 4.8 percent of all dismissals.[84]

The only noticeable effect of the exclusionary rule has been on drug, weapons possession, and gambling cases. This is understandable since these crimes involve the most problematic evidence-gathering questions. Even in drug cases, the rule's effect is marginal at best. Sheldon Krantz and colleagues found that in Boston motions to suppress evidence were made in only 13 percent of all drug and gambling cases and only 16.4 percent of those motions were successful. Thus, it succeeded in only 2 percent of all the original drug and gambling cases.[85]

The potentially disturbing aspect of the exclusionary rule is the possibility that it might encourage police lying. In the first study of the rule's impact, Dallin Oaks noted the "dropsy" phenomenon. There was an increase in the number of officers claiming that the defendant had dropped the narcotics on the ground, thus allowing the officer to obtain it legally.[86]

The dropsy phenomenon and its counterparts in other areas of the criminal process raise fundamental questions about the impact of rules. If, as some critics argue, formal rules only encourage creative evasion, then the attempt to control discretion may be both ineffective and, in some respects, positively harmful. There is another side to the issue, however, which emphasizes the long-term positive effects of the exclusionary rule. We will examine this phenomenon shortly.

LIBERAL DREAMS. Liberal dreams that the Supreme Court alone could reform policing, along with the rest of the criminal justice system, have also been unfulfilled. Even many supporters of the exclusionary rule have pointed out that at best it is an extremely weak enforcement mechanism.[87] As a sanction, it is reactive, coming into play only when there is a criminal prosecution. Yet no more than half of all arrests ever come before a magistrate. More important, criminal law enforcement represents only a part of police work—between 20 and 30 percent of a patrol officer's activities.[88] Thus, sanctions on the use of illegally obtained evidence leave the vast bulk of police work completely untouched.

The Impact of Miranda

The initial studies of the impact of *Miranda* raised questions about its effect on routine police work. They found that defendants regularly waived their rights to silence and to an attorney and talked with detectives.[89] Neal Milner's study of four small police departments in Wisconsin, however, reached a somewhat more hopeful conclusion. In those departments that were more professionalized, *Miranda* had the least significant impact on arrests and convictions and the officers were least hostile to it. This suggests that the basic thrust of the decision was compatible with professional police practices.[90]

All these studies, however, were conducted in the immediate aftermath of the *Miranda* decision. The police were scrambling to adjust to the new requirement and, by all accounts, officers were extremely hostile to it. Regrettably, there are no studies of the long-term response which would take into account changes in training, supervision, and general familiarity with the requirements of the decision.

The long-term accommodation to *Miranda* involves a number of unanswered questions. One possibility is that police officers have become extremely adept at complying with the formal requirements of the warning while inducing suspects to waive their rights and to talk. This is a more subtle form of evasion than the dropsy phenomenon, since it doesn't involve outright perjury. On the other hand, compliance may have become routinized, with officers generally halting interrogations when suspects refuse to talk. They know that failure to do so could risk loss of the case. In short, the deterrent effect may work. The warning may be a somewhat empty formality but it may also establish some limits on the conduct of interrogations, eliminating the grosser forms of coercion. Given the long history of brutal police interrogation practices, this is an accomplishment that should not be dismissed as trivial.

The Problem of Empty Formalism: A Look at Search Warrants

The problem of empty formalism cannot be readily dismissed, however. It is a general problem facing all formal rules in every aspect of the criminal justice system. The problem can be stated in the following terms: Do rules degenerate into an empty ritual which respects the letter of the law but not the spirit of justice? Since the answer may not be a simple yes or no, a more subtle way of posing the question might be: How empty is empty formalism?

Studies of the search warrant process offer some insight into this matter. The Fourth Amendment mentions two kinds of searches: those with and those without a warrant. There has long been a consensus of opinion that searches under a warrant are preferable to warrantless searches. The warrant functions as a rule in the terms used here. It holds the officer accountable by requiring him or her to specify the evidence to be seized, the source of the information, and the reliability of the informant. The judge who reviews this information and issues the warrant functions as a check on police discretion.

Few people have any illusions about the warrant process. Critics have long pointed out that reliance on informants is fraught with problems.[91] Informants have their own motives and generally inspire little trust. After all, the best sources of information are people who are either engaged in criminal activity or close to others who are. Some become adept at manipulating their handlers.[92] The standard statements by detectives that the informant has provided valuable information in the past

are seen as self-serving. Finally, many observers feel that local judges
are largely uncritical. By virtue of personal contact or a shared set of
assumptions about crime, they generally accept whatever the police tell
them and issue the warrant.

A study of the warrant process by the National Center For State
Courts (NCSC) found a very mixed picture. In general, the Fourth
Amendment's warrant requirement "often appeared to operate much as
intended." It inhibited "impulsive" searches by police and produced
a "higher standard of care than would otherwise be the case."[93] A
study of Chicago narcotics detectives, meanwhile, found that the 1961
Mapp decision had encouraged a greater reliance on the use of warrants
and discouraged the more problematic warrantless searches.[94]

The NCSC report warned, however, that it would be a "gross overstatement" to say that the warrant process worked as intended. There
are numerous ways of getting around both the command of the Fourth
Amendment and the specific requirements of the warrant process. Not
only were most searches in the NCSC study warrantless, but most were
"consent" searches. While a consent search is constitutional, there are
always questions about exactly how voluntary the consent is. As in so
many areas of policing, the imaginative officer can find ways of obtaining the necessary consent.

Some of the most disturbing testimony about search warrants came
from judges. Whereas some judges routinely failed to scrutinize warrant
applications closely, others expressed concern about their ability to
scrutinize them in a meaningful fashion. The heart of the judge's problem is determining the reliability of the information presented in the
warrant application. The NCSC study found that most of the affidavits
they examined "were often barely distinguishable from one another."
They were simply "boilerplate" that could be put together by cutting
and pasting from old affidavits.[95]

Confidential informants posed the greatest problem. The typical af-
fidavit declared the "information provided by this informant has resulted
in at least——arrests. . . . Informant has never given false or misleading
information." It requires enormous naïveté to accept such statements
at face value. It was particularly significant that in every case where a
judge ordered the informant produced, the prosecutor dismissed the
charges.[96] We can view this from two perspectives. On the one hand,
it tends to confirm all the doubts about the reliability of confidential
informants. Why else would prosecutors be so reluctant to produce

them? On the other hand, it offers some modest grounds for confidence in the warrant review process. Asking that the informant be produced does seem to check questionable searches. The important question, of course, is how often judges take this step.

Not So Empty Formalism: Positive Effects of the Exclusionary Rule

Formalism may not be entirely empty. There is good evidence that the exclusionary rule, to take one noted example, has had positive long-term effects on policing.

In the thirty-year battle over the exclusionary rule, conservative politicians have engaged in rhetoric about criminals being set free. The debate among the scholars, meanwhile, focused on attempts to measure the deterrent effect of the rule through statistical tests. How many cases were "lost," or suppressed, because of search and seizure problems?[97]

Despite this enormous public interest, there is only one detailed study of how the exclusionary rule affects day-to-day detective work. Myron Orfield interviewed narcotics officers in the Chicago police department in the mid-1980s. This was an excellent choice, since it has been well established that the rule affects drug cases far more than any other category of crime. If it has any effect, good or bad, this is where to find it.[98]

Orfield's findings contradict all the objections to the exclusionary rule and provide persuasive evidence that it has had a profound and continuing effect on improving the quality of police work. He identified five major institutional reforms resulting from the exclusionary rule. First, there was a significant increase in screening of warrants by prosecutors. In the terms established by Kenneth C. Davis, this represents an important check on discretion. It is also a quality-control measure. Relations between police and prosecutors were expanded to include general advice and formal training by the state's attorney's office.

Second, the police department instituted an officer-rating system that included a measure of cases lost through suppression of evidence. Officers reported that more than two suppressions in major cases in one year could easily jeopardize chances for promotion. The question of performance evaluation is extremely important and deserves further research. Another study of felony arrests found that supervisors were little interested in the "quality" of arrests, measured in terms of their ultimate outcomes.[99] If Orfield's findings have general applicability, then we could conclude that rules work because compliance becomes important to an officer's career. If, on the other hand, supervisors are generally uninterested in compliance, we are forced to a different conclusion about the efficacy of rules.

Third, police training improved substantially. One officer who had joined the Chicago police department in 1954 did not recall any discussion of the law of search and seizure. Formal training began in the 1960s and was increased from eight or nine to fourteen hours in the early 1980s. Moreover, training now included the actual writing of warrant applications.

Fourth, the department instituted the use of a monitoring device. Whenever evidence was suppressed, officers were required to complete a Court Disposition and Attendance Form, which asked them to explain the reasons for the suppression. This was followed by an internal review session or discussion with supervisors about the problem.

Fifth, the exclusionary rule produced a significant increase in the use of warrants. Veteran officers recalled that in the early 1960s they "seldom" used warrants. Two decades later, nearly all preplanned searches involved warrants. The impact on the quality of searches was dramatic. Searches with warrants rarely led to the suppression of evidence.

Narcotics officers reported that the exclusionary rule had affected their work. Virtually all reported that the experience of testifying in court, especially losing a suppression hearing, was the best training they ever got. They also reported that they rarely had evidence suppressed for the same reason, indicating that they in fact learned something from the previous experience. They not only learned much about the substantive law and the techniques for drafting successful warrants, but they acquired a definite preference for the use of warrants.

On the negative side, officers reported that in most of the cases where their evidence had been suppressed, they *had* understood the law. They chose to risk a bad search in order to get the drugs off the street. This suggests that officers are undeterred by the exclusionary rule when they are not interested in conviction. At the same time, it suggests that when they are interested in conviction, they know the law and understand the risks of bending it.

Direct and Indirect Effects of the Supreme Court

Some caution must be used to avoid generalizing too broadly on the basis of Orfield's study of one department (although the fact that it involves a department not known for its level of professionalism does suggest that things could be even better in other departments with better reputations). With this caveat in mind, however, his study is richly suggestive about the direct and indirect changes in policing resulting from the landmark Supreme Court cases of the 1960s. Far too much attention has focused on the precise holding of particular decisions and their progeny. Other effects may have been pervasive and lasting.

First, the Court's decisions focused public attention on police decision making and its impact on individual liberty. This raised the level of public awareness of the constitutional aspects of police work to an extraordinarily high level. A survey of public awareness of individual rights, on the occasion of the bicentennial of the Bill of Rights, found that although only 33 percent of respondents could correctly identify the Bill of Rights, 80 percent knew that they had a right to remain silent if arrested.[100] No one has yet studied the impact of citizen awareness of rights as a "check" on police behavior: To what extent are police officers constrained by the fact that a citizen verbally asserts a right? The "rights revolution" of the past twenty-five years has been accompanied by the growth of the "rights industry," a network of civil rights and civil liberties organizations along with innumerable private attorneys specializing in civil rights work. The existence of this "industry" represents a resource that the citizen can call upon. Does it make a difference that police officers know (or at least believe) that a local ACLU or NAACP office might come to the aid of this particular citizen? With respect to the long-term effect of law on police behavior, these still-uninvestigated questions are enormously important.

Second, the Court stimulated wide-ranging reforms in the education, training, and supervision of police officers.[101] The law enforcement accreditation movement is one response to court intervention that now has a life of its own. Third, as Orfield's research suggests, the intervention of the courts has altered the context of the working environment of policing.[102] The principle of accountability—that there are limits on police powers, that those limits can be set down in writing (whether a court decision or a departmental rule), and that officers should be routinely expected to answer for whether they comply with those rules—has been established, at least as an ideal.[103] This principle is an established fact of life for a new generation of police officers.

Conclusions

In the end, what have we accomplished? After more than thirty years of intensive agitation, litigation, research, and reform, have we brought police discretion under control? A fair assessment would be that we have made a start. We have succeeded in imposing *some control* over *some decisions*. Many—even most—important decisions remain untouched. Nor can we say with absolute certainty that the rules that do exist work as intended (although the research on the deadly force rules is very persuasive). It would be easy to focus on how much has not been accomplished and to cite current headlines about police misconduct (the beating of Rodney King) as evidence that no improvements have been made. This would be a mistake. Rather, we should examine the positive gains that have been made and attempt to draw some lessons about the possibilities for further progress. The principal accomplishments and failures of the past thirty years can be summarized as follows.

First, and most important, we have brought the issue of police discretion into the open. It is now out of shadows and into the realm of public debate. This alone is an enormous accomplishment. Unlike thirty years ago, we now have a realistic understanding of what police officers do as well as a reasonable understanding of why they act the way they do and the problems that are associated with discretion. Although we are impressed with the difficulty of controlling discretion, this is an improvement over the blissful ignorance that prevailed thirty years ago.

Second, we have succeeded in establishing the principle of accountability. If we do not fully implement this principle in practice, at least we know what our ideal is. Police officers should be held accountable for their actions. There are things they must do and things they must not do. And we have a network of rules designed to implement those commands. The most important thing is that the principle of accountability is recognized by police officers, criminal suspects, and citizens alike. Every junior high school student knows that suspects are entitled to their "*Miranda* rights." They often have the details wrong, but the principle that there are limits on police officer behavior, and penalties for breaking those rules, is firmly established. To an extent that we understand only imperfectly at present, we may have succeeded in altering the context of the police subculture, establishing both the principle and the mechanics of accountability as facts of life in police work.

Given the lawless context of policing thirty years ago, this is also no small achievement.

Third, we have succeeded in controlling a number of critical police decisions and, as a consequence, curbed some of the grosser forms of abuse. The control of deadly force is a major achievement. The emerging controls over pursuits also promises to be a major step forward. The rules over search and seizure and interrogations, while more difficult to document, have probably reduced some of the worst police behavior.

Fourth, the important area of arrest remains very problematic. It is the most important substantive decision police officers make regarding individual liberty. We have taken a small but significant step forward with respect to controlling discretion in domestic violence situations. We are not yet convinced that the new rules will succeed on a routine basis. But at least we have a realistic sense of why they might not work and what it might take to make them work. Consideration of the arrest decision reminds us that there are many other decision points that remain free of any meaningful controls.

In conclusion, then, there are grounds for cautious optimism. The situation is not totally hopeless. We have made a start in bringing police discretion under control. These small beginnings provide useful lessons for future reform efforts. Nor does the current posture of the Supreme Court mean there is no hope for controlling police discretion. Administrative rulemaking, prompted by vigorous political advocacy, remains a viable avenue of reform.

3

The Two Bail Reform Movements

Politics and Bail Reform

Nowhere is the impact of shifting political winds on criminal justice policy more evident than in the case of bail. In the space of little more than fifteen years the bail issue went through three different phases, with each change driven by a change in the political climate.

Until the early 1960s there was virtually no interest in the problems associated with bail. A national bail reform movement suddenly emerged in the 1960s, emphasizing justice for the poor and seeking to reduce pretrial detention of criminal suspects. The bail reform movement captured the attention of the White House, the Congress, the news media, and a national network of reformers and scholars. Within the space of just a few years, it stimulated dozens of innovative bail programs in local jurisdictions, the landmark federal Bail Reform Act in 1966, and bail reform laws in several states.[1]

Just as this movement was reaching its peak, however, the political winds shifted. In response to rising crime rates, interest in crime control replaced concern for poor defendants. The result was a second bail reform movement, seeking preventive detention laws designed to allow judges to deny bail to defendants deemed "dangerous" to the community. The shift in the national mood was marked by a 1970 preventive detention law for the District of Columbia. The second bail reform

54

movement was at least as successful as the first. By 1978, twenty-three states had some form of preventive detention; by 1984, the total had reached thirty-four states.[2] In 1984, Congress passed a federal preventive detention law which the Supreme Court declared constitutional three years later.[3]

A Brief History of Bail as a Discretion Problem

Both bail reform movements sought to control judicial discretion in bail setting. The basic questions remained the same: Which defendants secure release before trial? On what criteria? The first bail reform movement saw the problem as the detention of too many people. Specifically, the money bail system discriminated against the poor, forcing them to remain in jail awaiting trial. Caleb Foote's pioneering research found that in addition to the indignities of being held in jail, persons detained were more likely to be convicted and, when convicted, more likely to be incarcerated than those defendants who were released. The second bail reform movement defined the problem in terms of too many people obtaining pretrial release. Research focused on the amount of crime committed by persons out on bail. Although the two reform movements had very different social policy goals, both defined the problem in terms of the discretion of the bail-setting judge.

Both bail reform movements confronted the tension between law and practice. On the one hand, the Anglo-American legal tradition asserts a right to bail in all noncapital cases. The exact nature of that right has long been a matter of debate, however. The Eighth Amendment to the U.S. Constitution prohibits "excessive bail" but does not explicitly guarantee an absolute right to bail. Nor does the Eighth Amendment offer any standards for determining what constitutes excessive bail. The Eighth Amendment notwithstanding, bail practices in the United States have historically resulted in the pretrial detention of many suspects. Traditionally, this has been accomplished covertly with the judge setting a bail amount that is clearly beyond the means of the defendant. Thus the nominal "right" to bail is honored in principle with detention assured in practice.[4]

Caleb Foote almost singlehandedly launched and defined the terms of the contemporary debate over bail with his pioneering 1954 study of bail practices in Philadelphia.[5] He found a stark contrast between constitutional ideal and actual practice. About 75 percent of all suspects did not obtain pretrial release. In addition to the denial of a presumptive constitutional right, detention imposed other penalties. Detention itself was a form of punishment. The condition of many local jails was and still is deplorable. Unlike prisons, local jails are not equipped for long-term detention and typically have fewer services and recreational facilities. Detention, moreover, increased the likelihood of conviction and subsequent imprisonment. Nearly three-quarters (72%) of those detained in Philadelphia were convicted, compared with only 52 percent of those who obtained their release. Of those convicted, 59 percent of those detained were given a prison sentence, compared with only 22 percent of those who had been released.[6] Finally, a number of experts argued that excessive pretrial detention contributed to the problem of jail over-crowding. As recently as 1982, some 57 percent of all people in jail on any given day were there awaiting trial.[7]

The widespread detention of defendants before trial was not inad-vertent. It reflected a conscious decision on the part of judges to detain those people deemed ''dangerous,'' in terms of their propensity either to commit crimes while out on bail or to flee and not appear in court. This factor introduced an additional criticism of bail practices: that predictions of ''dangerousness'' were routinely made without any em-pirical foundation and were based on supposition, stereotypes, and out-right bias.[8] Some reformers objected to the excessive detention of defendants but did not object to a rational, empirically based system of selective pretrial detention.[9]

Because the law (until recently) did not authorize pretrial detention for the purpose of protecting the community, judges did it covertly. The simplest expedient was to set money bail at a figure they were sure the offender did not have. One study in the mid-1970s found that bail for armed robbers averaged $3,075 in Detroit, $7,719 in Chicago, and $23,686 in Baltimore.[10] Virtually all armed robbers are poor and it is a reasonably safe bet that the average Baltimore robber does not have $2,300 (assuming the existence of a 10% bail plan). Nor are those robbers in Detroit or Chicago who have a higher than average bail likely to have sufficient money available to make bail.

The practice of detaining defendants through high bail is another illustration of the covert decision making that has traditionally pervaded the entire criminal justice system. The most shocking and influential revelations of the American Bar Foundation survey—with respect to police discretion, plea bargaining, and other decision points—involved the process by which officials made low-visibility decisions that were not authorized by the law and were in many instances questionable or blatantly illegal.[11]

The Bail Decision

Decision Points

Like so many other decisions in criminal justice, the bail decision is far more complex than appears at first glance. It is not a simple either–or, bail–no bail decision by a judge. In practice it is an extremely complex process, involving a number of decisions, several different decision makers, and a number of considerations.

The basic judicial decision in all but a handful of cases is whether to set monetary bail or to release the person without financial considerations. Historically, judges have always been able to release defendants on their own recognizance, even without specific statutory authorization. The first bail reform movement sought to control that decision in two ways. First, new bail laws declared as a matter of social policy that release on recognizance was the presumptive decision. They directed judges to choose that option unless there were extenuating circumstances. Second, bail reform attempted to make decisions empirically sound by providing accurate information about the defendant. Generally, this involved the creation of a pretrial services agency whose staff would collect and verify information about the defendant's criminal and social history.

Both nonmonetary and monetary bail options involve considerable discretion. For the person released on his or her recognizance, the judge can impose a number of conditions: limiting travel, requiring employment, undergoing treatment, and so on. Some of the most important bail reforms have involved creating social service agencies to facilitate these goals. In the case of money bail, the judge has nearly unlimited discretion as to the dollar amount. The only exceptions to this are jurisdictions that have adopted fixed bail schedules. This reform, however, has been limited to misdemeanor cases. The unlimited discretion as to the dollar amount has been the traditional window of opportunity for covert preventive detention.

Decision Makers

Whereas the judge has the formal authority to set bail, studies of the bail-setting process have found that in practice other officials play some role in influencing the decision. The relevant actors are the police, the prosecutor, the defense attorney, other court officials (clerks, bailiffs, etc.), and, in certain cases, the bail bondsman.[12]

Police officers can influence bail decisions in two important ways. First, the arresting officer's decision as to the officially recorded offense shapes the decisions of all the other actors. All the studies of bail have found that the seriousness of the offense is a major factor—perhaps *the* most important one—in decision making.[13] Thus the officer's decision to formally arrest someone for assault rather than rape is likely to result in a series of more lenient decisions: a greater likelihood of obtaining pretrial release, a greater chance of having charges dismissed or bargained down to a misdemeanor, a vastly reduced chance of going to prison, and so on. These considerations add perspective to the subject of police discretion. As Chapter 2 indicated, the basic decision to arrest is essentially ungoverned by any formal controls. In the event of an arrest, the decision as to the "offense" is also ungoverned.[14]

Police officers also influence bail decisions through the information they provide to the judge. Derogatory information about the suspect's character, behavior at the time of arrest, or the crime itself—information which the officer can easily manipulate—substantially reduces the likelihood of pretrial release.[15]

Virtually all studies of bail have found that the prosecutor is the dominant nonjudicial figure in the bail-setting process. First, the prosecutor determines the formal charge, reviewing and often revising the charge filed by the arresting officer. The prosecutor is also the judge's primary source of information about the defendant and the offense, filtering the information that comes from the police. The prosecutor informs the judge about the strength of the evidence, which judges generally interpret as a sign of probable innocence or guilt.[16] Most important of all, the prosecutor makes recommendations about bail: release or no release and the dollar amount. This is enormously influential because judges generally follow these recommendations— 80 percent of the time according to one study.[17] The prosecutor also plays the leading role in the handling of appeals for reduction in bail.

The defense attorney is probably the weakest of the nonjudicial figures in bail setting. Judges tend to reflexively defer to the judgment of the prosecutor.[18] Perhaps the most important aspect of the defense attorney's role is the simple fact that he or she is there. The changing role of the defense attorney over the past thirty years represents a hidden revolution in the criminal justice process. At least through the 1950s many felony defendants (perhaps as many as half) went to trial without an attorney.[19] As a result of the Supreme Court's 1963 decision in *Gideon v. Wainwright*, felony defendants now receive at least some nominal representation. The main impact of this change with respect to bail setting is that it probably helps curb the worst abuses. There is someone present to challenge grossly excessive bail or derogatory information that is completely without factual basis. The manner in which criminal defense is provided may make a significant difference. Wice found that defense attorneys were present in about 25 percent of all initial bail settings, but they were present 50 percent of the time in jurisdictions with large public defender systems.[20] In short, a large and professionalized public defender system may provide better representation in bail decisions than a mixed public and private system.[21]

Finally, there are other courthouse employees who, in some jurisdictions, have some influence over bail setting. These officials traditionally included clerks, secretaries, and bailiffs. Paul Wice, for example, found that in some busy urban criminal courts, where cases are handled on an assembly-line basis, many judges rely on these secondary officials to collect and assemble the information about the case. This seemingly routine clerical task becomes critical to bail setting when the information in question involves the nature of the charge. In Detroit, for example, Wice found that judges relied on the arraignment officers for recommendations on bail.[22]

The role of these other courthouse personnel has been greatly enhanced by the first bail reform movement. The principal institutional change was the creation of pretrial release agencies with staff who would collect and verify information about the defendant. Thus the bail decision would have a factual basis instead of being based on supposition or bias. But, of course, everything hinges on the quality of that information, which, in turn, depends on the professionalism of the pretrial release agency's staff.

The Bail-Setting Process

With many different officials involved, bail setting is very much a group decision. Frederic Suffett described it as an exchange relationship among the various members of the courtroom work group.[23] Basically, judges prefer to share the responsibility through a process of negotiation. Prosecutors traditionally ask for high bail and defense attorneys respond by asking for lower bail. The net result is a rough consensus as to the amount of bail. Suffett is quick to point out that not all the players are equal in this negotiation–exchange process. The prosecutor carries far more weight with the judge and prevails about 80 percent of the time.

The underlying purpose of seeking consensus is to spread the responsibility should something go wrong, for example, the defendant committing a serious crime while out on bail or fleeing altogether. Judges insulate themselves from criticism for having released a "dangerous" offender by pointing out that other key actors, particularly the prosecutor, agreed to it. Suffett's findings were consistent with those of other studies of bail setting: considerations of public safety dominate decisions, and "dangerousness" is defined in terms of the seriousness of the pending charge and the criminal record of the defendant.

Roy B. Flemming's comparative study of bail setting in Detroit and Baltimore illustrated how different institutional arrangements can increase or decrease the exposure of bail-setting officials to community pressures about getting tough on crime. He found a relatively very low rate of release on recognizance in Baltimore (11.8% of all felony defendants) compared with Detroit (48.8%), even though the Baltimore bail process had been extensively "reformed" on two occasions. This resulted partly from the political vulnerability of the people actually setting bail. Reform in Maryland put responsibility for bail setting in the hands of court commissioners, appointed by the chief judge of the statewide court system. In practice, the commissioners felt extremely vulnerable to political pressures, particularly pressures to get tough with criminals. Judges in Detroit, on the other hand, were more independent and less vulnerable to the same kind of pressures.[24]

Predictions of Dangerousness

The decision to detain a defendant before trial is essentially a prediction about that person's future behavior. The judge is predicting that the person is likely to commit another crime if released and/or fail to appear in court on the present charge.

The bail decision is not unique in this respect. Many, if not most, decisions in the criminal justice system involve a prediction, either implicitly or explicitly.[25] Arrest decisions are often influenced by officer predictions about whether the victim will cooperate with the prosecution or how the prosecutor and/or judge will respond to the case. The decision to prosecute is often based on a prediction about the probability of conviction. Sentencing decisions also contain an important predictive element. Probation tends to be granted to those convicted offenders the judge believes will not pose a serious threat to the community by committing additional serious crimes. The parole release decision has historically been the most overtly predictive of all decisions. The decision that the offender is "rehabilitated" reflects a judgment that he will not commit any more crime. A disproportionate share of all research in the area of corrections from the 1930s through the 1960s was devoted to improving predictions.[26]

All of the empirical studies of bail have found that these predictions are based primarily on two criteria: offense seriousness and prior record.[27] At the same time, however, the empirical research on bail has consistently found that these criteria are not accurate predictors of "failure," in terms of new crimes while out on bail or failure to appear. Failure-to-appear rates are generally very low and many failures are unintentional. Crime on bail was also relatively low. A 1970 study by the National Bureau of Standards found that only 11 percent of all defendants were rearrested while on bail. This included persons charged with both felonies and misdemeanors. Felony defendants were more likely to be rearrested (17%) but only half of those arrests were for another felony. In other words, only 7 percent of all felony defendants were rearrested for another felony.[28] The most recent national survey found that 18 percent of all felony defendants in the fifty-seven largest counties in 1988 were rearrested while on pretrial release. Only 3 percent of the total were arrested for a violent offense and 6 percent were arrested for a drug offense.[29]

Studies of preventive detention indicated that only 5 percent of defendants who would be potentially eligible for detention without bail would be rearrested for a violent crime. A Boston study estimated that 14.5 percent would be rearrested for some offense, but only 5.2 percent for a violent crime.[30] Evaluations of the 1984 federal preventive deten-

tion law found that failure-to-appear rates were extremely low beforehand (between 1.3 and 2.1% in four district courts) and remained just
as low after the law went into effect. Rearrest rates were also low.
Before the law went into effect, the highest rearrest rate in the four
districts studied was 2.4 percent.[31] These data supported the liberal
criticism of traditional bail-setting practices to the effect that bail decisions were empirically unsound and that judges "overpredict" by
detaining many people who do not pose any genuine risk.

Decisions and Detention Resources

Flemming argued that bail-setting decisions are highly constrained by
existing resources, specifically the capacity of the local jail. If for
political or legal reasons (a court order limiting the number of inmates,
for example) it is not possible to detain a high rate of defendants,
detention rates will be lower. Decisions, in other words, are not made
in a vacuum and bail reformers have erred by focusing on bail-setting
procedures and ignoring the larger context of resources. He concludes
that limiting the capacity of the jail might be the most effective way of
reducing pretrial detention.[32]

Controlling Discretion in Bail Setting

Common sense might suggest that discretion in bail setting would be
relatively easier to control than some other decisions. Unlike most police
decisions, the bail decision is highly "visible": it occurs in open court
and leaves a written record. This visibility presumably heightens accountability and serves to control discretion. And as Suffett's research
indicates, judges do feel that their bail-setting decisions are exposed to
public view—although the impact on bail decisions is complex and
troublesome.[33]

Additionally, bail setting includes an adversarial element, where the
judge hears competing bail recommendations from the prosecutor and
defense attorney. One of the most troublesome aspects of hidden decision making is the absence of even the opportunity for an adversarial
confrontation, where facts can be tested and assumptions challenged.

Defining discretionary decisions in criminal justice in terms of their
relative visibility sheds some interesting light on bail setting. The relatively high visibility of the bail decision gives it much in common

with sentencing. This may help to explain why both bail reform and sentencing reform have generally been addressed legislatively. Police discretion and plea bargaining, on the other hand, are extremely low-visibility decisions, hidden from public view. This may account for the fact that they have been addressed primarily through administrative regulations rather than legislation.

Greater visibility should improve the chances of formal control. The first step in any control process, after all, is to identify the decision point and the relevant decision maker(s). The control of plea bargaining, as Chapter 4 will explain, is enormously complicated by the fact that the disposition of a case involves three officials and the defendant. The advantages of visibility with respect to the bail decision may be more apparent than real, however. The evidence of twenty-five years of bail reform suggests that the decision may be as elusive and resistant to control as the more hidden decisions in the criminal process.

The attempts to control discretion in bail setting take several forms: abolition, guided discretion, and expanded discretionary options. Some reforms seek to abolish discretion by denying bail to certain categories of offenders. A few have developed fixed schedules of bail amounts. Others attempt to guide discretion by declaring a presumptive outcome, although leaving the judge with discretion regarding the actual decision. Some of the most prevalent reforms seek to influence judicial discretion by defining certain options explicitly and creating procedures for providing the judge with more information on which to make bail decisions. The underlying assumption is that the availability of information will lead to more rational decisions.

The First Bail Reform Movement: Discretion Guidance

The first bail reform movement burst onto the American scene in the early 1960s. Until then, there had been little public interest in bail problems and no serious prospects for reform.[34] Caleb Foote's account of the fate of his studies illustrates the dramatic shift in the political climate. His 1954 study of bail in Philadelphia documented the fact that 75 percent of all defendants were unable to secure their release before trial and those detained were more likely to be convicted and imprisoned than those who did secure release.[35] The dean of the University of Pennsylvania Law School was very impressed with Foote's article and had it reprinted and distributed to judges, prosecutors, law professors, and the news media. According to Foote, there was absolutely no response. He later said that by 1960 only a madman would have predicted a serious bail reform movement.[36]

Then, suddenly, everything changed. The Vera Institute of Justice launched the Manhattan Bail Project in 1961 with little, if any, fanfare. It was designed to facilitate the release of defendants on nonfinancial conditions by identifying those who had strong community ties, in the form of jobs or family ties, and therefore were unlikely to flee the jurisdiction.[37] The idea quickly captured the imagination of national leaders, including the new attorney general, Robert Kennedy. The money bail system was critically examined by the Attorney General's Conference on Poverty and the Administration of Justice in 1963 and in even more detail by the 1964 National Conference on Bail. Cosponsored by the Vera Institute, the latter conference gave a powerful endorsement to its approach to bail reform. Attorney General Kennedy opened the conference by telling the delegates that they had a "special responsibility to represent those who cannot be here, those who are poor, those who are unfortunate—the 1,500,000 persons . . . who are accused of crime . . . who are yet unable to make bail." Chief Justice Earl Warren immediately followed with an endorsement of the "immensely significant" Manhattan Bail Project.[38]

The impact on public policy was swift. By 1965 there were an estimated forty-eight local programs based on the Vera model.[39] In 1966 Congress passed the Bail Reform Act—the first new federal bail law since 1789—which declared release on recognizance the presumptive bail decision. Meanwhile, many states revised their bail laws. Bail reform took several forms: legislation similar to the federal law defining a presumptive right to release on recognizance; the creation of local bail services agencies based on the Vera model to interview defendants and make bail recommendations; creation of 10 percent plans, under which defendants could obtain release by posting only 10 percent of the formal bail amount; the development of bail schedules specifying the amount of bail for specific offenses.

The first bail reform movement was a product of a new political context driven by three powerful forces. The civil rights movement heightened national consciousness about racial discrimination in every part of society. This, in turn, stimulated a new concern about poverty, which culminated in the 1965 Economic Opportunity Act. The impact of money bail on the poor was one of the newly defined social problems.[40] At the same time, the Supreme Court was aggressively examining the criminal process and establishing new standards of due process and equal protection.[41]

The result was a sense of national outrage at the money bail system and the emergence of a national consensus on the need to ensure justice for the poor. Reformers denounced prevailing bail practices as "checkbook justice" and local jails were condemned as "the new poorhouses." Ronald Goldfarb titled his attack on the bail system *Ransom*.[42] One index of the strength of the national consensus was the fact that Congress passed the 1966 Bail Reform Act with a unanimous vote in the Senate and only fourteen opposing votes in the House of Representatives.

Bail Reform as Discretion Control

From the standpoint of controlling discretion, the first bail reform movement primarily attempted to guide discretion. Release on recognizance (ROR) was not really a new option. It had always been available and judges had used it. The 1966 federal Bail Reform Act attempted to guide discretion by declaring a *presumption* in favor of ROR. The law stated that "any person charged with an offense, other than an offense punishible by death, shall . . . be ordered released pending trial on his personal recognizance . . . unless the officer determines, in the exercise of his discretion, that such a release will not reasonably assure the appearance of the person as required." By clearly stating a presumption in favor of ROR, the law went even further than the Manhattan Bail Project, which had inspired it. The Vera Institute's program was designed to facilitate ROR but did not explicitly require it. The law provided further guidance by spelling out the criteria judges were to use in making bail decisions:

> The judicial officer shall, on the basis of available information, take into account the nature and circumstances of the offense charged, the weight of the evidence against the accused, the accused's family ties, employment, financial resources, character and mental condition, the length of his residence in the community, his record of convictions, and his record of appearance at court proceedings or of flight to avoid prosecution or failure to appear at court proceedings.

It is important to note that while the law stated a presumption in favor of release, it did not assert an absolute right to bail. It should also be noted that the law applied to the federal criminal justice system, including the District of Columbia. Although it was a highly influential model, it did not affect directly the vast majority of criminal cases that are the responsibility of state and local courts.

State and local bail reforms incorporated similar efforts to guide discretion. Goldkamp reported that by 1978 twenty-four states had laws expressing a preference for release on recognizance, and twenty-two mandated release on the least restrictive condition. From the standpoint of bail reformers, however, there was a lot less to most of these laws than appeared at first glance. Most of the laws also stated or implied that the purpose of bail was to protect the community from dangerous offenders. Concern about crime control, then, was never absent and the first bail reform movement sowed the seeds for the second.[43]

The major institutional innovation of the first bail reform movement was the creation of pretrial services agencies with staff who would interview arrestees, obtain the necessary information on their background, attempt to verify the information, and make bail recommendations to the judge. To guide discretion, many used a formal point system. In Philadelphia, for example, a defendant received one point for having lived for three years or more in the Philadelphia area, or three points for having lived at the present address for one year; four points for living with his family and having contact with another family member, but only one point for living with a nonfamily friend or having contact with his family; four points for being employed at the present job for one year, with a statement that the employer will take him back, but only one point for employment in the present job for four months (or six months in the present and former job). The defendant would then lose points for prior criminal activity (minus seven for an adult felony conviction) and bad moral character (minus two each for current drug addiction or alcoholism). A total of six points was necessary for a positive ROR recommendation (Fig. 3.1).[44]

For misdemeanors, some states established rigid bail schedules, specifying the amount for each crime. This, of course, was as a more drastic form of discretion control, effectively abolishing it. California had created a bail schedule for misdemeanants in 1945. A 1973 law directed judges to develop bail schedules for felonies. The law contained an important exception, however. Police were given authority not to apply it to any defendant they thought should not be released. Thus judicial discretion was curbed for most defendants, but the critical discretionary decision regarding allegedly dangerous offenders was simply transferred

TO BE RECOMMENDED FOR RELEASE ON OWN RECOGNIZANCE, A DEFENDANT NEEDS:

1. A local address which can be verified, *AND*
2. A total of five points, verified by references, from the following:

RESIDENCE

3 Present address one year or more
2 Present residence 6 months, *OR* present and prior 1 year
1 Present residence 3 months, *OR* present and prior 6 months

1 Five years or more in Nine Bay Area Counties

FAMILY TIES

3 Lives with family, *AND* has contact with other family members in area
2 Lives with family, *OR*, has contact with family in the Bay Area
1 Lives with a nonfamily person

EMPLOYMENT

3 Present job one year or more
2 Present job 3 months, *OR* present and prior job 6 months
1 Current job, *OR* intermittent work for 1 year
1 Receiving unemployment compensation or welfare
1 Supported by family, or savings

PRIOR RECORD (within the last 15 years)

2 No convictions
1 One misdemeanor conviction
0 Two misdemeanor convictions, *OR* one felony conviction
−1 Three or more misdemeanor convictions, *OR* two or more felony convictions
−2 Four or more misdemeanor convictions, *OR* three or more felony convictions

FIGURE 3.1. Criteria for release on recognizance. (Generic form adapted from the original Manhattan Bail Project system)

from the judge to the police. This may well have made the decision less visible than before.[45]

Impact of the First Bail Reform Movement

The results of the first bail reform movement were mixed, and by the mid-1970s, many of the leading reformers were extremely disillusioned. Patricia M. Wald, one of the leading advocates of the 1966 federal bail reform act, looked back in 1972 and found "a decade of promise without fulfillment."[46] This conclusion, however, reflected the inflated expectations characteristic of reformers. It is more useful to assess bail reform from the perspective of modest expectations and determine what was accomplished and what was not.

At a threshold level, the first bail reform movement had one major accomplishment: it brought the entire issue of bail-setting discretion into the open. Bail-setting practices were debated, the existence of discretion was acknowledged, and reform efforts were focused on controlling decision making. This paralleled the opening up of the subjects of police discretion and plea bargaining during the same period. Given the tradition of neglect and refusal to acknowledge either discretion or the problems associated with its exercise, this was no small accomplishment.

A second major accomplishment was that the percentage of defendants detained before trial dropped. In some jurisdictions, the reduction was substantial. John Goldkamp found that in Philadelphia the percentage of defendants held for more than twenty-four hours dropped from 75 percent in 1954 (Foote's data) to only 25 percent in 1975. Those who were detained, moreover, remained in jail for significantly shorter periods of time.[47]

Nor was Philadelphia atypical. The National Bail Survey found that in most cities more defendants were released before trial; more were released on nonfinancial conditions; and in the case of money bail, the amounts were generally lower than before. In the twenty big cities studied, the percentage of felony defendants not obtaining pretrial release fell from 52 percent in 1962 to 33 percent in 1971.[48] Seventeen years later, the national figure was unchanged, with 34 percent of all felony defendants detained until their cases were disposed of.[49]

The decline in pretrial detention between 1962 and 1971 included some particularly dramatic reductions in particular cities: from 54 to 13 percent in Minneapolis; from 67 to 26 percent in San Diego. Two of the twenty cities still had high detention rates: in Boston it was unchanged (61 vs. 62%); in Kansas City it declined from 78 to 63 percent.[50]

Defendants obtaining release through nonfinancial resources increased from 5 percent of the total to 23 percent, according to the National Bail Survey's 1971 data. By 1988 that had increased to 35 percent of all defendants (thus, 34% were detained, 31% obtained release through financial means, and 35% obtained nonfinancial release).[51]

There was little change in the dollar amounts of bail, but substantially more defendants with bail in the $1,000 to $2,900 range succeeded in raising it and obtaining their release.

The most dramatic effect of reform occurred in Washington, D.C., where the 1966 Bail Reform Act applied. By 1977 only 1 percent of all criminal defendants were unable to obtain release.[52] This probably resulted from the explicit presumption of release in the federal law and from the fact that the District's pretrial services agency was large and, by reputation, highly professional (which probably meant that the relevant information was collected in a timely and detailed fashion).

Reform, in short, succeeded in accomplishing one of its basic goals: reducing pretrial detention, with all of its negative consequences, for many criminal defendants.[53] That was a significant accomplishment.

To a certain extent, the reduction in the *percentage* of defendants detained was hidden by the fact that the total *number* of pretrial detainees increased. Part of Wald's pessimism was due to the fact that by 1972 there were more people in the New York City and Washington, D.C., jails than before bail reform. This was a result of the sharp rise in serious crime during the period. Wald's pessimism on this point was misplaced. Reform did accomplish a major part of its goals; it was offset by developments unrelated to bail reform.[54]

Several observers, however, have suggested that the increase in the percentage of defendants obtaining their release might have occurred without the benefit of reform. Given the increase in crime and arrests, judges might have released people they would not have previously released simply to make room for the flood of arrestees. Wald concluded that bail reform probably resulted in the release of ''good risk defendants who might otherwise have had to pay a bondsman or go to jail.''[55] Wayne Thomas found that some cities with no formal pretrial release program released a high percentage of defendants on their own recognizance. In ''unreformed'' Rhode Island, 50 to 55 percent obtained pretrial release, a figure that was higher than all but one of the jurisdictions with a ''model'' pretrial release program.[56] Thomas concluded that the ''use of nonfinancial releases was not contingent upon the intervention of a pretrial release program.''[57]

In a broad review of court reform, Malcolm Feeley also reached the pessimistic conclusion that reform was ''redundant''; the same results would have been obtained without reform.[58] Feeley's pessimism also may be somewhat overstated. His perspective reflects a tough-minded evaluation of the claims of reformers. But he also noted some reduction in discrimination in pretrial release. In unreformed Rhode Island, for example, "blacks were at a noticeable disadvantage in obtaining ROR," despite the generally high rate of pretrial release.[59] Reform in Baltimore, on the other hand, did reduce arbitrariness and discrimination. (Unfortunately, the National Bail Study did not address the critical question of race discrimination; moreover, the current National Pretrial Reporting Program does not report data on race and bail.)[60] Reduction in racial discrimination is an important achievement, given the fact that one of the basic criticisms of unfettered discretion is that it permits prejudicial attitudes to influence decision making.

Failures of the First Bail Reform Movement

Despite the reduction in the percentage of defendants detained and some apparent lessening in discrimination, the first bail reform movement fell short of many of its goals. There were three basic failings. First, creating an ROR option did not necessarily control discretion; it remained an option that judges were free to reject. Second, the goals of reform were undermined by administrative problems, particularly the lack of resources. Finally, and perhaps most important, there is some persuasive evidence that reform did not substantially alter the fundamental dynamics of the bail-setting decision.

The first two problems were evident in New York City, where the innovative programs of the 1960s had been reorganized and institutionalized by the 1980s. Staff members with the Criminal Justice Agency interviewed defendants in the holding cell and then sought to verify the information about community ties. The defendant's score became the basis of a bail recommendation to the judge. (Meanwhile, the police sent the defendant's fingerprints to the New York State Identification Department for information regarding criminal history.) If the information could not be verified, no recommendation for ROR was made. Because of the high volume of cases, each defendant's case received about one hour of attention, including both interview and verification. Obviously, the shortage of staff resources precluded recommendations for many defendants.[61]

Even more important from the standpoint of controlling discretion, however, is the fact that the judge was free to reject the bail recommendation. In this sense, the recommendation is not really a *control* over discretion at all. The data, moreover, clearly indicates that judges frequently rejected the recommendation. Judges granted release in only 58 percent of the cases where the staff recommended ROR—and in 54 percent of the cases where there was a qualified recommendation. Equally interesting, judges granted ROR in 40 percent of the cases where the staff made no recommendation for release.

The critical factor in the bail recommendation process is the nature and quality of the information available to the judge. One of the major goals of bail reform was to replace uninformed supposition and bias with facts. In New York City, the pretrial release report did not include information on offense seriousness. Nonetheless, judges obtained that information independently and there is good reason to believe it was a significant factor in their decisions.

In Philadelphia, information about the offense and prior record was part of the pretrial report. John Goldkamp's evaluation of bail reform in Philadelphia is particularly important for two reasons. First, it is the most rigorous evaluation of bail reform in any local jurisdiction. Second, Philadelphia represented a "model" of bail reform and the result was a bail process "at its best."[62] Nonetheless, Goldkamp found that decision making was similar to that in unreformed jurisdictions. Bail decisions were dominated by the seriousness of the charge, which was used to predict both the possibility of failure to appear and the likelihood of committing a crime while on release.

Instead of altering traditional bail practices, reform may only have strengthened them. Goldkamp found that the scores designed to measure defendants' community ties "did not appear to be influential in determining pretrial custody."[63] Instead, when Philadelphia judges wanted to detain someone, they simply selected the information—about the offense or the defendant's prior record—that would justify doing so. In short, judges used reform procedures to subvert the goals of reform.[64] Feeley observes that bail reform may have only provided a "veneer of science and rationality."[65]

A 1988 survey of bail practices nationwide found that seriousness of the offense continued to be a major factor in bail outcomes. While 34 percent of all felony defendants were detained before trial, the rates were consistently higher for murder (61%), rape (45%), robbery (48%), and burglary (47%). In short, nearly half of all persons arrested for a predatory "high-fear" crime remained in jail while waiting for trial.[66] Prior record had a consistent effect on pretrial release. The percentage detained rose steadily as the record of prior criminal activity worsened:

only 23 percent of those with no prior conviction were detained, compared to 34 percent with a misdemeanor conviction, 48 percent with a nonviolent felony conviction, and 54 percent with a violent felony conviction.[67] These data are consistent with a large and growing body of research that indicates the powerful effect of offense seriousness and prior record on all decisions in the criminal justice system.[68]

A final set of problems involves the use of money bail. In the end, bail reform did not impose any controls over the decision on the actual dollar amount for persons charged with felonies. Even where 10 percent plans have been instituted as a reform, it is possible for judges to set bail at a high enough level to ensure detention. News media regularly report on judges setting bail in the amounts of $100,000 or even $1 million—figures clearly designed to prevent release. Data from the 1988 National Pretrial Reporting Program confirmed these suspicions. Persons charged with violent crimes were more likely to be detained than those charged with property crimes. Rape (45%) and robbery (48%) suspects, meanwhile, were more likely to be detained than persons charged with assault (31%). Judges consistently set high bail amounts for the more serious offenses. Persons charged with violent offenses were far more likely to face a bail amount of $10,000 or higher, and particularly amounts of $20,000 or higher.[69]

Bail reform also may have institutionalized discrimination against the very poor in another way. Assessments of community ties rely heavily on employment records. Defendants with jobs, however menial or ill-paid, gain points under this system while the unemployed, especially the long-term unemployed, do not. Thus *some* poor people benefited from bail reform but the very poor found themselves up against a formidable hurdle. They were not necessarily worse off. Reform did not backfire in the sense of creating unintended consequences; it simply stopped short of its goal of eliminating economic status as a consideration in bail release. Goldkamp concludes that bail reform appears equitable on the surface—in the sense that persons charged with the same crime have the same bail figure—but "proves to be inequitable in practice."[70]

In sum, the full impact of the first bail reform movement was mixed. It could claim some significant gains in reducing the overall percentage of defendants detained and some apparent reduction in racial discrimination. But it fell far short of the goal of ensuring the right to bail for all defendants regardless of economic status. From the standpoint of discretion control, it did not fundamentally alter the dynamics of bail decisions. In fact, the net result may have been a sharper distinction between what Goldkamp called the "two classes" of accused. More of those defendants charged with relatively less serious offenses, with no serious prior record, and some evident community ties now obtain release. But those who fall on the other side of the line—accused of a serious offense, with a prior record, and with weak family ties and no employment record—are no more likely to obtain their release than before.

The Age of Diminished Expectations: Bail Guidelines

A more recent approach to bail reform, the development of guidelines for bail setting, reflects substantially diminished reform expectations. The guidelines approach seeks to guide discretion by providing a matrix indicating the recommended bail decision based on seriousness of the offense and prior record.

The guidelines approach was first developed for parole decision making but has found its most significant application in sentencing (see the discussion in Chapter 5).[71] Guidelines are developed on the basis of empirical analysis of current practices and are essentially designed to provide more consistent decision making (primarily by eliminating or discouraging decisions that deviated from the norm). This represents the admirable goal of achieving greater equality. Critics, however, have raised the objection that, because guidelines are based on an empirical analysis of past practices, they simply sanction the status quo and freeze it in place.[72]

The most elaborate experiment with bail guidelines was undertaken in Philadelphia. The two-factor matrix was based on offense seriousness and probability of failure, as measured primarily by prior criminal record and any record of prior failure on pretrial release. As the offender's score moves toward the high-risk corner of the matrix, the bail recommendation moves from release on recognizance to progressively higher amounts of money bail. Quite obviously, this approach institutionalizes traditional practices. It does this in the face of the empirical evidence that offense seriousness is not correlated with the risk of either failure to appear or crime on bail. By capitulating to traditional practice, the guidelines approach abandons the high ideals of the first bail reform movement and reflects a new age of diminished expectations.[73]

An evaluation of the use of the bail guidelines in Philadelphia found mixed results. The guidelines did produce greater equity in bail setting. Defendants facing similar criminal charges were more likely to receive similar bail decisions from judges using the guidelines than were defendants in a control group where judges did not use the guidelines. In this respect, guidelines guided discretion and promoted greater fairness. The guidelines did not, however, produce lower rates of failure to appear or lower rates of crime on pretrial release. Rearrest rates, for example, ranged from a low of 5 percent to a high of 19 percent among judges using the guidelines compared to a low of 5 percent and a high of 16 percent among judges not using the guidelines. In other words, the criteria in the decision-making matrix did not produce more accurate predictions of failure.[74]

The Second Bail Reform Movement: Preventive Detention

The second bail reform movement defined the problem in terms of public safety. Judges, the argument went, released too many dangerous criminals on bail, allowing them to victimize law-abiding citizens. This criticism is a classic illustration of the conservative, crime control, anti–civil libertarian perspective of the last two decades: excessive concern for individual rights produces direct harm to the community as a whole. The advocates of preventive detention were not deterred by the empirical research indicating that detaining more people would not reduce crime. Like so many criminal justice reforms, the "lock-'em-up" strategy was fuelled by something akin to religious zeal rather than scientifically verifiable evidence.[75]

Because of the strength of conservative crime control ideology in the 1970s and 1980s, the second bail reform movement was extremely successful in rewriting the law of bail. The specific reform proposal, preventive detention, involved granting judges explicit authority to deny bail to criminal defendants they deemed dangerous to the community. From the standpoint of the control of discretion, this approach had several ramifications. At first glance, it defined a new option for judges, empowering them to deny bail to certain categories of suspects. State laws varied widely in terms of who could be detained and on what grounds. In practice, these laws did not control discretion at all. At most, they only guided it.

The detention alternative was, of course, not a new one at all. As every knowledgeable observer of the bail process recognized, judges had always detained people they thought dangerous. The research by Suffett and others found that detaining people believed to be dangerous—as measured by the offense charged and prior criminal record—was the dominant factor in bail setting.[76] For all practical purposes, then, preventive detention laws simply provided legal justification for traditional practices. These laws have the virtue of making public a covert decision-making process.

The 1970 District of Columbia Preventive Detention Law

The first victory for the second bail reform movement was a 1970 law authorizing preventive detention in Washington, D.C. (officially the District of Columbia Court Reform and Criminal Procedures Act). The law granted judges the right to deny bail to defendants deemed a danger to the community or likely to flee to avoid appearance in court. In response to criticisms by civil libertarians, the law also created elaborate procedural safeguards, which, as we shall see, appear to have severely limited the use of the law.

Politically, the law had enormous significance. Coming only four years after the 1966 Bail Reform Act, and embodying a completely different philosophy, it was the clearest indicator of the sudden shift in the political climate. Violent crime had risen sharply since the early 1960s and this had a significant impact on public attitudes. The wave of urban riots between 1964 and 1968, together with public reaction to protests against the Vietnam War and the rise of a drug subculture, hardened public attitudes toward crime. Both Richard Nixon and George Wallace had successfully exploited public fear of crime in the 1968 presidential election campaign. Street crime in the District of Columbia was an extremely sensitive political issue. The District is the one jurisdiction with responsibility for ordinary street crime (particularly the "high-fear" crimes of robbery, rape, and burglary) over which Congress can legislate. Thus the 1970 law had an important symbolic role as a convenient way for members of Congress to go on record as being tough on crime. And at the same time, it served as a model for the Nixon administration's promise to establish "law and order."

Despite the enormous fears among civil libertarians, a curious thing happened: the D.C. preventive detention law was rarely used. In a 1983 review of bail reform, Malcolm Feeley described it as "nearly dormant."[77] Non-use was apparently related to the procedural protections it included. The law authorized detention without bail for up to sixty days of a person charged with committing a violent crime. The defendant was entitled to a formal hearing to determine that substantial probability of guilt exists and to make sure that no other less restrictive release procedure could guarantee public safety. The defendant had to have been convicted of a crime in the preceding ten years, be a narcotics addict, or currently be on bail, probation, or parole. The hearing allowed the defendant to challenge any of the evidence against him. Finally, the defendant has a right to be released on bail if the trial is not held within sixty days.

In the first six months, prosecutors requested detention hearings in only twenty of six thousand felony cases. These resulted in nine actual hearings and eight detentions. Two others were detained as a result of judicial initiative, for a total of ten. Five of these were later released on appeal or reconsideration; a sixth was released when the grand jury refused to indict him. Thus a grand total of four people were fully detained under the law.[78]

An important part of the context of the 1970 law was that it amended the 1966 Bail Reform Act, which, with its explicit presumption of release on recognizance, made the District of Columbia arguably the most ''reformed'' jurisdiction in the country. A 1977 cross-city comparison of case processing indicated that only 1 percent of all felony defendants in the District failed to obtain pretrial release; 49 percent were released on nonfinancial conditions and another 40 percent on money bail (the disposition of the remaining 9% could not be determined). The 1 percent detention rate compared with 3 percent in Detroit and 41 percent in Salt Lake City.[79]

Assuming that the 1 percent detention rate prevailed during the period of the evaluation of the preventive detention act (1970–1971), we can estimate that a total of sixty defendants were detained during the period (1% of 6,000). Assuming that four of them were detained under the new law, fifty-six were detained because they could not raise bail. This helps explain why the law was so infrequently used. The judge and the prosecutor easily reach a tacit agreement to detain a defendant without recourse to the complex and time-consuming procedures of the preventive detention law: the formal request for a detention hearing, the hearing itself, the inevitable appeal, and so on.

The evidence on the D.C. preventive detention law has mixed implications. On the one hand, it adds some support to the argument that complex procedures designed to protect individual rights may only invite covert evasion (in this instance, by using high money bail to achieve detention). At the same time, it suggests that the existence of a new option may not mean that judges will actually use it very often.

The 1984 Federal Preventive Detention Act

In 1984 Congress passed a law authorizing preventive detention for all federal criminal cases. The law (officially the Comprehensive Crime Control Act) allowed judges to deny bail where the prosecutor could demonstrate that no other procedure would ensure the safety of individuals or the community. The law created specific criteria to guide judges in denying bail: the nature of the offense, the weight of the evidence against the defendant, the history and characteristics of the defendant, and the nature and seriousness of the danger posed by possible release. Judges are required to inform defendants of the basis for detention and of their right to an expedited appeal.

In *United States v. Salerno* (1987), the Supreme Court upheld the constitutionality of the law, holding that the government had a legitimate interest in preventing crime and that this interest is heightened when it "musters convincing proof that the arrestee, already indicted or held to answer for a serious crime, presents a demonstrable danger to the community."[80]

The impact of the 1984 law has been far different from that of the 1970 District of Columbia law. Many more people are being detained under its provisions than Congress had anticipated. The director of the U.S. Marshalls Service said it was having a "dramatic" impact on the entire federal criminal justice system, particularly in terms of jail overcrowding.[81] Because of the great concerns about both the constitutional implications and the practical impact of the law, a number of studies have been undertaken. The data from these reports reveal several basic patterns in bail setting.

First, the number of persons detained was large and increased significantly after the Supreme Court's 1987 decision. In 1987, the Administrative Office of the United States Courts reported that 2,733 persons were detained in the first six months and 3,486 in the last half of the year; 4,135 were detained in the first six months and 4,470 in the last six months of 1988. Much of this increase was due to the increase in the number of drug arrests, the category where detentions were most often requested.[82] The percentage of cases where detention

was granted remained fairly stable. Between 70 and 75 percent of all
hearings resulted in detention during the two-year period. The percentage of detainees who were subsequently convicted remained high
and stable at around 85 percent.[83]

Nonetheless, the heavy use of the law did not result in a great increase
in the overall percentage of defendants detained. A national survey by
the federal Pretrial Services Agency found that the percentage of defendants held before trial for any reason increased from 24 to 29 percent
as a result of the law.[84] A General Accounting Office study of four
federal district courts found a similar increase, from 26 to 31 percent.
In both studies, the percentage released by one method or another
experienced a corresponding decline, from 62 to 58 percent.[85] A separate
study of the impact of the law in California federal courts, on the other
hand, found no increase in the overall detention rate.[86]

The distribution of the reasons for detention suggest the real dynamics
of the law's impact. All the 26 percent detained before the law took
effect were detained because they were unable to raise their cash bond.
Of the 31 percent who were detained after the law took effect, half (or
16% of the total) did not pay their cash bond and half (15% of the total)
were detained under the preventive detention provision of the law. These
data suggest that the primary effect of the law was to give judges legal
authority to do what they formerly did covertly. A Justice Department
study concluded that "pretrial detention has largely been substituted for
bail as a means of detaining defendants."[87] Under the new law, however, the reason for the detention was openly stated and the defendant
had an opportunity to challenge that reason directly.[88]

The third major finding has particularly important implications for
the advocates of preventive detention. The law had little impact on the
rate at which defendants either failed to appear in court or were rearrested
for new crimes while on release. The failure-to-appear rates ranged
between 1.3 and 2.1 percent in the four districts studied. The failure
rate declined in one district (from 3.8 to 1.6%) but increased in two
others.[89]

The data on rearrest showed a similar pattern. Overall rates were
extremely low beforehand and remained low. They declined in two
districts but increased in two others. Even in the worst performing
district under the old law, the rearrest rate was only 2.4 percent. Under
the new preventive detention law, moreover, rearrests generally involved relatively minor crimes. More than half involved arrest on a

misdemeanor. These data were consistent with the findings of earlier studies and gave additional support to the argument of preventive detention opponents that the entire issue of crime by persons on bail had been grossly exaggerated.

The reason failure-to-appear and rearrest rates did not increase, of course, was that the overall detention rate changed very little. The types of defendants judges believed to be high risks were already being detained. In short, a major change in the law of bail—which included an explicit revision of longstanding assumptions about the constitutional right to bail—produced relatively minor changes in actual practices.

Conclusions

The evidence of the two bail reform movements seems to lead to the same conclusion: formal controls at best have only limited capacity to control bail-setting discretion. Reflecting community attitudes as well as their own personal views, criminal court judges appear determined not to release certain offenders they regard as dangerous. Dangerousness is defined primarily in terms of the seriousness of the offense charged and the defendant's prior criminal record. This practice continues in the face of substantial research indicating that it is not possible to predict future criminality on the basis of prior criminal record. It is only a slight overstatement to describe the situation in terms of judges saying "rules be damned; we know who's dangerous and we're not going to release them."

These pessimistic conclusions should not deflect our attention from other real, although admittedly modest gains of thirty years of bail reform. Along with police discretion, plea bargaining, and many other decisions, the bail-setting decision has become visible. It is out in the open, we have reasonably good data on actual practices, we are aware of the problems associated with it, and policy is a matter of public debate. This represents considerable progress over the state of affairs thirty years ago.

Nor should we overlook the substantive accomplishments of the first bail reform movement. Many offenders who in years past would have been detained in jail simply because they were poor are now able to obtain their release. As a result, they are spared the pain of imprisonment and the higher risk of conviction and possible further imprisonment.

To be sure, these gains are modest, and most might have occurred without an elaborate bail reform movement, but they are gains nonetheless.

The consequences of the second bail reform movement are of a more ambiguous nature. Although conservatives have dominated public policy-making for the last twenty years, and can claim credit for numerous laws and a major Supreme Court decision, they have not achieved their principal social policy goal. Preventive detention has not reduced crime. Moreover, there is persuasive evidence that it cannot. After more than half a century of research, the best minds in criminology have not been able to develop diagnostic tools that predict criminal behavior with any precision. In this respect, the preventive detention movement has not achieved its own goals.

With respect to the control of discretion, however, the second bail reform movement has succeeded in moving an important decision into the open. Civil libertarians regard this issue with decidedly mixed feelings. On the one hand, they are appalled at the spread of preventive detention laws and the consequent denial of the consequent denial of the constitutional right to bail. On the other hand, the laws do not change actual practice and there is much to be said for bringing this covert decision to light. Judges, it seems, have always detained defendants they thought were dangerous. Historically, they achieved this result covertly. The first bail reform movement failed to end the practice. The second bail reform movement at least made the decision overt and, in the case of the 1984 federal law, provided a means of challenging a detention decision. If visibility and openness are worthy goals—and a necessary precondition for rational change—then this represents a measure of progress.

The influence of offense seriousness and prior criminal record on bail setting deserves some comment. Studies of the administration of justice have found that these two factors pervade the entire criminal process. Repeatedly, they are major factors, often the principal factors, influencing the exercise of discretion. This is true with respect to arrests, plea bargaining, and sentencing. The evidence suggests the profoundly pessimistic conclusion that formal controls may have very limited ability to override the power of these factors.

4

The Plea-Bargaining Problem

The Politics of Plea Bargaining

Among all the discretionary decisions in the criminal justice system, plea bargaining is most often the focal point of general public dissatisfaction with the criminal justice system.[1] The idea that most cases are settled by "deals" is a convenient symbol of everything that people believe is wrong with the justice system.

Public discontent takes two forms, reflecting the political divisions over crime and justice issues. Many people believe that plea bargains allow dangerous criminals to beat the system and go free. Alarmists claim that only 1 percent of all criminals go to prison (Fig. 4.1). While it is true that most offenders are not punished, the 1 percent figure is extremely misleading and incorrectly focuses on plea bargaining.[2] The real weaknesses in the criminal process are the failure of victims to report 63 percent of all crimes and the fact that the police make arrests in only about 20 percent of those that are reported. And, as Chapter 2 indicated, about half of these arrests are dismissed (Fig. 4.2). Nearly all the remaining cases result in a conviction, usually through a guilty plea.[3] Whether justice is done through those pleas is a question this chapter will address in due course. For the moment, however, it is important to emphasize that plea bargaining is not the primary cause of the failure of the criminal justice system to punish wrongdoers.[4]

Nonetheless, the belief that plea-bargaining "deals" allow offenders to get off easy remains strong. Adherents of this view believe that the

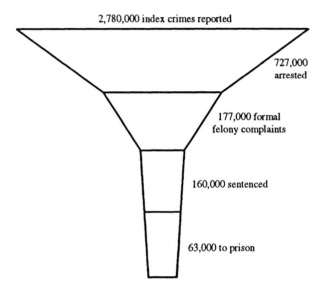

2,780,000 index crimes reported

727,000
arrested

177,000 formal
felony complaints

160,000 sentenced

63,000 to prison

FIGURE 4.1. Funneling effect from reported crimes through prison sentence. (The President's Commission on Law Enforcement and Administration of Justice, *Task Force Report: Science and Technology* [Washington, D.C.: Government Printing Office, 1967], p. 61)

solution is to ban plea bargaining, to foreclose this discretionary option altogether. Some plea-bargaining bans are incorporated into mandatory-sentencing schemes, which dictate a mandatory prison sentence for certain crimes (usually drugs or use of a weapon) and prohibit plea bargaining to a lesser offense as a way of evading prison.

For many others, the problem with plea bargaining is that it represents a mockery of justice. Donald Newman's pioneering work on the subject found that a wide variety of "considerations" entered into the guilty plea process, many of which had little to do with strict standards of culpability. In many cases, guilty pleas allowed officials to subvert the law, since defendants could avoid mandatory or other severe sentences, or a criminal law could be nullified altogether. Plea

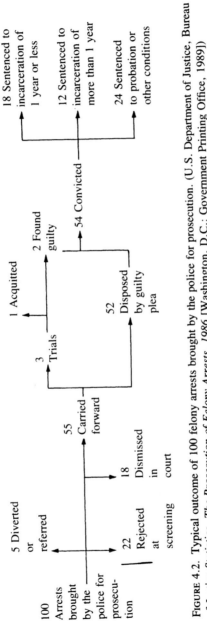

FIGURE 4.2. Typical outcome of 100 felony arrests brought by the police for prosecution. (U.S. Department of Justice, Bureau of Justice Statistics, *The Prosecution of Felony Arrests, 1986* [Washington, D.C.: Government Printing Office, 1989])

bargains also allowed preferential treatment for allegedly "respectable" defendants and dismissive treatment of allegedly "disreputable" victims. Prosecutors could either punish the police for apparently illegal behavior or cooperate with preferential treatment of informants. Although plea bargaining greatly facilitated the individualization of punishment—the primary goal of the indeterminate sentence system—there were no controls over these decisions.[5] The historic absence of controls over prosecutorial decisions led other commentators to call the plea bargain the "single most unreviewed decision" in the entire criminal process.[6] Historically, however, there have been many decisions of critical importance that have been essentially unreviewed. The point here is not to determine which is the most unreviewed but to underscore the fact that very important decisions by prosecutors have been free from controls.

Many critics focus on specific due process and equal protection problems, arguing that the entire process is coercive and produces outcomes that are either arbitrary or discriminatory. According to this view, prosecutors systematically "overcharge" and then "deal down" to what should have been the original charge. Defendants are coerced into waiving their privilege against self-incrimination, the right to confront their accusers, and the right to a trial. In what might be described as the "nightmare" version of plea bargaining, even the defense attorney is part of a conspiracy to induce a guilty plea. Instead of being the defendant's advocate, the defense attorney is concerned primarily with maintaining good working relations with the other members of the courtroom work group and shares their views on the importance of moving cases along. To this end, they bluff (or simply lie to) their clients, thus coercing them to accept deals they have arranged. Albert Alschuler concluded that the defense attorney is often the "source of abuse" of the defendant.[7]

With respect to the right to trial, there is some evidence that the criminal justice system does punish defendants who refuse to play the game and insist on a trial. Although not entirely conclusive, some studies have found that defendants who are convicted at trial receive more severe sentences than those who plead guilty.[8] There is also the problem of the *perception* of justice. Interviews with convicted offenders indicate that they believed they would be sentenced to longer prison terms as a penalty for refusing to play the game. A comment from a prisoner interviewed by Jonathan Casper captures defendants' skepticism about the quality of public defenders: "Did you have a lawyer when you went to court the next day? No, I had a public defender."[9] Convicted felons perceive public defenders as part of the courthouse group.[10] Many other people share their perception that plea-bargaining "deals" are inherently unfair.

With respect to outcomes, many people believe that plea bargaining discriminates against the poor and racial minorities. The famous 1973 Spiro Agnew plea bargain, which allowed the vice president of the United States to avoid prison, reinforced the belief that the rich and powerful can always beat the system (although the more recent ten-year prison term handed out to financier Michael Milken suggests otherwise). The fact that blacks are overrepresented in prison raises serious questions about whether there is a pattern of racial discrim-ination in the criminal process and the extent to which plea bargaining is the primary locus.

There is conflicting evidence on the question of whether there is racial discrimination in the charging decision. Spohn, Gruhl, and Welch found some evidence of discrimination against Hispanics, blacks, and males in Los Angeles County. They looked at both the decision to accept or reject felony charges (where "rejection" could involve either reduction to a misdemeanor or dropping charges al-together) and the subsequent decision to dismiss or not dismiss charges after they had been filed. Evidence of discrimination was found at the first decision point (rejection–no rejection). There was no evidence of racial discrimination, however, at the second (dismiss–no dismiss). They speculated that the second decision point is more "visible," since it occurs (at least nominally) in court rather than in the privacy of the prosecutor's office. Visibility brings into play social norms against race discrimination.[11]

Using statewide California data, however, Joan Petersilia found that blacks and Hispanics were more likely to have charges dismissed, at both stages, than whites. Although it appeared at first glance that racial minorities were receiving favored treatment, she conceded the possibility that the higher rate of dismissals represented a correction to questionable police practices. That is, the police may be arresting more blacks and Hispanics on the basis of less stringent standards of evidence. Prosecutors then reject many of these weak evidence cases.[12]

Concern about the coerced violation of constitutional rights and dis-crimination against the poor and racial minorities has caused great unease about plea bargaining among liberals—an unease that has led some to call for its abolition.

Plea Bargaining as a Process

Plea bargaining was actually the first discretionary decision to be identified by observers of the criminal process. All the crime commission studies in the 1920s and 1930s expressed alarm over the "mortality" of cases between arrest and conviction. They viewed this not only as a retreat from the ideal of the jury trial but also as a sign that vast numbers of criminals were avoiding punishment.[13] These early studies could not come to grips with the attrition of cases because they did not understand the general phenomenon of discretion. Thus they attributed case mortality to inadequately trained prosecutors, or political interference, or simple lack of prosecutorial will.

Attempts to control plea bargaining are confounded by the fact that it does not involve a single decision. It is best understood as a *process* that includes a number of decisions. In fact, it is impossible to distinguish plea bargaining apart from the general prosecutorial process.[14]

The standard definition of plea bargaining—a system of negotiations leading to a plea of guilty—is incomplete because it does not include the most important decision of all: the decision to dismiss charges altogether.[15] It is more useful to think of plea bargaining as a process of testing the evidence that begins immediately after arrest and can lead to a number of different outcomes: dismissal, plea to one or more charges, plea to the top charge or lesser charge, or trial.

Thinking of plea bargaining as a continuing process immediately dramatizes the central problem in trying to control it: it is not really a decision *point* at all. It is not a single decision that can be isolated and subjected to formal controls. Instead, it involves a series of decisions, over a period of time, by different officials. By definition, *bargaining* assumes the participation of at least two people. Plea bargaining involves at least four individuals: prosecutor, defense attorney, judge, and defendant. In some jurisdictions, police officers have a significant role. And in recent years, victims' rights advocates have demanded that the victim be given a voice as well.[16]

The matter is further complicated by the great variation in how cases are prosecuted in different jurisdictions. In some areas police officers play a major role.[17] A formal grand jury indictment is required in some jurisdictions. In fact, there are at least three decision points that could properly be described as the "charging" decision: booking, the filing of initial charges, the filing of formal charges. The importance of each decision point varies from jurisdiction to jurisdiction.[18]

The involvement of different officials seriously complicates control efforts. Formal controls focus on particular officials: the police officer's decision to shoot; the judge's decision on bail. The matter is far more complex when several officials are involved. A control placed on one—say, a ban on prosecutors' ability to accept pleas to lower charges—may only push the important decision into the hands of other officials. There is an adage about discretion in the criminal process says that you can never really control or eliminate it; you only move it around. Restricting it at one point only pushes it upstream or downstream in the criminal process. Much of the evidence we will review supports this idea. The plea-bargaining process is maddeningly complex. In this respect it is fundamentally different from most police discretionary decisions, for example, which can be isolated conceptually and practically. The arrest decision may be difficult to control but at least it can be pinpointed. This is not the case with plea bargaining.

The Courtroom Work Group: A Bureaucratic Perspective

The participation of several officials means that decisions are constrained by group norms. It has been well established that the operations of local criminal courts are heavily influenced by the informal norms established by the courtroom work group. Over the years, prosecutors, defense attorneys, judges, and other court officials, establish common understandings about two basic issues: how routine cases will be handled and what the expected punishment is for various crimes. The latter is commonly referred to as the "going rate."[19] As a result, in local criminal courts that have been studied in detail, outcomes have been found to be highly predictable, given certain facts about the crime, the strength of the evidence, and the defendant's prior record. Also, these informal norms are capable of effectively resisting any significant change in operating procedures imposed from without. Feeley found that courtroom work groups were very successful in negating the intent of speedy trial laws, for example.[20]

Courtroom work groups have important consequences for the control of plea bargaining. Group norms serve as a powerful constraint on prosecutorial discretion. Prosecutors are not entirely free to act as they might like; decisions have to be negotiated. The prosecutor who deviates from the group's norms risks the same sanctions as the uncooperative defendant. The contrast with police discretion is instructive. Whereas police officers generally make critical decisions alone, prosecutors operate in a group setting where they must contend with often conflicting interests.[21]

The bureaucratic setting of plea bargaining also makes formal control efforts more difficult. Common sense suggests that group norms are more powerful than individual attitudes. It is one thing if one official resists a change; it is quite a different matter when a group of people who regularly work together resist a change.

A Comment on "Adversarial" Justice

Much of the traditional hostility to plea bargaining arises from the belief that it violates the ideal of an adversarial system of justice: that the defendant is innocent until proven guilty and that the state must prove that guilt in an open adversarial proceeding. Trials, according to this view, are adversarial and therefore necessarily relatively just. This is the point that prompted the crime commissions of the 1920s and 1930s to express concern about the "mortality" of cases. Somehow, it seemed, we had lost sight of the ideal.[22] Much of the contemporary discontent with plea bargaining rests on a similar belief that a contested adversarial process is a better way of determining truth in a criminal case than a negotiated process.

The sentimental view of the adversarial criminal trial does not reflect reality. Even our language about "adversarial" and "negotiated" procedures does not necessarily describe what happens in a particular case. Many plea negotiations are bitterly contested, whereas in some trials the defense barely contests the charges at all. In the former, the prosecution has to do far more to prove the defendant's guilt than in the latter. Even the nominally objective data do not accurately reflect what really happened. In some jurisdictions, cases officially go to trial but are best described as a "slow plea": the end result is actually the product of a negotiating process. Categorizing such proceedings as a "contested trial" is very misleading.[23]

Decision Points

The Decision to Charge or Dismiss

The first and most important decision in the prosecution of a case is whether to file criminal charges. The charge–dismiss decision ranks with arrest as one of the two most important decisions in the criminal justice process. Fifty years ago, Attorney General (and later Supreme Court Justice) Robert Jackson observed that "the prosecutor has more control over life, liberty, and reputation than any other person in America.[24] Although we might argue that the police officer's arrest decision is more consequential, the power of the prosecutor is undeniable. The implications of the decision not to charge for both the individual suspect and the criminal justice system are obvious: the individual is not indicted and the criminal justice system has one fewer case. Other commentators have pointed out that the traditional measures for holding prosecutors accountable for their actions are extremely limited.[25] They can always be voted out of office, but this is more often the result of political forces that have little to do with the handling of routine criminal cases.

The importance of the charge–dismiss decision is not simply theoretical. At least half of all arrests do not result in criminal prosecution. A multijurisdictional study of felony cases found dismissals in about half of all cases. This ranged from a low of 31 percent in Cobb County, Georgia (suburban Atlanta), to a high of 76 percent in Los Angeles County. There were significant differences between jurisdictions on when cases were dropped. In Salt Lake City, 20 percent were rejected at the initial screening and another 25 percent dropped later (for a total attrition rate of 45%). In New Orleans, 57 percent were rejected at the initial screening and only 7 percent later.[26] An earlier INSLAW study found that 21 percent of all cases in Washington, D.C., were rejected by prosecutors and another 29 percent were dismissed later.[27]

Petersilia's analysis of California felony cases found that the police released 11 percent of all people arrested, prosecutors refused to file charges on another 15 percent, and another 18 percent were either dismissed or acquitted in court. This meant that 44 percent of all arrests did not result in a conviction and most of those were the result of a dismissal at some point.[28]

Petersilia's study reveals an important complicating aspect of the data on case processing. As already indicated in Chapter 2, the police never present many cases to the prosecutor. The person is arrested, officially booked only in some unknown number of cases, and then released. The available studies of case processing do not necessarily give us reliable figures on the true dismissal rate because we are not sure about the baseline figure. If we say that prosecutors dismiss 42 percent of all cases, the question is, 42 percent of what figure? This might include all arrests or it might include only those presented to the prosecutor.[29]

Charging practices have important side effects. In his national survey of plea-bargaining practices, William McDonald found that police officers adapted to formal case-screening procedures on the part of prosecutors. When Seattle prosecutors imposed a high evidentiary standard for accepting cases, the police began prescreening cases more closely. As a result, about 90 percent of their arrests were accepted for prosecution.[30] This phenomenon adds a new perspective on the question of whether controls simply move discretion around. Controls imposed at one point undoubtedly have some effect on other decision points. But there are several possible effects. The controls may simply displace discretion in a way that offsets their intent, or they may force other decision makers to adapt their behavior to conform to these new controls.

The Decision on the Top Charge

Once the suspect is charged, a number of other decisions follow. This is the process that is usually referred to as plea bargaining. Negotiations fall into two general categories: charge bargaining and sentence bargaining.

The question of the "top charge" is often the source of attacks on plea bargaining by conservatives. They argue that too many offenders are allowed to plea to a lesser offense and thereby "get off easy." The robbery defendant pleads guilty to a larceny; the rape suspect pleads guilty to an assault; the burglary suspect pleads guilty to larceny; and so on. In practice this process is often a form of sentence bargaining, since the prevailing "going rate" for assault is far less than for rape.

The Decision on the Number of Charges

People who are arrested are often suspected of having committed several crimes. They may have committed several crimes over a period of time, or they can be charged with several different crimes as part of the same transaction. A particular criminal act often involves several lesser and included offenses: a robbery includes a larceny from the same person and an assault. Apart from the question of the top charge, the prosecutor has complete discretion as to the number of charges to file. Another aspect of this phenomenon is the potential applicability of a habitual criminal statute. Typically, these laws allow the prosecutor to file an additional criminal charge, with a substantially longer prison term, against the defendant who qualifies (typically with two or more prior felony convictions). Despite the prevalence of such laws, however, they are rarely used.[31]

One of the longstanding criticisms of plea bargaining is the allegation that prosecutors routinely "overcharge"; that is, they file additional charges to use as bargaining chips. Trading away one of these charges, it has been said, is "giving you the sleeve from your vest."

The issue of overcharging is extremely complicated. The term has several meanings. "Horizontal" overcharging involves filing charges against the suspect for a number of separate criminal acts (e.g., several burglaries the suspect may or may not have committed). If this involves wholly fabricated cases, where there is absolutely no evidence against the suspect, then it is clearly illegal and outrageous. McDonald, however, found no evidence of this form of overcharging. More common is the filing of charges where there is some evidence against the suspect but where the prosecutor has no real intention of prosecuting. This practice may be unfair but it is not illegal.[32]

"Vertical" overcharging involves filing the most serious possible charge for a particular criminal act (e.g., filing first-degree murder charges where the homicide was probably second-degree murder). The problem is not one of fabricating a case against an innocent suspect. Rather, it is filing a charge for which there is some evidence but where the prosecutor has no real intention of prosecuting on that charge. As some have put it, the prosecutor will "file high and deal down."

Both the American Law Institute's *Model Code of Pre-Arraignment Procedure* (1975) and the National Advisory Commission on Criminal Justice Standards and Goals (1973) condemned the practice of filing charges that are not ordinarily filed or on which there is no clear intent to prosecute.[33] (The ABA *Standards*, however, contain no similar injunction.)[34] General prohibitions in criminal justice, however, have little impact. Specific policies controlling the charge decision, and their impact on overcharging, are discussed later.

The Decision on the Sentence

Much plea bargaining is really sentence bargaining.[35] Where evidence is strong and the question of guilt not an issue, the only remaining issue is the sentence. Sentence bargaining can take several forms. The most direct is a straightforward agreement about a sentence recommendation by the prosecutor and/or a commitment from the judge. In some instances, charge bargaining is really a form of sentence bargaining. Some cynics have referred to this as "making the crime fit the punishment." An understanding is reached regarding the appropriate sentence and then a formal charge is selected that will yield the desired result.[36] Sentence bargaining through charge bargaining is also a traditional way of avoiding particularly harsh sentences. A guilty plea to assault, for example, avoids the usually automatic prison term for a robbery conviction. The filing or nonfiling of habitual criminal charges is also a form of sentence negotiations, with the prosecutor agreeing not to seek the heavy sentence such charges would entail.

Prosecutor- and Judge-Shopping

Although not usually included in discussions of plea bargaining, judge-shopping represents a discretionary decision that affects the ultimate disposition of a case.[37] In most local jurisdictions, it is known that there is great variety among judges, reflecting their attitudes about particular crimes. Some are known as tough on crime. (The judge in the Watergate scandal, John Sirica, was well known as "Maximum John" for his harsh sentencing practices.) Some are known to be tough on certain kinds of crime—drugs or crimes with weapons—and not others. Obviously, manipulating the court schedule to pick a judge known to be tough on the crime at hand allows the prosecutor to structure the parameters to his or her advantage. For the defense attorney, the process works in the opposite direction.

The opportunities for judge-shopping vary from jurisdiction to jurisdiction. They are greatly reduced in jurisdictions with formal and impersonal court-calendaring systems.

Even prior to judge-shopping, there are opportunities in some jurisdictions for the police to engage in prosecutor-shopping. The detectives in one jurisdiction reported making judgments about the toughness and competence of the different assistant prosecutors. The local district attorney's office rotated the assistant prosecutors through different assignments. Thus, it is sometimes possible to avoid certain prosecutors by holding back a case—on the presumably legitimate grounds that the investigation has not been completed—and wait for a different, preferred, prosecutor the following week.[38] As is the case with judge-shopping, choosing the more aggressive prosecutor sets the parameters of any eventual plea bargain.

Abolishing Plea Bargaining

Public disenchantment with the practice of plea bargaining probably reached its peak in the fall of 1973 when Vice President Spiro Agnew, accused of accepting bribes, avoided a possible prison term by being allowed to enter a nolo contendere plea to a lesser charge. It is not clear, however, whether public outrage was directed at the bargain itself, the spectacle of the vice president of the United States caught redhanded, or the Watergate scandal, which was unfolding at the same time.[39] Nonetheless, the Agnew scandal popularized the idea of abolishing plea bargaining.

The idea of "abolishing" plea bargaining represents a visceral reaction, a gut-level view that there is something inherently wrong with settling criminal cases through "deals." Abolition received its first serious endorsement in 1968 from Albert Alschuler. A few years later, he strengthened his condemnation, arguing that "no mechanism of control seems adequate to control the dangers" of plea bargaining.[40] Abolition received an even greater boost in 1973 when the National Advisory Commission on Criminal Justice Standards and Goals recommended that it be abolished by 1978.[41] Needless to say, this goal was not achieved.

The standard defense of plea bargaining has always been that it is necessary to handle the enormous volume of cases. The criminal courts would "collapse," it is said, if plea bargaining was abolished and every case had to go to trial. This is a pragmatic rather than a principled defense. Opponents of abolition often concede many of the problems with plea bargaining but argue that there is no realistic alternative.[42]

Abolition proposals recur in the history of the discretion controversy. The first law review article on police discretion found it to be illegal and called for its abolition.[43] The popularity of "flat-time" or determinate sentencing in the mid-1970s also reflected a belief that sentencing discretion had to be eliminated.[44] Generally, the passion for abolition quickly fades. Closer examination usually reveals that the decision at issue is exceedingly complex and that abolition is neither feasible nor desirable. A general consensus has developed that discretion is inevitable and when properly controlled serves some useful purposes.[45] With only a slight variation, plea-bargaining control efforts have followed this trajectory.

There have been several attempts to ban plea bargaining. The most significant was in Alaska, where the attorney general banned it in the entire state. Other attempts to eliminate the practice have been limited to specific types of cases, such as drug cases or crimes involving the use of a weapon.

Abolishing Plea Bargaining in Alaska

Alaska's attorney general, Avrum Gross, officially banned plea bargaining on July 3, 1975. A memorandum to all local district attorneys instructed them to "refrain from engaging in plea negotiations with defendants designed to arrive at an agreement for entry of a plea of guilty in return for a particular sentence." Gross approved charge reductions in some situations but advised that they should not be done "simply to obtain a plea of guilty." Exceptions to the ban were possible but had to be approved by the attorney general's office.[46]

It should be noted that the unique structure of the state's legal system made Gross's action possible. All the local prosecutors were under his direct supervision. A similar step would not be possible in other states where local prosecutors are elected and thus formally independent of the state attorney general.

The impact of the Alaska ban was surprising. Contrary to the dire predictions of most experts, the Alaska criminal justice system did not collapse. There was only a modest increase in jury trials, from 6.7 to 9.6 percent of all cases that reached a verdict. This was a smaller percentage than in most jurisdictions where plea bargaining existed.

The Myth of Case Pressure

Why didn't the Alaska system collapse? The best answer is that the role of case load pressure as the primary cause of plea bargaining has been grossly exaggerated. Historical evidence indicates that the jury trial disappeared long before the emergence of today's crowded urban criminal courts. The crime commissions of the 1920s noticed that jury trials were rare events. Milton Heumann found that they had been rare in nineteenth-century Connecticut courts. Not only were they equally rare in both high-volume and low-volume courts, but the "high-volume" courts of the period had an extremely low volume of cases by today's standards.[47]

The myth of case pressure is extremely relevant to the effort to control plea bargaining. If guilty pleas are not required by case pressure, then some other factors must explain their prevalence. Any effort to control plea bargaining must confront these factors.

What did happen in Alaska? The short answer is, not much. There were subtle adaptations, but no fundamental changes. The evidence does provide some insight into the question of whether limiting discretion at one point simply forces it to reappear somewhere else.

The Alaska data indicate that eliminating plea bargaining did not push discretion upstream and produce an increase in dismissals. The rate of dismissals remained high, at slightly more than 50 percent of all cases, but did not change significantly and was similar to rates in other jurisdictions.[48]

A more surprising result was that cases moved through the courts faster than before. The disposition time in Anchorage was cut in half, from a mean of 192 months to 89 months. This contradicted all the dire predictions that the criminal courts would "collapse" because of a backlog of cases.

This result may not be as contradictory as it first appears. There is supporting evidence from New Orleans, where case disposition time also dropped when the district attorney imposed a rigorous case-screening procedure.[49] The explanation may be that case disposition time is reduced when uncertainty is eliminated or reduced. In New Orleans, tighter case screening weeded out weak evidence cases. These are the cases that traditionally involve the most extensive charge bargaining. Left with only strong evidence cases ("dead-bang" or "slam-dunk" cases in standard jargon), both prosecutors and defense attorneys can reach an agreement more quickly. The ban on plea bargaining in Alaska probably had the same effect: by foreclosing a major option it fostered quicker settlement.

The results in Alaska and New Orleans are significant because attempts to *mandate* faster disposition through speedy-trial laws have been regarded as failures. Malcolm Feeley's study of speedy-trial laws found that members of courtroom work groups were highly successful in subverting the intent of those laws.[50] This result is consistent with the failure of most "mandated" changes in the criminal justice system (mandatory sentences, etc). With respect to case disposition time, it is possible that although officials cannot be forced to settle cases faster, that result can be encouraged by eliminating alternatives that consume a lot of time, such as charge bargaining. For this reason alone, limitations on plea bargaining, especially charge bargaining, may have an unintended but salutary effect on the criminal process.

Another adaptation to the ban on plea bargaining in Alaska, however, is cause for concern. The ban increased sentencing disparity. The sentencing differential was three times greater than in any of the six jurisdictions studied by McDonald. Going to trial increased sentence lengths by more than 300 percent. In effect, discretion was shifted downstream to the sentencing judge.[51]

Developments in New Orleans provide additional supporting evidence. With the stricter screening procedures weeding out the weak cases, there was less charge bargaining over the remaining strong evidence cases. This shifted the bargaining initiative to the judge, who induced pleas by deals over the sentence. McDonald found that sentencing differentials generally were narrowest in those jurisdictions where charge bargaining dominated and greatest where sentence bargaining dominated.[52]

McDonald concludes that the real choice is not between plea bargaining and no plea bargaining, but between the location of the bargaining. Eliminating charge bargaining only increases sentence bargaining. The choice is not without consequence, however. Greater sentence disparity, the apparent consequence of increased sentence bargaining, is itself a serious problem. In many respects it may be a greater problem than alleged abuses associated with plea bargaining. In passing, we should note that reducing sentencing disparities is one of the principal goals of sentencing reform, especially through the device of sentence guidelines. Sentencing reform is examined in Chapter 5, but it is worth noting at this point that these two attempts at discretion control may be working at cross-purposes.

Plea Bargaining as Routine Activity

One of the main reasons why the number of trials in Alaska did not increase substantially and the criminal courts did not collapse is that plea bargaining is essentially a very routinized activity involving people who are factually guilty.

To grasp this point, which is central to understanding plea bargaining, it is necessary to recast the image of plea bargaining. It is misleading to think of plea "bargaining" in terms of a marketplace or street bazaar. Typically, there is not much bargaining at all. Malcolm Feeley suggested that the proper metaphor is the supermarket, which does a high volume of business with fixed prices.[53] The key to maintaining a high volume of business in the criminal courts is the eventual elimination of the most important element of uncertainty: guilt or innocence. Guilty pleas are common because virtually all of the surviving cases involve people who are factually guilty. Many critics of plea bargaining and the entire criminal justice system have great difficulty swallowing that conclusion; therefore, it is important to explain the empirical basis for it.

Guilty pleas are the end result of the funnel effect in the criminal process (see Fig. 4.2). Cases are screened out in large numbers at various stages of the process. Only an estimated 37 percent of all crimes are reported in the first place. Only 20 percent of those are cleared by arrest. Perhaps as many as half of those arrests are subsequently dismissed. The figures are somewhat different for each crime. Figure 4.3 presents the funnel effect for robbery. The net result is that for every 100 robberies there are only 14 arrests and perhaps 9 prosecutions.

The process of attrition weeds out those cases where the evidence is weak and/or where the victim is unwilling to pursue the case. This leaves only a very small number of cases; in courtroom jargon they are referred to as the dead-bang cases: not only is the defendant factually guilty but the evidence is very strong.[54] There is no real contest over guilt or innocence and, because the "going rate" for this particular crime is well established, there is little to negotiate in terms of the ultimate punishment.[55]

The most recent multijurisdictional study of plea bargaining found a high degree of consistency and predictability in the process. Even al-

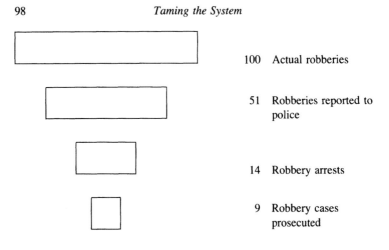

FIGURE 4.3. The attrition of robbery cases in the criminal justice system. (Bureau of Justice Statistics, *Criminal Victimization in the United States, 1989* [Washington, D.C.: Government Printing Office, 1991]; Federal Bureau of Investigation, *Crime in the United States, 1990* [Washington, D.C.: Government Printing Office, 1991]; Bureau of Justice Statistics, *The Prosecution of Felony Arrests, 1988* [Washington, D.C.: Government Printing Office, 1992])

lowing for variations based on local work group norms, about 80 percent of all plea-bargained cases fell within tightly defined sentencing clusters. Out of 5,600 cases, only 15 percent received a reduction in the top charge. Another 25 percent received a reduction of one or more secondary charges, but the authors concluded that these concessions by the prosecutor were largely symbolic, with no real substantive benefit to the defendant. Plea bargaining, in short, is not a bazaar, filled with negotiation, coercion, and wildly varying outcomes. Instead, it is a supermarket, doing a high volume of business, with fixed prices and predictable outcomes.[56]

The view of plea bargaining as a highly routinized and predictable activity has important implications for efforts to control the process. On the one hand, bargaining is not as wild and arbitrary as some critics have suggested. Instead, it is heavily controlled, albeit informally, by the bureaucratic setting and the influence of group norms. Or, to put it more directly, prosecutorial discretion may not be misused as badly in plea bargaining as so many people believe.

Other Attempts to Ban Plea Bargaining

Although Alaska is the only jurisdiction that has attempted a complete ban on plea bargaining, there have been several bans affecting specific types of crimes. These experiments offer additional evidence on the difficulty of banning plea bargaining by fiat.

The 1976–1977 Michigan Felony Firearms Law provided mandatory prison terms for gun-related crimes. The law was advertised under the slogan of "one with a gun gets you two." The prosecutor for Wayne County, which includes Detroit, supplemented the law with a policy of not dropping weapons charges in return for a guilty plea, thus banning charge bargaining.[57]

These two reforms produced no significant changes in the sentencing of murderers and armed robbers. Convicted armed robbers continued to get an average of six years in prison. The impact was negligible because prosecutors had not been trading away weapons charges in the first place. They were tough on armed robbers and had not been letting them beat the system through plea bargains.

There was a significant change with respect to less serious crimes, however. The new policies produced longer minimum prison sentences for persons convicted of felonious assault. Apparently, people charged with that crime had been able to plead to a lesser offense or bargain for a relatively light sentence. Other evaluations of sentencing reforms have also found that measures designed to get tough with serious offenders result primarily in harsher sentences for persons charged with moderately serious offenses. Some observers have labeled this process the "hydraulic," or "trickle-up," effect.[58] The criminal justice system, in short, is already pretty tough on serious offenders (i.e., persons convicted of a violent crime and/or with a substantial prior criminal record) and reforms designed to close alleged loopholes primarily affect less serious categories of crimes and offenders.[59]

Another notable attempt to ban plea bargaining was included in a highly publicized and very draconian drug law enacted by New York State in 1973. At the time it was celebrated as "the nation's toughest drug law." Among other things, the law banned pleas to lower charges for anyone charged with a Class A-1 drug offense (which carried a

mandatory sentence of fifteen to twenty-five years to life imprisonment).
Anyone charged with a lesser drug felony could not plead to a
misdemeanor.[60]

An evaluation of the law found strong evidence that it shifted discretion in the criminal process, with results that undercut the law's
intent. The percentage of drug arrests resulting in indictment dropped
from 39 to 25 percent. At the same time, convictions fell from 86 to
80 percent of indictments. The net result was that the overall percentage of drug arrests resulting in convictions fell from 33.5 to only 20
percent—a substantial 40 percent drop. The evaluation labeled this
process "leakage": cases that were previously plea bargained down
were either dismissed or beaten through acquittal.

Another ban on plea bargaining occurred in Hampton County, Iowa,
where a local prosecutor promised to make "no deals with dope
pushers." The no-deals policy, however, produced fewer drug convictions. Before the new policy, there were 107 guilty pleas in 109 drug
cases, with 88 (or 82.2%) pleading to reduced charges. A year after
the policy went into effect, all defendants in drug cases pled to the top
charge, but there was a 60 percent reduction in the number of indictments
(falling from 157 to 63).[61] Charge bargaining was apparently eliminated,
but it only shifted discretion to the charge-filing decision. A reform
designed to get tough with criminals resulted a lower overall level of
prosecution.

The various attempts to ban plea bargaining do not inspire optimism
about abolition as a solution to the problem of prosecutorial discretion.
In the case of Alaska, there was little significant change of any sort. In
the crime-specific bans, abolition apparently only moved discretion to
another point, with results that subvert the intent of the reform.

Regulating Plea Bargaining

Paralleling developments with respect to police discretion, a consensus
of opinion has emerged on the point that eliminating plea bargaining is
futile and that regulation is the more realistic approach. The principal
objective is to bring plea bargaining out of the closet and to raise its
visibility in the expectation that scrutiny by more people will curb the
worst abuses. Some reforms seek increased visibility through formal

procedural regulations. Others address the charging decision directly, with indirect effects on plea negotiations. Still other reforms specify procedures for the plea-negotiating process itself.

Controlling the Charging Decision

New Orleans

When Harry Connick (father of the popular singer) became New Orleans district attorney in 1974, he created a new Screening Division to control the charging decision.[62] Under the new procedure, an assistant DA reviews all cases and makes a decision to charge or dismiss. If the decision is to dismiss, the assistant DA must explain why in writing. To make the system work, Connick had to alter the system of status and rewards in the DA's office, elevating the traditionally low status of "the desk" relative to trial work, which had traditionally been the high-status center of the action. Among other things, Connick transferred lawyers with more experience to the screening division.

At the simplest level, Connick's reform was a conventional process of bureaucratization. It created a new layer of bureaucracy (or at least enlarged the role of an old one) and established a formal procedure for holding officials accountable for their actions. The requirement of a written explanation for dismissing cases is a classic exercise in bureaucratic paperwork.

The primary purpose of Connick's reforms was to tighten the screening of cases and improve the efficiency of the DA's office. The New Orleans DA's office had a longstanding practice of screening out few cases and when Connick took office he found over 7,500 "open" cases. One went back to 1936. He quickly dismissed about 5,000 old cases and his procedures reduced the number of new cases accepted by 20 percent.

The new screening procedures had an indirect but nonetheless significant effect on plea bargaining. For all practical purposes, it eliminated charge bargaining. Screening eliminated cases that were weak because the evidence was questionable and the chance of conviction was low. This left the trial attorneys with sure winners and they had little need or inclination to bargain for pleas to lesser offenses. This may also have reduced the problem of overcharging. With no need to bargain over the charge, there was no need to stack the deck.

The consequences of eliminating charge bargaining are complex and ambiguous in their meaning. "Law and order"-minded conservatives might not be happy with the fact that a lot of arrestees are not prosecuted. Under the old procedure many would have pleaded guilty to a lesser charge. At the same time, however, Connick's reform essentially systematized a process that informally characterizes most plea negotiations. All of the research on plea bargaining has found that the strength of the evidence is the key variable.[63] Connick's reforms made a sharper distinction between strong evidence and weak evidence cases.

Yet, as also occurred in Alaska, reducing the frequency of charge bargaining enhanced sentence bargaining. Discretion moved downstream to the sentencing judge. McDonald found judges playing a larger role in outcomes in New Orleans, and this resulted in greater differentials in sentences. Sentencing differentials were greater there than in any of the six jurisdictions he studied.

The net result of the reform of the charging decision in New Orleans, in terms of social policy, is ambiguous. If conservatives would be upset at the higher rate of dismissals, liberals would be troubled by the increase in sentencing disparity. As McDonald suggests, the idea of "banning" plea bargaining has been presented in overly simplistic either–or terms. In practice, the choice is not between bargains or no bargains. It actually lies between different kinds of bargains, with different consequences. The choice is between charge bargaining and sentence bargaining, between bargaining dominated by the prosecutor and bargaining in which the judge plays a major role.

King County, Washington

A somewhat similar process occurred in King County, Washington, which includes Seattle.[64] The district attorney's office developed a set of written policies governing the filing of charges. One rule instructed assistant prosecutors not to engage in charge bargaining where weapons were used or even present. Another rule required that in the case of rape, robbery, and residential burglary, sentence recommendations had to include "some loss of liberty." Discretion was not abolished completely: assistant district attorneys could deviate from the sentence recommendation policy but only with the approval of a senior prosecutor. Even then, they could bypass the mandatory sentence recommendation only in three circumstances: where evidence problems made conviction unlikely; where the defendant provided information leading to conviction of others responsible for more serious crimes; or where a lesser sentence was required by considerations of "mercy."

The impact of these policies on charge bargaining appears to have been substantial. Among the six jurisdictions studied by McDonald, the disposition of cases in Seattle most closely resembled New Orleans. Charge bargaining (i.e., where charge bargaining or dismissal was the only factor in the disposition) was less significant than in any other city. Sentence bargaining (where a sentence recommendation alone was the only factor) was extremely important (and second only to New Orleans).

Reflections on Bureaucratizing the Prosecutor's Offices

The reforms in New Orleans and Seattle represent a rather conventional form of bureaucratization. Some general observations on this process are in order. First, there are some interesting parallels with the attempts to control police discretion. The development of formal procedures (written policies, reporting requirements, review by supervisors) is more common in larger cities. This parallels developments in policing where the biggest departments were the first to adopt restrictive shooting policies and, in general, to have elaborate standard operating procedure systems. Second, bureaucratization initially alienated front-line personnel but eventually obtained compliance with new rules. Assistant prosecutors resented controls that limited their traditional discretion, challenged their self-image as professionals, and imposed more paperwork. Despite these grumblings, however, it appears that staff members generally complied with the new requirements. McDonald detected significant differences in the outcome of cases in different prosecutorial offices based on their degree of bureaucratization.[65]

At the same time there is an important difference between bureaucratization in police departments and prosecutorial offices. Police discretion is essentially a "low-visibility" phenomenon. Officers act alone and out of view of independent observers, including supervisors. Prosecutors, on the other hand, work in a group setting. The key decisions are bargains, negotiated with others. The fact that plea negotiations occur in the back room rather than in open court may mean that they have low visibility with respect to the public, but they are highly visible to other courthouse officials. One result is that controls over prosecutors' discretion tend to push the discretionary power to other members of the work group. The central problem with police discretion is asserting any kind of control over low-visibility decisions. The problem with prosecutorial discretion is controlling the behavior of several officials.

Even with all these problems in mind, bureaucratizing prosecutors' offices may yield other benefits. McDonald found a qualitative difference in those offices with greater formal controls. Not only was charge bargaining lessened, but there were fewer charges filed by the police.[66] This is an important consideration, given the concern about abuse of overcharging. Where prosecutors stick with top charges, the police may feel they do not have to stack the deck with additional charges. In terms of making the charging process fairer and more consistent, this is a gain.

This point has some broader implications. As noted earlier, one of the standard criticisms of the discretion control effort is that controls often only shift discretion elsewhere with the result that the intent of the new controls is subverted. The effect on decision makers upstream and downstream may not always be such subversion. In some instances a new control may force other decision makers to alter their behavior in a positive way. We do not yet have a good picture of the full dimensions of these systemwide effects. The control of discretion has been attempted on a piecemeal basis. Each decision is attacked as if it existed in isolation from other decision points. This can be explained in terms of the politics of reform: a crisis defines a "problem"; a self-constituted reform group mobilizes to attack the problem; a specific reform is proposed; and so on. Although we understand intellectually that the criminal process is a "system," the politics of reform have not encouraged a systemwide approach to discretion control.

McDonald also noted that cases in the bureaucratized offices were disposed of more quickly and that there was more likely to be a formal record of the plea agreement. These, too, are gains. Case processing, as already noted, is speeded up by narrowing the range of bargaining alternatives. Production of a written or electronically stored record, a natural concomitant of bureaucratization, serves to open up the process (a written record or a printout is necessarily "visible," compared with an informal verbal agreement) and reduce the possibility of misunderstandings (and formal appeals based on those misunderstandings).

The potential for even more formal control over the charging decision exists. One model is the case evaluation system developed in the 1970s by PROMIS (Prosecutor's Management Information System). The procedure is very similar to the one developed earlier for bail setting. Prosecutors use a evaluation form to assign points based on the nature of the case and the characteristics of the defendant. Defendants charged with the more serious crimes and/or with more serious criminal histories are identified as being ineligible for charge reduction and/or recommendations for lenient sentence.[67]

Reforming Plea-Bargaining Procedures

The majority of plea-bargaining reforms that have been proposed and implemented are essentially procedural in nature. That is, they attempt to regulate how plea negotiations are conducted in the expectation that this will reduce undesirable outcomes. In the terms used here, a ban on plea bargaining or even a limitation on charge bargaining would be considered a substantive change in plea bargaining. We now turn our attention to the various procedural reforms.

Ensuring a Factual Basis of the Plea

The initial concern about plea bargaining in the early 1960s focused on the problem of the accuracy of guilty pleas.[68] This involved two possible abuses: (1) factually innocent persons might be convicted, and (2) guilty pleas to crimes wholly unrelated to the crime the defendant actually committed made a mockery of justice. These concerns led to a major revision of the Federal Rules of Criminal Procedure. Rule 11 was revised in 1966 to require the judge to "address the defendant personally" to determine that the plea was voluntary and that "there is a factual basis for the plea." Rule 11, however, did not provide a standard against which to measure that factual basis. Rule 11 was further revised in 1975 to include more detailed instructions for the judge.

McDonald identified a variety of measures used in his six local jurisdictions to determine factual accuracy. These included asking the defendant directly if he or she committed the offense; asking other questions about the offense; and requiring the prosecutor to produce either evidence or a witness. New Orleans relied almost entirely on direct questions to the defendant (82% of all cases), while Norfolk, Virginia, asked the district attorney to produce evidence (38% of all cases) or a witness (25% of all cases).[69]

The lack of a factual basis for a plea may not be the real issue, however. The problem is not the murderer who pleads guilty to larceny.

Rather, it is that some robbers (who are factually guilty of that crime) are allowed to plead to the lesser offense of larceny or that some people who in fact committed a rape are allowed to plead to assault. Such pleas result in significantly less serious penalties and are the cause of public complaints that criminals are "getting off easy." In these instances, however, there is a genuine factual basis for the plea. A robbery necessarily includes a larceny. The problem is whether such pleas are justified. Requiring judicial inquiry into the factual basis, however, will not curb the problem of excessive charge bargaining.

McDonald tried to measure the impact of judicial inquiry into the factual basis of pleas but found the data too ambiguous to permit a judgment. He measured how frequently judges rejected pleas, on the assumption that this reflected judicial determination of a defective plea. The overall rejection rate, 2 percent, was extremely low, with no jurisdiction higher than 5 percent. These figures could be interpreted to mean that nearly all pleas are sound or that the process is just an empty formality. The requirement of judicial inquiry may serve as a general check on the process and eliminate gross abuses.[70]

Increased Judicial Involvement

Rule 11 and its state counterparts increase judicial involvement in the plea negotiation process. This represents a general reform strategy, based on the assumption that judges are more concerned about fairness and the integrity of the judicial process than conviction-oriented prosecutors and will serve as a check on prosecutorial behavior.[71]

General practice now seems to include fairly extensive judicial involvement. McDonald found that only 11 percent of the defendants had their pleas accepted without any direct inquiry from the judge—and virtually all of those were in misdemeanor cases. Over three-quarters (78.2%) of the defendants were addressed individually by the judge.[72]

Even more critical than the question of a factual basis for the plea is whether it represents a "knowing" and voluntary waiver of rights. It is important because, whereas there may be relatively few instances of a factually innocent person pleading guilty to something he did not do, coerced pleas could well be a routine practice. This matter involves several distinct questions. The first is whether the defendant knows what rights he or she is waiving. These rights include the right to trial, to remain silent, to confront witnesses, and to appeal. In all the jurisdictions studied by McDonald at least one right was generally mentioned, although it was usually the right to a jury trial. Some jurisdictions generally mentioned three or more rights, but El Paso and Norfolk rarely mentioned that many.[73]

There is good reason to question the efficacy of this form of judicial inquiry, however. Although designed to ensure fairness, judicial inquiry comes at the end of a negotiating process that may well have been very coercive. A defendant can be carefully coached to provide the proper answers to the judge's questions. Thus, the ritual of judicial inquiry could be merely an empty formality.

McDonald concluded from interviews with defendants that most did in fact understand what they were doing. To say that the pleas were "knowing," however, is not the same as saying that they were voluntary. This highlights the civil libertarian concern about the potentially coercive aspects of plea bargaining: whether defendants knowingly waive certain rights because they feel they must. There is in fact evidence of a "trial penalty" in the criminal process whereby defendants who do not agree to plead guilty are punished with more severe sentences.[74] On this point, McDonald's interviews yielded particularly troubling responses. Most of the defendants he interviewed (77%) felt they had to accept the deal and would be punished if they did not.[75] Many stated that they never saw their lawyer until just before trial and that they were threatened with more charges by the police or with a harsher sentence by the judge.[76] It is important to note that these defendants, like those Jonathan Casper interviewed, did not claim to be factually innocent.[77] They complained about fairness and the kind of deal they got.

Pretrial Conferences

Another device for bringing plea bargaining out into the open is the requirement of a formal pretrial conference. There have been several experiments with this approach. In one instance conferences speeded up the processing of cases but had no effect on the percentage of guilty pleas.[78] In another jurisdiction, prosecutors and defense attorneys found the conference a nuisance, resisted it, and eventually had it abolished.[79]

Conferences may serve another positive function, however. An evaluation of formal pretrial conferences—which included the judge, prosecutor, and defense attorney, with the defendant permitted to attend and the victim invited to attend (about half of the victims did attend)— found that it had a favorable impact on both defendants' and victims' perceptions of the process. There was no change, however, in the disposition of cases or the ultimate sentences.[80] Given the widespread perception that plea bargains are unfair—on the part of both defendants and the public—this is a modestly important improvement.

Written Plea Agreements

Yet another reform is the signed plea agreement. The terms of the bargain are committed to writing and the defendant signs a statement verifying that the agreement is voluntary. McDonald found this to be a rather common practice: the specific terms of pleas were set forth in 71.1 percent of all cases in the six cities. Practices varied widely from jurisdiction to jurisdiction, however. All plea agreements were set forth in writing in Tucson and in 98.6 percent of the cases in Seattle; but this was true in only 43.3 percent of the cases in New Orleans and in none of the cases in El Paso.[81]

As is the case with judicial inquiry, however, the signed agreement is the end product of a negotiating process. Putting it in writing may eliminate misunderstanding later but does not curb any coerciveness in the first instance.

Conclusions

In terms of controlling discretion through formal rules, the subject of plea bargaining inspires considerable pessimism. Attempting to abolish plea bargaining outright appears to be futile. Controlling the decision to charge through bureaucratic means, on the other hand, produces very mixed results. In some instances it moves discretion upstream or downstream, with results that are not necessarily desirable. Procedural reforms, meanwhile, do not touch the substance of negotiated pleas. Plea bargaining, in short, is an extremely elusive phenomenon which cannot be reduced to a single decision point that can be isolated and controlled.

This may be an overly pessimistic conclusion. The attempt to control discretion in plea bargaining has yielded some gains. As is the case with police discretion and bail setting, we have succeeded in bringing out into the open a critical decision affecting individual liberty. We now have a realistic understanding of what goes on between arrest and trial. Knowledge is wisdom and if we have a strong appreciation of the enormous difficulties in controlling plea bargaining, at least we are no longer susceptible to being seduced by simplistic reform proposals.

Nor should we discount the importance of some of the modest reforms in prosecutorial practices. The bureaucratization of prosecutors' offices is in some important ways a positive step. Minimally, establishing formal controls over the charging decision represents a recognition that an important decision is being made, that there should be some uniformity in those decisions, and that individual prosecutors should be held accountable for their decisions. Increased judicial involvement in plea negotiations may be very much an empty formality, but is is a vast improvement over no judicial scrutiny at all. Finally, putting plea agreements in writing adds an important element of certainty to the process, eliminating potential misunderstanding and providing a basis for possible appeals.

These observations lead us to rethink that much-maligned phenomenon known as *bureaucratization*. Bureaucratization is not a static phenomenon. The word itself denotes a process of change, a movement toward a more complex form of organization. Current practice at any given moment is measured in terms of what sociologists have defined as an ideal type of bureaucratic arrangement. In today's criminal courts, the process of bureaucratization involves major changes in the courtroom work group. Most of the research on the criminal process, and plea bargaining in particular, puts great emphasis on the powerful influence of local work group norms on the processing of cases.

From a historical standpoint, one of the most important events in the emergence of the contemporary courtroom work group is the expanded role of the defense attorney. The presence of a defense attorney (even if only in some minimal formal respect) is itself a product of a revolution in constitutional law. It is now an overused cliché to say that the decade of the 1960s was a time of social and political "revolution." Too often, the term is used to describe utterly superficial changes in clothes or hair styles. In some respects, however, there may be a great deal of truth to this cliche.

One fundamental change in American criminal justice was the role of the criminal defense attorney. In the 1963 *Gideon v. Wainwright* decision the Supreme Court ruled that every criminal defendant facing felony charges had a right to an attorney.[82] The *Gideon* decision alone would have had a near-revolutionary impact on local criminal justice systems, but the Court extended the Sixth Amendment right to counsel in other important ways as well. In 1964 it ruled that suspects in the custody of the police had a right to counsel if they were to be interrogated.[83] Two years later, in *Miranda*, the Court ruled that the police had to affirmatively advise suspects of their right to an attorney.[84] Finally, in 1972, the Court held that defendants in misdemeanor cases where there was the possibility of imprisonment were entitled to a lawyer.[85] The decisions involving the Sixth Amendment right to counsel were but one part of a much broader "due process revolution" affecting the entire criminal justice system, which, in turn, was but one part of a more pervasive "rights revolution" that affected every institution.[86]

Gideon and the decisions that followed had a profound effect on the institutional arrangements of the criminal justice system. The provision of criminal defense was a patchwork, catch-as-catch-can system. While a few cities had public defender systems, most jurisdictions relied on a mixture of private and court-appointed counsel. The net result was that many persons facing felony charges, often with the possibility of long prison terms, went to trial without a lawyer. A rereading of Donald Newman's classic studies of plea bargaining dramatizes the extent to which our standards of fairness have changed. One is astounded at the casual reports that many defendants never had a lawyer. In the context of the times, Newman's 1966 comment (based on 1956–1957 field research) that "in the serious or doubtful cases, trial judges ordinarily assign counsel with great care, where possible selecting 'good' lawyers," was intended to be reassuring.[87] By contemporary standards, however, it only dramatizes the extent to which defendants in routine felony cases either had no counsel or an assigned counsel of dubious qualifications. Newman's earlier study, based on 1951–1952 field research, reported that nearly half of all felony defendants had no lawyer. The 1955–1956 field research found that "many, perhaps most guilty plea defendants waive counsel."[88]

All that has now changed. As a consequence of the Supreme Court's decisions, the public defender has become a permanent institutional presence in the criminal process. Although there are considerable variations in how defense attorneys are provided—with some jurisdictions relying entirely on public defenders and others using a mix of public and assigned private attorneys—the presence of legal representation now appears to be universal.[89] This can be considered the outcome of bureaucratic change to fulfill a rights mandate. To comply with the right to counsel asserted by the Court, local officials had to provide defense counsel on a systematic basis. In most urban jurisdictions, where a disproportionate percentage of serious felony cases are prosecuted, there are now public defender systems, with full-time defense counsel.

There is much discontent with the quality of defense provided by public defenders. Considerable evidence suggests that the effort is pro forma at best. Defense attorneys often meet their clients just before appearing in court. Faced with heavy case loads, they have little time for thorough (or perhaps even adequate) case preparation. And unlike the private defense attorney, who depends on his or her reputation for success, the public defender has no direct incentive to provide a particularly vigorous defense. A study of Cook County, Illinois, reported public defenders stating that none of their supervisors cared about their "won/loss" performance.[90] These factors lend support for Casper's cynical joke about having a public defender instead of a lawyer.[91] At the same time, however, studies of case outcomes have found that after all relevant variables have been controlled, it does not make much difference whether the defendant has a private attorney or a public defender.[92]

The role of the public defender again raises the question of empty formalism. Has compliance with a basic constitutional right resulted in little more than an empty ritual? Possibly. There is another way of looking at the matter, however. Criticisms of public defenders may be misconceived, reflecting the old romantic image of the criminal process as a spirited adversarial contest. A more realistic view is that the criminal process is administrative and highly routinized. In this context, the public defender may serve an important function merely by virtue of his or her presence. I am tempted to call this the "warm body" theory of criminal defense. The mere presence of a defense lawyer functions as a "check" on the prosecutor, preventing the worst abuses from occurring. Given the bureaucratic setting of the criminal courts, this form of check may be more effective than any written rule or directive. Finally, the proper standard by which to measure this is not the unrealistic ideal of contested trials but the historical reality of the pre–1963 period, when many defendants had no lawyer at all.

5

Sentencing Reform

The Politics of Sentencing Reform

In a remarkable burst of reform, criminal sentencing in the United States underwent sweeping changes between the mid-1970s and 1990. Nearly every state and the federal government revised its sentencing laws during the period. Although some of the changes were minor, several were radical departures from past practice. As one commentator observed, at the beginning of this period it was possible to talk about *an* American system of criminal sentencing; by 1990 there were several different approaches to sentencing.[1]

Reform was accompanied by a searching philosophical debate over the purpose of criminal sentencing.[2] This debate reexamined first principles to a degree that had not occurred since the creation of the modern penitentiary two hundred years ago.[3]

Sentencing Discretion and the Indeterminate Sentence

As was the case with other areas of the criminal process, discontent with sentencing focused on discretion.[4] It was inevitable, then, that sentencing reform would be radical in the sense of challenging first principles. The status of discretion in sentencing was completely different from discretion in every other part of the criminal process. In policing, plea bargaining, and elsewhere, discretion was the great unmentionable, a subject that officials refused to acknowledge. The first

112

task facing reformers in these areas was to force public recognition that discretion existed.

Not so with sentencing. Discretion was not only visible under the indeterminate sentence; it was celebrated as the cornerstone of sentencing policy. When first introduced, the indeterminate sentence was a great reform, resting on the premise that offenders could be effectively rehabilitated only by individualizing their sentences. Individualization could be achieved by granting broad discretion to judges and parole boards. Discretion as to the appropriate sentence, length of prison term, and parole release date represented the very essence of the system.

All of the sentencing reforms of the past fifteen years have struck at the core of that system. They were designed to curb discretion, with the trend of change steadily in the direction of greater determinacy.

Criticisms, Left and Right

Both liberals and conservatives attacked the indeterminate sentence and the underlying philosophy of rehabilitation,[5] although for different reasons. Within each political camp, moreover, there were different views as to the exact nature of the problem and the proper solution.

Liberals were the first to question the indeterminate sentence. In 1959 law professor Francis Allen suggested that the rehabilitative ideal had been "debased" in practice, with very dangerous consequences. Humanitarian rhetoric about rehabilitation masked a punitive reality, and the entire system of decision making was characterized by "procedural laxness and irregularity."[6] Although couched in very moderate, thoughtful terms, Allen's criticisms had radical implications. The Supreme Court's due process revolution, which soon followed, reflected his point about procedural laxness. In time, others would articulate explicitly radical attacks on the indeterminate sentence.

As important as it was for so many other parts of the justice system, the due process revolution did not challenge the indeterminate sentence directly. Instead, there were important decisions governing particular aspects of the correctional process: due process standards for probation and parole revocation decisions. The prisoners' rights movement, meanwhile, produced procedural protections for prison discipline decisions. The prisoners' rights movement, in turn, stimulated the accreditation movement in corrections. The resulting standards have institutionalized an elaborate set of rules over decision making by prison officials.[7] With the exception of the death penalty, however, routine felony sentencing was not directly affected by the Court.

The line of thinking opened by Allen reached its peak with the publication of an American Friends Service Committee report, *Struggle for Justice*, in 1971.[8] Reflecting the impact of both the social upheavals of the 1960s and its Quaker sponsorship, the report was profoundly critical of imprisonment and the entire criminal justice system. It found no credible scientific evidence to support sentencing and parole decisions. The report went even further and described the pervasive discretionary decision making as "awesome in its scope." In a separate chapter on the issue, it stated its readiness "to strike at the core [of the problem]— discretionary power."[9] In an abolitionist mode, it suggested that "the elimination of discretion would make the lives of the bulk of the clients of the criminal justice system more tolerable."[10] Unchecked discretion resulted in arbitrary sentences and racial discrimination. At the same time, the correctional "treatment" process was little more than a cynical game in which prisoners jumped through certain hoops to prove that they were rehabilitated. Judge Marvin Fraenkel added another influential voice with his 1972 book, *Criminal Sentences: Law Without Order*, in which he condemned the lack of controls over judicial sentencing power.[11]

As interest in sentencing reform increased, not all liberals wanted to go as far as *Struggle for Justice*. Norval Morris spoke for those who wanted to retain the principle of rehabilitation while curbing its abuses.[12] Others wanted to substitute a philosophy of just deserts for rehabilitation as the underlying rationale and retain some limited discretion for judges.[13] A few diehards, mainly correctional officials, tried to keep the faith, arguing that rehabilitation had never really been tried. They had a point. There had never been any real investment in prison treatment programs, which consumed only 5 to 10 percent of prison budgets at most. Correctional "treatment," however, was in disrepute, even among liberals. One veteran correctional official summed up the "treatment" of parole supervision by asking, "Who needs a doorbell pusher?"[14]

Conservatives had their own criticisms of sentencing. Their main argument was that the prevailing system of sentencing had failed to control crime.[15] Some argued that correctional treatment programs did not work. This view was summarized by Robert Martinson's highly publicized (although generally misinterpreted) study, which argued that few if any correctional treatment programs were demonstrably effective.[16] Other conservatives challenged the concept of rehabilitation on philosophical grounds and revived the ideas of punishment, deterrence, and incapacitation as justifications for sentencing. James Q. Wilson spoke for many conservatives when he declared in 1975 that "wicked people exist. Nothing avails except to set them apart from innocent people."[17] Finally, many conservatives argued that the broad discretion conferred on judges and parole authorities by the indeterminate sentence resulted in inadequate crime control. Judges sentenced offenders to overly short prison terms and/or parole authorities released them too early.

The 1971 Attica prison uprising galvanized the growing discontent on both sides of the political spectrum and prompted the creation of two highly influential study commissions which set the framework for the emerging debate over sentencing. The deliberations of the Committee for the Study of Imprisonment quickly moved far beyond the question of imprisonment per se and extended to the very nature of criminal sentencing. This resulted in publication of *Doing Justice* in 1976, nominally written by Andrew von Hirsch.[18] The same year, the Twentieth Century Fund created the Task Force on Criminal Sentencing and published its report, *Fair and Certain Punishment*, which recommended replacing the indeterminate with determinate sentencing.[19] Several states quickly adopted radical revisions of their sentencing laws and the national sentencing reform movement was under way.

A Historical Note on Sentencing
Before the Indeterminate Sentence

Underlying the criticisms of the indeterminate sentence was a vague and highly romanticized view of criminal sentencing in an earlier era. Because many reformers imagined that determinate sentencing would be a return to some a better system that had been mistakenly discarded, it is worth examining this view of the past.

According to the standard view, the indeterminate sentence represented a radical shift from a system of "determinate," or "fixed," or "flat-time" sentences to one based on the principle of indeterminacy. When the judge said three years in prison in the nineteenth century, the offender served three years.

There is absolutely no reason to believe this is what actually happened. In practice, the system of punishment was highly indeterminate, although not officially so. First, it is clear that the harsh punishments prescribed by law were systematically mitigated. Although many crimes carried the death penalty, relatively few people were either sentenced to die or executed. Plea bargaining was well established by the mid-nineteenth century and probably existed in one form or another even earlier.[20] Death sentences and prison terms for routine felonies were mitigated through extensive use of pardons and commutations. Governors complained loudly about the stream of family members and friends beseeching them for pardons. There is good reason to believe that their unhappiness over this burden was an important factor in the development of the indeterminate sentence, which transferred the decision to an administrative agency.[21]

That transfer highlights the relevant point about the history of sentencing discretion. A more accurate view of criminal justice history is that discretion has always pervaded the criminal justice system.[22] As historian Lawrence Friedman suggests, innovations have generally involved the formal ratification of existing practices.[23] In many instances, a new administrative agency was created to handle decisions that had long been made informally. A few examples illustrate the point. Although the history of probation is usually told in terms of the story of the humble Boston shoemaker John Augustus in the 1840s, the evidence suggests that there was a long history of nonprison sentences, often including restrictive conditions. The assumptions and practices embodied in the first juvenile court in 1899—the idea that juveniles should be treated differently, the disposition of cases in a manner substantially different from adult cases, the assumption that juveniles were not hardened criminals but people who could be rehabilitated through relatively mild sanctions, and so on—also had long histories.

The implications of this evidence are clear. If it is true that discretion always pervaded the system of punishment, then there is no discretion-free golden age to return to. The indeterminate sentence did not create broad discretionary authority; it institutionalized it, gave it official legal sanction, and in the process expanded it significantly. Current reforms may do nothing more than shift the locus of discretion once again.

Two criticisms of the indeterminate sentence are worth noting, however. First, the indeterminate sentence appears to have resulted in longer prison terms than had been the case before.[24] Judges and parole boards used their expanded discretionary power to confine more people for longer periods of time. Thus the historical evidence suggests that although a certain degree of discretion is inevitable, its scope can be controlled.

Second, one of the major problems with the indeterminate sentence was that it divided the sentencing process between two authorities: the judge and the parole board.[25] This probably invited problems. In principle, divided responsibility is unwise. In this particular case it created a situation where each authority tries to guess what the other really has in mind. Thus the judge says, if I give him three years, the parole board will let him out in eighteen months; to make sure he really does three years in prison I need to give him six. Eliminating discretionary parole release, concentrating the decision in the hands of the judge, and limiting the range available to the judge—as some recent sentencing reforms have done—may have a salutary effect.[26]

In short, the historical evidence strongly suggests that a certain degree of discretion is inevitable; the exact nature of its use, however, may be subject to control.

Decision Points and Decision Makers

Sentencing is no exception to the rule—explored in the earlier chapters of this book—that particular decisions are highly complex and often involve multiple decision makers. Sentencing has its unique aspects of this problem. It is helpful to divide sentencing decision makers into three groups. First, there are the two decision makers who, under the indeterminate sentence, have formal authority over criminal sentences: judges and parole boards. Second, there are officials "downstream" who have some ability to affect the length of prison terms. Third, there are officials "upstream" whose decisions determine the parameters for judicial decision making.

Judges and Parole Authorities

Criminal sentencing is nominally the responsibility of the judge. The single most important decision is whether to sentence the convicted offender to prison. In terms of its impact on the individual, this decision ranks with the police officer's decision to arrest and the prosecutor's decision to charge as one of the three most consequential decisions in the criminal justice system.

The decision on probation is itself a complex one. First, the judge does not make the decision in isolation. In some cases it is the product of a plea bargain in which the judge may or may not have played a major role. A sentence recommendation by the prosecutor is often *a*— if not *the*—major influence. The judge's probation–prison decision is also heavily influenced by the presentence investigation (PSI). This is the primary source of information available to the judge about the offender. One study found that judges followed the PSI recommendations 96 percent of the time.[27] The nature of these reports depends on the quality of the probation staff, the thoroughness and accuracy of the investigations, and the inclusion of a strong sentence recommendation.[28]

Nor is probation a simple matter. Typically, a sentence of probation includes certain restrictions. These generally involve employment, participation in some kind of treatment program, restrictions on travel or personal associations, reporting to the probation officer, the length of the probationary period, and so on. The judge has broad discretionary authority over these matters.

In addition, there is the decision to revoke probation. Although the judge has the formal authority to make that decision, it is enforced by probation officers. In this respect, probation officers play a law enforcement role; the decision to revoke probation is identical to the police officer's arrest discretion. And until fairly recently, that discretion was completely free of controls.[29] The Supreme Court's decision in *Mempa v. Rhay* (1967), guaranteeing a probationer's right to counsel at a revocation hearing, was part of the Court's larger due process revolution and one of the first important limits of discretionary decision making in the correctional area.[30]

One of the major features of criminal sentencing in the United States is the very stark choice that judges face between probation and prison.[31] The consequences for the offender are, as indicated previously, enormous. Norval Morris and Michael Tonry, two of the leading authorities on sentencing, recently made a forceful argument on behalf of intermediate punishments (fines, community service, etc.) that would give judges more flexibility and could be more closely tailored to the offender.[32] Suffice it to say at this point that this proposal would enormously complicate the matter of sentencing discretion, adding yet another range of options. It is regrettable that their discussion does not directly address how to control those decisions.

In the event of a decision to imprison the offender, the actual length of the prison term is an extraordinarily complex matter under the indeterminate sentence. Judges have enormous discretion, but it is constrained by a number of formal and informal factors. First, judges operate within the limits of the relevant statute. This varies from state to state. For most crimes there are specified minimum and maximum terms. A possible range of one to fifty years is not unusual, however. In many instances there are limits such as mandatory minimum sentences.

After the judge has pronounced sentence, the decision on the actual length of a prison term is controlled by a number of factors. Formal responsibility is vested in the paroling authority. The pre-1976 California law was unique in that it carried the medical model of correctional treatment to its logical conclusion by making all prison terms indeterminate. The Adult Authority had complete power over the length of the sentence. The decision to grant early release from prison on parole is, obviously, one of enormous consequence. Much of the fury directed at the indeterminate sentence concerned the fact that these all-important decisions about the "rehabilitation" of a prisoner were made without any scientific basis.[33]

The paroling authority's decision regarding release is in turn affected by a number factors. Most important is the operation of "good-time" laws which directly affect the date of parole eligibility. This and other downstream factors will be discussed shortly.

As with probation, parole release includes various restrictions and the possibility of revocation for violating those conditions. This includes two important discretionary decisions. The first involves the exact nature of the restrictions and the second involves the power to revoke parole and return the offender to prison. Parole revocation was another of the many hidden discretionary decisions that remained free of any meaningful controls until the 1960s. The Supreme Court introduced a limited range of due process protections in parole revocations with the *Morrissey v. Brewer* (1971) decision.[34]

Controlling Sentences Upstream

As Chapter 4 indicated, much plea bargaining is really sentence bargaining. Suffice it to say here that the various decisions comprising plea bargaining are a part of the sentencing process. Norval Morris goes so far as to say that "charge and plea bargaining is our primary sentencing technique.''[35] Because plea bargaining is a group decision-making process, with the judge playing a greater or lesser role, depending on local custom, any significant change in the law of sentencing will have a major impact on the plea-bargaining process. One of the most important issues in sentencing reform is the extent to which the move toward greater determinacy produces major changes in plea bargaining. Does limiting the sentencing discretion of judges only shift the important decisions upstream to the prosecutor?

Modifying Sentences Downstream

The length of a prison term is also affected by decisions downstream in the criminal process. The most important is the practice of shortening sentences by granting prisoners credit for ''good time.'' Because the primary effect of good time under the indeterminate sentence is to advance the date of initial parole eligibility (although not necessarily guaranteeing release at the first opportunity), it should be seen as a part of the overall sentencing process.

The laws on good time are complicated and vary from state to state.[36] Generally, there are two kinds of good time: automatic and discretionary. In some states both operate simultaneously. Automatic good time accrues as a matter of right, with the prisoner earning so many days of credit for every month served. Because this involves no exercise of discretion, it is of little concern here. Discretionary good time, however, is important. The prisoner earns this kind of good time for participating in institutional programs (education, etc.) and for maintaining a record of good behavior. This necessarily involves a series of discretionary decisions by prison officials that ultimately affect the length of a prison term.

The same decisions affect the length of prison terms in another way. Under the indeterminate sentence, a prisoner's record of institutional conduct is a major factor in parole release decisions.[37] Quite independent of formal good-time credit, a record of good behavior is seen as evidence of rehabilitation. Conversely, the prisoner with numerous disciplinary actions in his or her file is presumed to be not ready for release.

The ''record'' of institutional conduct, however, is a purely bureaucratic phenomenon, indicated by officially recorded actions. A correctional officer makes a decision to formally ''write up'' the inmate for some violation of prison rules. This critical discretionary decision is identical to the police officers' decisions: a crime enters the official records only when an officer completes a crime report; an arrest enters the official records only when an arrest report is completed.[38] As Chapter 2 indicated, police officers routinely exercise discretion in not filling out such reports. In the prison setting, citing a prisoner for many official violations (the equivalent of police harassment on the street) is almost certain to lengthen the prison term.

The prisoners' rights movement has had a significant effect on these critical decisions. In *Wolff v. McDonnell* (1974) the Supreme Court held that prison inmates are entitled to a measure of due process when faced with revocation of statutorily authorized good time. In these and other disciplinary actions, inmates are entitled to notice of the charges, a hearing, a written statement of the evidence, and the right to present evidence on their own behalf. The Court did not grant them the right to cross-examine their accusors or to be represented by legal counsel in the disciplinary hearings.[39]

The overall impact of the prisoners' rights movement has been similar to the impact of earlier rulings on the police. First, the rulings asserted a set of rights that were not clearly defined beforehand. These rights greatly limited the power of officials. James B. Jacobs, perhaps the leading expert on the subject, comments that one of the major effects of the prisoners' rights movement was to limit the power—or at least the sense of power—of prison officials.[40] Second, the rulings accelerated the bureaucratization of the prisons. The holding in *Wolff* and innumerable other prisoners' rights decisions were subsequently incorporated into the American Correctional Association *Standards for Adult Correctional Institutions.*[41] The *Standards* are the functional equivalent of the police standard operating procedure manual. Among other things, the current *Standards* require prison officials to advise new inmates of their rights in the form of a written statement of inmate rights and responsibilities.[42] This can be seen as the prison equivalent of the *Miranda* warning.

The full impact of the prisoners' rights movement on decision making in correctional institutions is not clear. Some have argued that the formal bureaucratic apparatus of control is as repressive as the earlier informal methods, although without the physical brutality.[43] The essential point here, however, is that numerous critical decisions affect the length of prison sentences, that those decisions have been traditionally "hidden" from view, and that a network of controls has only recently emerged—although with uncertain effect.

A final point needs to be made regarding the latent functions of both parole and good time. Historically, both have been used to control institutional behavior and to control the size of prison populations. They are instruments for institutional control because they give prison officials some means of rewarding good behavior and punishing misbehavior.[44] A second function has been to control the size of prison populations— no small matter given the chronic problem of prison overcrowding. The problem was complicated even further in the 1970s and 1980s as prisoners' rights suits often resulted in court orders limiting the number of prisoners in an institution. A new procedure has emerged to control the size of prison populations: emergency release laws. These "backdoor" solutions to prison overcrowding specify that when the population reaches a certain level above capacity, parole release dates are automatically advanced (persons convicted of certain violent crimes are usually not eligible, however).[45]

"Back door" or "escape valve" procedures are not discretionary decisions, but they are an important part of the entire context of decision making about sentences. The practical effect is that even under a theoretically "fixed" sentencing system, the offender may not serve the sentence meted out by the judge.

A Brief History of Sentencing Reform

Sentencing reform over the past fifteen years has not been a unified movement by any means. The depth of public and professional discontent generated a broad philosophical debate and many reform ideas. Some of those ideas have been implemented, while others were cast aside. Some of the first reforms were immediately regarded as missteps by most observers. Many of the new laws that were enacted do not represent new ideas at all. By the early 1980s, after continued debate and evaluation of some of the first reforms, a consensus of opinion began to emerge that the best method of controlling discretion was through sentencing guidelines which indicated a presumptive sentence but left the judge some limited discretion.

With one notable exception, the attack on sentencing discretion has followed the same trajectory one finds in other parts of the criminal justice system. Early on, there were calls for the abolition of discretion. In the case of sentencing, this took the form of flat-time or determinate sentencing along with the abolition of parole. Abolition soon gave way to more modest proposals to limit but not abolish the discretion of sentencing judges through sentencing guidelines.[46]

The sentencing guidelines/presumptive sentencing approach resembles the discretion control measures emerging in other parts of the criminal justice system. The common elements include accepting discretion as a fact of life, attempting to regulate it through written rules, and creating formal procedures for holding officials accountable for their actions. In Kenneth C. Davis's terms, this embodies the principles of confining, structuring, and checking discretion.[47]

The exception to this general rule is discretionary parole release, which has been abolished in about ten states and the federal criminal justice system. This stands as the one instance in the entire criminal justice system where the idea of abolition has succeeded and still retains intellectual respectability.[48]

The following review of some of the major sentencing reforms of the past fifteen years is not intended to be comprehensive. It is selective and designed to highlight some of the major achievements and failures of the broader reform movement. Nor does it concentrate on the social policy issues that have preoccupied sentencing reformers, such as the impact of sentencing on crime or prison populations. The focus here is on sentencing reform and the control of discretion. One major item is deliberately omitted: the federal sentencing guidelines that went into effect in November 1987.[49] While they represent a major reform, they have been deeply embroiled in political controversy and legal challenges[50]—far more than any state sentencing reform—and it is not possible to draw any conclusions about their overall impact as of this writing.

Flat Time and Other Initial Missteps

Flat-Time Sentencing

The first drastic reform proposal to appear in the mid–1970s was the concept of flat-time sentencing. In the minds of its advocates, flat time meant just that: the judge would impose sentences of a fixed number of years and/or months and the offender would serve exactly that amount of time in prison. This was designed to abolish the discretionary power of both the judge and the parole authority.

Critics described flat time as a "throwback to the early nineteenth century.''[51] Perhaps. Flat time was based on a romanticized view of nineteenth-century practices where, some reformers believe, sentences were in fact flat, fixed, or determinate. But as I have already argued, there is little basis for this view. Sentences were extremely indeterminate.

During its brief period of popularity, flat-time sentencing enjoyed the support of many liberals and conservatives. Liberals assumed it would solve the problem of arbitrary and discriminatory sentences; conservatives thought it would prevent the early release of dangerous offenders. This odd political coalition, which was strongest in California, soon fell apart—primarily when the liberals discovered that in the prevailing political climate they could not control the legislative process.[52]

Flat time did not survive long as an intellectually respectable idea. Commentators argued that there was a need for some flexibility in sentencing to take into account differences in the severity of a crime and the characteristics of different offenders.[53]

Sentencing Reform in Maine

The first important sentencing reform occurred in Maine in 1975. The new law was often described as determinate sentencing, but most knowledgeable observers saw it as a misstep.[54] From the standpoint of discretion control, it was both a step forward and a step backward. Most important, it abolished discretionary parole release. Yet events soon indicated that perhaps parole had not been abolished after all. This was a result of the new law's failure to adequately control the sentencing discretion of judges.

In some respects, the Maine law actually aggravated the problem of judicial discretion. It made sentencing ''determinate'' in the sense that judges were to impose prison terms of fixed lengths. The law, however, only prescribed a maximum limit, with no guidance as to the actual length. Thus for Class B felonies, the judge could impose a fixed term of anywhere up to ten years; for Class C felonies, a fixed prison term of up to five years. The abolition of parole, meanwhile, eliminated the normal mechanism for mitigating very long sentences.[55]

In the end, judges adapted to the new law by making extensive use of so-called split sentences. These involve a short period of incarceration followed by probationary supervision. By the mid-1980s these were the most common sentences and had become known as ''judicial parole.''

This development is a classic illustration of the ability of the criminal justice system to develop creative adaptations to circumvent new rules that drastically upset existing practices.

Mandatory Sentencing: An Old Idea in New Garb

Perhaps the most popular sentencing reform of all was the idea of mandatory sentencing. In one form or another, virtually every state adopted some limited form of mandatory sentencing, usually applying it to drug offenses, drunk driving, or crimes committed with a weapon. With respect to discretion, mandatory sentencing was another form of abolition: the legislature would strip judges of all discretion by requiring a prison sentence and/or a mandatory minimum prison term.

Mandatory sentencing was nothing new in the 1970s. Indeterminate sentencing laws across the country had typically included some mandatory provision. Knowledgeable observers also knew that such provisions were regularly circumvented. The ABF survey uncovered many examples in the 1950s. One involved a Michigan law mandating a minimum prison term for armed robbery. As Frank Remington relates the story, Michigan parole board officials routinely began parole hearings with the comment, "I see you were convicted of unarmed robbery in Detroit. What caliber of gun did you use?" Inmates typically replied, "A .38 caliber revolver."[56] The absence of any note of humor in these exchanges suggested that the charade was quite routine. The ABF survey research indicated that some charge bargaining was motivated by a desire to evade mandatory sentences.[57]

Evaluations of some of the more famous mandatory sentencing laws of the 1970s confirmed what many observers already suspected: that it is a meataxe approach that only invites circumvention. Generally, the various adaptations undermine the original goals of the law. A few well-known examples illustrate the point.

In 1973 New York State passed what was then advertised as "the nation's toughest drug law." The law attempted to get tough with drug dealers through long and mandatory prison sentences and restrictions on plea bargaining. Class A-I drug dealers (major dealers), for example, faced a mandatory minimum prison sentence of 15 to 25 years and a maximum of life imprisonment. Class A-II dealers (midrange dealers: people who either sold ⅛ ounce of heroin or possessed 1 to 2 ounces) faced mandatory minimum prison terms of 6 to 8½ years and a maximum of life imprisonment. Anyone arrested for either of these two crimes could not plead guilty to a lesser crime.[58]

The law had little discernible impact on either drug use or predatory crime in New York City. With respect to the control of discretion, it appears to have displaced it to other decision points in the processing of drug cases. The result was an increase in "leakage," or attrition of cases. The percentage of drug arrests leading to indictment between 1972 and 1976 declined from 39 to 25 percent. The percentage of those indictments resulting in conviction fell from 86 to 80 percent. Thus the percentage of all drug arrests leading to conviction fell from 33.5 to 20 percent—a substantial decline in overall drug enforcement. For those who were convicted, however, the new law did achieve its goals of producing more severe punishments. The percentage of convicted offenders going to prison rose from 33 to 55 percent (it seems that some loopholes in the "mandatory" provisions remained). The percentage of convicted offenders receiving a prison term of three years or longer increased from 3 to 22 percent.[59]

Another highly publicized mandatory sentencing law produced somewhat different results. A 1976 Michigan felony firearms law mandated a prison term for anyone convicted of using a weapon in the commission of a crime. The law was advertised under the slogan "one with a gun gets you two." The Wayne County (including Detroit) district attorney supplemented the law with a new policy of not accepting guilty pleas to lesser charges in weapons offenses. The law produced little change in sentencing practices. Armed robbers continued to to receive sentences of about six years in prison, as they had before. The law had little impact because, contrary to popular belief, officials had always been tough on armed robbery. Armed robbers were not beating the system either by pleading to lesser offenses or by receiving light sentences. In short, there was no discretionary loophole to close.[60] Other studies have also concluded that for serious crimes there is little meaningful charge bargaining: charges may be traded away but usually this is done in return for a plea to the top charge, which generally results in a prison sentence.[61]

Determinate Sentencing in California, 1976

Enactment of the California Determinate Sentencing Law (DSL) in 1976 (effective July 1, 1977) was a landmark in the sentencing reform movement, if not criminal justice history generally. California had long been a national leader in criminal justice reform—in police professionalism, in correctional treatment, and in sentencing.[62] The state often set the pace for reform elsewhere. With respect to sentencing, the old California law was the most indeterminate system of any state. Convicted felons received sentences with no fixed upper limit; they were committed to the care of the Adult Authority, which had the power to determine release dates.

The new Determinate Sentencing Law was a radical departure, replacing indeterminacy with legislatively defined presumptive sentences. The law offered the judge a range of three possible prison terms for each crime. As later amended, the convicted robber could be sentenced to two, three, or five years, with the middle term as the presumptive sentence. The judge could choose the higher sentence for "aggravated robbery" or the lower one for "mitigated robbery." The sentence could also be enhanced by one year each for a prior incarceration, use of a weapon, or infliction of serious injury. In an equally radical break with the past, discretionary parole release was abolished. Offenders would be automatically released at the end of their sentence and serve a one-year term under parole supervision. Sentences could be reduced by as much as one-third for good time.

The law represented a radical restriction and reorganization of discretion. The Adult Authority was the greatest loser, and the legislature the major winner. Judges actually gained some discretion, since they could now control the upper limit of sentences, but only within a narrow range. Some discretionary power was not touched, however. Most important, judges retained control over the all-important decision on probation versus prison.

Implementation Through Administrative Rules

The legislature also directed the California Judicial Council to issue a set of rules for implementing the new law. These rules are of particular interest here, since they cover the critical "hidden" discretionary decisions that affect sentencing.

The most important rules governed the criteria for sentencing the offender to probation rather than prison and procedures for using the various sentence enhancements. An evaluation of the law, however, found the rules regarding probation were nearly useless. They essentially listed every possible factor that might be considered, without indicating any priorities, and thus provided ''little guidance.''[63] The contrast with the police deadly force rules discussed in Chapter 2 offers an explanation of this failure. The deadly force rules work because they indicate clear priorities and the criteria to be used in handling specific situations.

Local district attorneys, meanwhile, adopted their own set of rules regarding probation and the sentencing enhancements. At this point, it becomes apparent that the California law was not as determinate as it appeared at first glance. The various enhancements required discretionary decisions by the prosector to bring them to the attention of the judge. In three of the jurisdictions studied by Casper, Brereton, and Neal, the district attorney adopted tough ''full-enforcement'' policies. All probation disqualifiers and sentence enhancement allegations would be filed; individual prosecutors were not to drop them simply to settle a case. In practice, however, substantial bargaining over enhancements developed. In particular, a weapons use enhancement might be dropped if the prosecutor anticipated difficulty in proving the facts about the weapon. In other instances, prosecutors would not file enhancements if they felt the presumptive sentence was sufficient punishment; this was, in effect, a form of sentence bargaining.[64]

The Impact of Determinate Sentencing

For most of the public and the professional community, the key issue concerning the impact of the California law involved incarceration rates. The evidence on this point was ambiguous. Convicted offenders were sent to prison at higher rates in the late 1970s, but this trend began before the law took effect and was symptomatic of the national trend toward more frequent incarceration. Similar trends were evident in states that did not revise their sentencing laws. Greater incarceration rates were primarily due to increased imprisonment of persons convicted of ''midrange'' crimes, offenders who would previously have received probation or a split sentence involving some jail time. In short, the DSL did not itself cause a major change in imprisonment rates.[65]

Perhaps most important, the DSL may have helped to curb racial discrimination in sentencing. A Rand Corporation study of 11,553 persons convicted in 1980 was unable to identify evidence of racial discrimination in either the decision to incarcerate or the length of prison terms.[66] Thus by drastically curbing judicial discretion, determinate sentencing may have furthered the goal of racial equity.

Nor was there any great impact on plea bargaining. Many observers predicted that the DSL would increase plea bargaining because the law shifted control over sentence length from the Adult Authority to the courtroom work group. There were some changes in both the rate and the timing of guilty pleas, but these were part of long-term fluctuations unrelated to the determinate sentencing law.

The law did not appear to change the relative influence of the various members of local courtroom work groups. The two courtrooms that had previously been "prosecutor-dominant" remained so, while the one "judge-dominant" jurisdiction was also unchanged. Contrary to predictions that the critical decision would shift to prosecutors, there was some indication that judges increased their influence in the formerly prosecutor-dominant courtrooms. This was because the law increased the significance of the probation versus prison decision, which the judge still controlled.

The most significant findings related to the use of the probation disqualifiers and sentence enhancements. Among all the persons sentenced to prison in 1979, for example, 44 percent had been prosecuted with an allegation of a prior prison term (thus triggering an enhancement). The rates for the three jurisdictions studied were 22 percent in San Bernardino, 59 percent in San Francisco, and 66 percent in Santa Clara—indicating substantial variation in local going rates. With respect to use of a gun, prosecutors were steadily less likely to drop such charges. The dropping of use of gun allegations declined in all three jurisdictions: from 60 to 40 percent in San Bernardino, from 64.7 to 22.8 percent in San Francisco, and from 48.9 to 40.8 percent in Santa Clara. This decline, however, was probably a symptom of the national trend toward getting tough with weapons offenses and not a result of the DSL. The net effect of the law seems to have been to narrow and focus the exercise of plea-bargaining discretion. Given the very restricted options on sentence length, the importance of the various enhancements and disqualifiers increased. One potential gain is that this situation would appear to create an opportunity for even tighter control over plea bargaining. Administrative regulations that meaningfully control the use of enhancements and disqualifiers would strike directly at the most important aspects of plea bargaining under the DSL.[67]

One other effect of the California determinate sentencing law is cause for some concern. The rate of parole failure increased dramatically. In 1977 some 65 percent of all parolees successfully completed their parole supervision; by 1986 only 34 percent did. Over 25,000 parole violators were returned to the California prisons in 1986. They served an average of 125 days and accounted for 10 percent of the total prison population. In fact, California had 40 percent of all the parole failures in the entire country by 1986.[68]

The reasons for this problem are not clear. Parole "failure" rates, of course, are often an artifact of discretionary decision making. It is possible that only the behavior of parole officers changed. Having lost much of their old authority, they could have compensated by over-enforcing the rules available to them. At the same time, it is possible that the behavior of parolees did worsen and that the abolition of dis-cretionary parole led to greater misconduct. In either event, further scrutiny of the new parole process is clearly warranted before a final judgment on the determinate sentencing law can be made.

The Minnesota Sentencing Guidelines

The Minnesota sentencing guidelines, authorized in 1978 and imple-mented in 1980, have emerged as perhaps the most significant of all the recent sentencing reforms. They embody the key elements of the emerging consensus about the effective control of discretion (in all areas of the criminal justice system) and, in the opinion of one expert, have been "a remarkable success" in terms of achieving their stated objectives.[69]

Minnesota opted for a system of legislatively prescribed "presump-tive" sentences. There are several key elements of the Minnesota ap-proach. First, criminal sentences are presumptive in the sense that judges are expected to follow the guidelines but may depart from them as long as they provide the reasons for doing so in writing.[70]

Second, the legislature defined a clear set of social policy goals which the guidelines were to implement. The first goal was to reduce if not eliminate disparities in sentencing. The guidelines specifically stated that "sentencing should be neutral with respect to the race, gender, social, or economic status of convicted felons."[71] The second goal was to control the size of prison population. The guidelines expressed a preference for incarcerating persons who were convicted of the more serious crimes and/or had substantial criminal histories and for not incarcerating persons who were convicted of property crimes. The Min-nesota guidelines are unique in terms of their explicit recognition of prison population as a factor in sentencing.

Third, after defining general principles and goals, the legislature delegated responsibility for developing the actual guidelines to a Sentencing Guidelines Commission. This approach, which is widely used in other areas of administrative law (and was also used to develop the federal sentencing guidelines), offers several advantages. A commission can employ a professional staff and conduct the necessary fact-finding free of direct political pressures and time constraints of a legislative session.

The sentencing commission approach is not without hazards, however. Whereas the Minnesota guidelines have been widely hailed, the federal guidelines have aroused great controversy, even though they were developed by a similar procedure. Everything depends on the principles articulated by the legislative body and, then, the ideological orientation of the commissioners and staff.

Implementation

Like the California determinate sentencing law, the Minnesota guidelines attempt to control discretion by drastically limiting the range of prison terms available to the judge. Unlike the California model, however, the guidelines embody a more elaborate formula based on the seriousness of the crime and the offender's prior criminal history. The resulting sentencing grid appears in Figure 5.1. Criminal history scores are computed by assigning the offender one point for each prior felony conviction (regardless of whether it resulted in imprisonment or probation), one for being on probation or parole at the time of the current offense, one for every four misdeanor convictions (or for every two gross misdemeanor convictions), and one for every two juvenile dispositions.

As Figure 5.1 indicates, anyone convicted of murder, first-degree sexual assault, or aggravated robbery is to be incarcerated. Some burglars will go to prison, depending on their criminal history: the first-time residential burglar will not be incarcerated, although a burglar with three points on the criminal history scale will go to prison. The person who has three prior convictions and is convicted of armed robbery faces a presumptive sentence of forty-nine months (four years and one month). The judge may sentence the offender to as few as forty-five months or as many as fifty-three. Allowing the judge a range of only four months either way is obviously an extreme restriction on sentencing discretion (especially compared with indeterminate sentencing systems that allowed a range of one to fifty *years*).

The Minnesota guidelines are officially described as being "advisory

Criminal history score

Conviction offense	Severity level	0	1	2	3	4	5	6 or more
Unauthorized use of motor vehicle Possession of marijuana	I	12*	12*	12*	13	15	17	19 18–20
Theft related crime ($250–$2,500) Aggravated forgery ($25–$2,500)	II	12*	12*	13	15	17	19	21 20–22
Theft crimes ($25–$2,500)	III	12*	13	15	17	19 18–20	22 21–23	25 24–26
Nonresidential burglary Theft crime (over $2,500)	IV	12*	15	18	21	25 24–26	32 30–34	41 37–45
Residential burglary Simple robbery	V	18	23	27	30 29–31	38 36–40	46 43–49	54 50–58
Criminal sexual conduct, 2d degree (a) and (b)	VI	21	26	30	34 33–35	44 42–46	54 50–58	65 60–70
Aggravated robbery	VII	24 23–25	32 30–34	41 38–44	49 45–53	65 60–70	81 75–87	97 90–104
Criminal sexual conduct, 1st degree Assault, 1st degree	VIII	43 41–45	54 50–58	65 60–70	76 71–81	95 89–101	113 106–120	132 124–140
Murder, 3d degree Murder, 2nd degree (felony murder)	IX	105 102–108	119 116–122	127 124–130	149 143–155	176 168–184	205 195–215	230 218–242
Murder, 2d degree (with intent)	X	120 116–124	140 133–147	162 153–171	203 192–214	243 231–255	284 270–298	324 309–339

Numbers in the table refer to the length and range of the presumptive sentence. Cells above the dark line represent the area of the grid in which the presumptive sentence is a stayed prison term. Below the dark line a prison term is the presumptive sentence. The presumptive durations of confinement are in months.

*One year and one day.

FIGURE 5.1. Minnesota's sentencing guidelines grid. (Minnesota Sentencing Guidelines Commission, *Sentencing Guidelines and*

to the sentencing judge.''[72] A judge may decline to use the guidelines under two conditions. First, the reasons for doing so must be stated in writing. This represents a check on discretion. Second, the guidelines permit departure from the presumptive sentence by (1) specifying factors that *may not* be used and (2) specifying mitigating and aggravating factors that *may* be used. Factors that may not be used include race, sex, and employment history. Mitigating factors include the victim being the aggressor in the criminal incident and the offender being a passive or minor participant. Aggravating circumstances include the victim being particularly vulnerable because of age or infirmity or other reason and major economic offenses involving multiple victims.

Impact of the Minnesota Guidelines

Evaluations of the impact of the Minnesota guidelines have found that they have been highly successful. First, judges generally comply with the guidelines. If the threshold question in the control of discretion is compliance, this is a significant achievement. Judges departed from the guidelines in only 6.2 percent of all cases in 1981. This rose to 9.9 percent by 1984, suggesting that some "slippage" occurred. Nonetheless, the fact that the departure rate remained below 10 percent is cause for optimism.

The guidelines were also quite successful in achieving their primary goal of reducing sentencing disparities. The impact of race and employment status were reduced, although not completely eliminated, as factors in the decision to incarcerate. This also must be counted as a major gain.[73]

Even more significant has been the apparent success of the guidelines in controlling the use of imprisonment. In 1989 Minnesota had the second lowest incarceration rate in the country, following only North Dakota (Table 5.1). The number of prisoners per 100,000 population was less than one-third the national rate and one-third the Midwest rate. Minnesota had a very low incarceration rate even in the early 1970s—and enjoyed a national reputation for a sound correctional policy. The commitment of the Minnesota guidelines to a policy of limited use of incarceration in effect codified this earlier policy. The most significant aspect of the guidelines is that they appear to have limited the use of imprisonment at a time when incarceration rates were soaring across the country. As the data in Table 5.1 indicate, the gap between Minnesota and both national trends and those in neighboring states widened

TABLE 5.1. Rate of Sentenced Prisoners in State and Federal Institutions, December 31, 1971–1989

Region and jurisdiction	Rate per 100,000 resident population																		
	1971	1972	1973	1974	1975	1976	1977	1978	1979	1980	1981	1982	1983	1984	1985	1986	1987	1988	1989
United States, total	96.4	94.6	97.8	103.6	113	123	129	135	135	139	153	170	179	188	200	216	228	244	271
Federal institutions, total	10.2	10.5	10.9	10.6	11	13	13	12	10	9	10	10	11	12	14	15	16	17	19
State institutions, total	86.2	84.1	86.8	93.0	102	111	116	123	126	130	144	160	167	176	187	201	211	227	253
Northeast	56.4	56.8	60.4	63.4	70	73	77	82	84	87	103	115	127	136	145	157	169	186	215
Connecticut*	63.3	59.3	54.2	47.6	59	62	53	70	69	68	95	114	114	119	127	135	144	146	194
Maine	45.1	46.3	43.8	50.4	60	57	61	53	58	61	71	69	75	72	83	106	106	100	116
Massachusetts†	38.3	32.1	34.3	38.4	42	46	48	49	50	56	65	77	79	84	88	92	102	109	122
New Hampshire	28.0	30.8	34.8	27.1	31	30	26	32	35	35	42	47	50	57	68	76	81	93	103
New Jersey	72.5	72.4	73.5	71.6	77	78	78	74	76	76	92	107	136	138	149	157	177	219	251
New York	65.0	64.0	71.4	78.5	89	98	108	114	120	123	145	158	172	187	195	216	229	248	285
Pennsylvania	44.7	52.6	55.0	56.9	60	56	56	65	67	68	78	88	98	109	119	128	136	149	169
Rhode Island*	40.5	36.1	43.2	48.7	41	53	56	56	63	65	72	82	92	92	99	103	100	118	146
Vermont*	46.5	30.0	40.3	51.5	51	64	57	76	62	67	84	84	72	74	82	81	91	98	109
Midwest	72.9	65.6	62.8	69.0	84	95	108	104	105	109	121	130	135	144	161	173	184	200	225
Illinois†,‡	52.4	50.4	50.3	55.9	73	87	95	96	95	94	113	119	135	149	161	168	171	181	211
Indiana†	82.9	72.8	63.4	57.5	73	79	80	82	98	114	138	152	164	165	175	181	192	202	217
Iowa†	53.6	45.5	49.0	51.6	63	66	70	70	72	86	88	93	92	97	98	98	101	107	126
Kansas	90.5	73.5	60.6	63.5	76	91	97	98	95	106	116	129	152	173	192	217	233	232	222
Michigan†	106.4	93.9	86.8	94.6	119	137	151	162	163	163	165	162	159	161	196	227	259	298	340
Minnesota	40.2	34.5	36.0	35.1	42	41	44	49	51	49	49	50	52	52	56	58	60	64	71
Missouri	76.8	74.7	79.4	88.0	92	105	111	116	113	112	131	147	162	175	194	203	218	236	269
Nebraska	69.1	62.8	66.0	67.9	80	93	83	80	71	89	104	99	91	95	108	116	123	129	141

North Dakota‡	21.3	28.8	24.9	20.7	27	26	30	21	19	28	33	47	51	54	55	53	57	62	62
Ohio‡	84.7	77.2	71.9	86.9	107	117	120	122	125	125	139	160	155	174	194	209	219	243	279
South Dakota	57.8	51.0	34.9	37.0	49	70	76	74	77	88	97	109	115	127	146	160	160	143	175
Wisconsin	55.4	44.9	47.2	56.4	65	71	72	73	73	85	93	96	102	105	113	119	126	130	138
South	123.9	124.5	128.3	135.0	150	161	169	181	196	188	201	224	225	231	236	248	255	266	292
Alabama	110.0	103.5	104.5	110.3	121	83	94	144	141	149	183	215	243	256	267	283	307	300	328
Arkansas	83.9	80.4	82.2	99.6	102	115	111	115	132	128	143	166	179	188	195	198	227	230	261
Delaware*	33.2	49.3	57.1	76.1	100	118	120	173	181	183	208	250	273	263	281	311	326	331	333
District of Columbia*†‡	349.2	340.8	324.2	289.2	326	334	330	383	433	426	467	531	558	649	738	753	905	1,078	1,132
Florida†	135.8	139.3	132.5	137.9	183	211	221	239	220	208	224	261	235	242	247	272	265	278	307
Georgia†	146.1	174.3	173.3	191.4	204	225	224	216	224	219	220	247	259	254	251	265	282	281	300
Kentucky	94.1	89.5	89.4	91.7	100	107	106	97	105	99	114	110	127	128	133	142	147	191	222
Louisiana	113.0	92.2	108.3	127.7	126	120	152	184	190	211	216	251	290	310	308	316	346	370	396
Maryland	124.9	139.3	144.0	155.0	169	192	198	193	187	183	218	244	277	285	279	280	282	291	323
Mississippi	82.7	83.1	75.5	91.8	103	91	67	110	141	132	177	210	211	229	237	249	256	277	293
North Carolina†	153.0	159.9	183.9	207.2	210	214	234	223	240	244	248	255	233	246	254	257	250	249	250
Oklahoma‡	144.2	139.7	120.4	108.5	114	133	129	146	147	151	169	201	212	236	250	288	296	323	361
South Carolina	118.4	121.2	130.1	158.4	198	230	239	243	237	238	251	270	276	284	294	324	344	369	416
Tennessee‡	86.1	81.9	84.2	90.9	109	114	127	134	151	153	171	173	187	154	149	157	156	157	213
Texas†	140.9	136.0	146.6	140.6	154	167	176	189	196	210	210	237	221	226	226	228	231	240	257
Virginia	108.9	106.3	107.9	105.1	110	126	142	157	158	161	165	177	177	185	204	215	217	230	263
West Virginia†	59.6	59.1	60.8	57.3	65	71	67	63	66	64	80	77	83	82	89	77	77	78	84
West	81.9	78.6	8.6	93.9	84	91	92	99	101	105	119	139	152	166	176	197	214	234	256
Alaska*	65.6	61.0	56.3	57.1	56	63	75	127	133	143	170	194	219	252	288	306	339	355	361
Arizona†	74.3	76.9	81.0	97.0	118	125	129	146	139	160	184	209	223	247	256	268	307	328	350
California†	87.4	83.9	96.7	105.6	81	85	80	88	93	98	114	135	150	162	181	212	231	257	283
Colorado‡	85.9	81.3	77.5	79.4	80	87	89	93	90	96	92	108	109	104	103	115	145	174	207
Hawaii*	33.7	38.8	37.3	38.6	42	39	44	57	58	65	77	88	103	124	134	142	141	136	142

TABLE 5.1 (*continued*)

Region and jurisdiction	Rate per 100,000 resident population																		
	1971	1972	1973	1974	1975	1976	1977	1978	1979	1980	1981	1982	1983	1984	1985	1986	1987	1988	1989
Idaho	48.9	49.6	54.6	65.6	71	82	87	91	92	87	99	107	121	127	133	144	144	157	180
Montana	35.4	39.5	43.5	45.6	50	73	81	87	96	94	104	114	104	121	136	135	147	158	165
Nevada	124.0	121.2	134.9	130.3	136	156	187	204	224	230	245	301	354	380	397	447	432	452	438
New Mexico	61.3	55.7	66.4	80.7	86	105	126	123	112	106	100	126	142	133	144	154	174	180	178
Oregon	93.5	84.4	74.7	88.3	108	122	122	117	122	120	124	146	157	170	165	176	200	215	235
Utah	53.3	51.2	44.7	46.1	54	60	64	69	68	64	73	77	77	84	98	108	110	115	137
Washington	82.4	77.1	77.1	86.2	96	109	118	122	113	106	125	148	155	156	147	147	134	124	142
Wyoming†	77.5	75.7	76.6	73.9	80	87	98	102	95	113	117	135	138	143	148	168	190	199	216

Note: Sentenced prisoners are defined as those serving sentences of more than 1 year. The data for the years 1971–1977 represent sentenced prisoners in the custody of state and federal institutions. The data for 1978–1989 represent sentenced prisoners under the jurisdiction of state and federal correctional authorities. Population estimates are provided by the U.S. Bureau of the Census. Data for 1985 and 1986 have been revised from previous presentations.

*Figures include both jail and prison inmates; jails and prisons are combined in one system.

†All data for Arizona, California, the District of Columbia, Georgia, Illinois, Indiana, Iowa, Massachusetts, Michigan, North Carolina, Texas, West Virginia (men), and Wyoming are custody, rather than jurisdiction counts. Florida's courts are based on custody data.

‡Counts of inmates by sentence length may be slightly incorrect.

Source: U.S. Department of Justice, Law Enforcement Assistance Administration, *Prisoners in State and Federal Institutions*, NPS Bulletin SD-NPS-PSF-2, pp. 20, 21; NPS Bulletin SD-NPS-PSF-3, pp. 16, 17; NS Bulletin SD-NPS-PSF-4, p. 18; NPS Bulletin SD-NPS-PSF-5, p. 13 (Washington, D.C.: Government Printing Office); U.S. Department of Justice, Bureau of Justice Statistics, *Prisoners in State and Federal Institutions*, NPS Bulletin SD-NPS-PSF-6, p. 16; NPS Bulletin SD-NPS-PSF-7, NCJ-73719, p. 14; NPS Bulletin SD-NPS-PSF-8, NCJ-80520, p. 16; NCJ-86485, p. 16 (Washington, D.C.: Government Printing Office); U.S. Department of Justice, Bureau of Justice Statistics, *Prisoners in 1982*, Bulletin NCJ-87933, p. 2; *Prisoners in 1983*, Bulletin NCJ-92949, p. 2; *Prisoners in 1984*, Bulletin NCJ-97118, p. 2 (Washington, D.C.: U.S. Department of Justice); and U.S. Department of Justice, Bureau of Justice Statistics, *Correctional Populations in the United States, 1985*, NCJ-103957, Table 5.4; *1986*, NCJ-111611, Table 5.4; *1987*, NCJ-118762, Table 5.4; *1988*, NCJ-124280, Table 5.4; *1989*, NCJ-130445, Table 5.4 (Washington, D.C.: Government Printing Office).

Source: Bureau of Justice Statistics, *Sourcebook of Criminal Justice Statistics, 1990* (Washington, D.C.: Government Printing Office, 1991), p. 605. Table adapted by *Sourcebook* staff.

TABLE 5.2. Incarceration Rates and Crime Rates, 1989, Minnesota and Other Upper Midwestern States

State	Incarceration rate*	Crime rate[†]
Minnesota	71	4,383.2
Wisconsin	138	4,164.8
Iowa	217	4,081.4
Illinois	225	5,639.2
Nebraska	141	4,091.6
Indiana	211	4,440.0

*Prisoners per 100,000 population.
[†]Reported index crimes per 100,000 population.
Source: Federal Bureau of Investigation, *Crime in the United States, 1989* (Washington, D.C.: Government Printing Office, 1990); *Bureau of Justice Statistics, Sourcebook of Criminal Justice Statistics, 1990* (Washington, D.C.: Government Printing Office, 1991), p. 605.

through the 1980s. A low incarceration rate, of course, could be the result of a low crime rate. Table 5.2 indicates that Minnesota maintained its low incarceration rate compared to its Midwest neighbors, despite having a higher crime rate than several of them.

With respect to the use of imprisonment, it is instructive to compare Minnesota with the states of Washington and California and the federal sentencing guidelines. The sentencing guidelines adopted by Washington in 1984 resembled Minnesota's in that they embodied a policy of incarcerating primarily serious offenders. The result was a 20 percent reduction in the incarceration rate—a change that ran counter to national trends.[74] In California, where the determinate sentencing law did not indicate a clear policy on incarceration, imprisonment soared. Not surprisingly, this also happened in the federal system, where the new sentencing guidelines embodied a preference for imprisonment. The evidence clearly suggests that determinate sentencing per se is a general tool for controlling sentencing discretion. That discretion can be guided either in the direction of greater or lesser use of incarceration, depending on the general goals determined at the outset by the legislature.

The evidence about the Minnesota guidelines has two important implications. First, it suggests an alternative to the national trend toward massive use of imprisonment. From the standpoint of the control of discretion—the primary issue here—it suggests that it is possible to control the discretion of sentencing judges. In particular, the evidence appears to indicate that formal rules can insulate judges from the pressure of popular sentiment and ensure that sentences reflect carefully considered social policy. This is an achievement of enormous significance.

There were some subtle changes in sentencing practices under the guidelines as time went on. The percentage of all convicted offenders who went to prison dropped substantially at first and then rose, almost reaching the preguidelines level. The average length of prison terms dropped by more than half. A number of complicating factors, however, deserve some discussion. The fact that the imprisonment rate returned to its previous level suggests some backsliding. This raises the specter of nullification through creative adaptation. The larger significance, however, appears to be that while judges were apparently affected to some extent by popular "lock-'em-up" sentiment, the guidelines did a very effective job of insulating them from most of that pressure.[75]

At the same time, there was a significant increase in the use of jail sentences as a part of "stayed" (i.e., nonprison) sentences, which increased from 44.7 to 66.1 percent of all nonprison sentences. The issue of stayed sentences deserves some comment. Under this procedure, the judge stays, or does not impose, the prison sentence and instead sentences the offender to a term in the county jail. Thus the offender does not go to prison but does suffer some form of incarceration, followed by a period of supervised probation (in California and other states, this is referred to as a "split sentence"). This highlights the fact that judges found a loophole where the guidelines did not control their discretion. Presumably, the problem could be remedied if the guidelines were revised to include specific limits on jail sentences. Further, this suggests that the guidelines did not completely insulate Minnesota judges from the lock-'em-up mood of the period.

The Minnesota guidelines had only a slight impact on plea bargaining. There was little change in the percentage of cases going to trial. Sentence bargaining decreased, as expected, since the guidelines limited the options available there. The number of multiple charges filed increased, but so did the rate of charge dismissals. The percentage of charge reductions decreased.[76] These changes, however, represented relatively minor adjustments. The most important point is that, as was the case in Alaska and California, a major change in the law did not significantly alter plea-bargaining practices.[77]

In summary, then, the Minnesota guidelines have been very successful in achieving their basic goals: judges generally complied with the guidelines, incarceration was reduced, the objectives were not greatly subverted by plea bargaining. Some sentencing disparities involving race and economic status remained, but this represented a continuation of preexisting patterns. Although there was some adaptation on the part of judges, it appears that the guidelines insulated judges from the strong social and political pressures for greater incarceration that affected sentencing in most states. In short, sentencing discretion was brought under control to a very high degree.

The success of the Minnesota guidelines provides a model for other states. One important caveat needs to be sounded, however. The guidelines did not fundamentally alter social policy in Minnesota. Rather, they institutionalized and codified a prior commitment to the limited use of imprisonment. This earlier commitment was the product of many years of work by community activists and political leaders. Over the past twenty years, other states have opted for a different social policy, one that favors heavy use of incarceration. Some relevant questions then arise: What made the difference in Minnesota? How did this commitment develop? What were the conditions of its success? How has it managed to survive at a time when other states were moving in a very different direction?

Abolishing Parole

Throughout the history of the discretion control movement, parole stands out as the great exception to the rule that abolition is neither possible nor desirable.[78] Maine was the first to act, abolishing parole as part of its comprehensive sentencing reform in 1975. Although the rest of Maine's sentencing reform was generally regarded as a failure, parole abolition remains. By 1984 at least eleven other states had also abolished parole. The federal system abolished it as part of the sentencing guidelines that took effect in November 1987. At least one state—Colorado—had second thoughts, however, and reinstated parole in 1985.

The net result has been a fairly significant change in the pattern of prison releases nationally. Between 1977 and 1987, the percentage of all prison releases that were discretionary dropped from 72 to 40.6 percent. Meanwhile, there was a corresponding increase in mandatory supervised releases, from 6 to 31 percent of all releases. The percentage of unconditional releases due to expiration of sentence remained the same, at 16 percent of the total.[79]

There has been some misunderstanding of what "abolishing" parole actually means. Under the indeterminate sentence, parole consists of several elements. Most important is the discretionary decision to release the offender from prison and place him or her into a supervised community setting. That release typically involves various conditions or restrictions. Determining the nature of those conditions is a secondary discretionary decision. The second major component of parole is the supervision of the offender in the community by a parole officer. This is the "treatment" that is designed to facilitate readjustment to a law-abiding lifestyle. One part of that supervision includes the power to revoke parole for violation of the conditions and send the offender back to prison. The target of the abolition movement was the discretionary release decision. As we shall see, the supervisory aspects of parole have survived in jurisdictions where discretionary release was in fact abolished.

In the face of rising discontent with criminal sentencing in the early 1970s, abolition was neither the first nor the only idea to receive serious consideration. The first major reform to be proposed involved parole release guidelines. Indeed, the work on parole guidelines provided much of the basis for the current interest in sentencing guidelines.[80]

The parole guidelines were designed not to change existing practices but to rationalize them and produce greater consistency. The guidelines were developed on the basis of past practices. This, it is important to note, is an entirely different approach from the one taken with the Minnesota guidelines, where the legislature defined clear social policy goals. The parole-decision-making grid is based on two factors: offense seriousness and a "salient factor score" representing the perceived risk of reoffending, which in turn was heavily weighted by prior criminal record. First developed by the U.S. Parole Board in the mid-1970s, parole guidelines were adopted by fifteen states over the next decade.

Parole guidelines eventually fell into disfavor, overtaken by other reforms. At the federal level, the sentencing guidelines (authorized in 1984 and implemented in 1987) abolished discretionary parole release altogether. Meanwhile, four states that had adopted guidelines also abolished parole, while several other states substantially re-revised parole as part of a general sentencing reform.[81]

The California Determinate Sentencing Law of 1976 is the best example of parole abolition. The law provides for an automatic release from prison after completion of a relatively fixed sentence, followed by a one-year term of supervised parole (subsequently amended to permit up to eighteen months on parole). The supervision includes the traditional functions of parole—enforcement of conditions of release, counseling, and so on—including the discretionary power to revoke parole in the event that conditions are violated. Revocation, however, can result in imprisonment of no more than six months. This represents a substantial reduction in discretionary power, since revocation under the indeterminate sentence law returned the offender to an indeterminate status with no formal limit.

The most thorough review of the question of parole abolition cautiously recommended it as a policy goal.[82] Eliminating discretionary parole release, von Hirsch and Hanrahan argued, would end the system of divided responsibility over the length of prison terms that was and is central to the indeterminate sentence. On the one hand, this would help focus control over the length of prison terms as a matter of social policy. On the other hand, von Hirsch and Hanrahan make a persuasive argument that the indeterminate sentence fostered a basically dishonest system of criminal punishments. The law advertised one thing, judges meted out something else, and parole boards modified it further. Prison sentences came to be measured officially in vast amounts of time, with everyone knowing that few offenders would actually serve the theoretical maximum. Parole abolition, then, would encourage honesty in sentencing and sentences that represented "modest real sentences."[83]

Conclusions

The sentencing reform movement of the past fifteen years has, arguably, produced the most fundamental changes to be found in any area of criminal justice. In no other area has there been such a broad-ranging debate over first principles and such sweeping changes in operating assumptions and practices. To be sure, major reform has been a patchwork affair; only some jurisdictions have completely overhauled criminal sentencing. It is still too early to draw any definitive conclusions about the impact of the sentencing reform movement. We are still somewhere in the early or middle stages of a historic period of change and we do not yet know where it will lead. It is possible, however, to draw some general conclusions about the direction of change to date.

The first and most important point is that the sentencing reform movement has produced a substantial reduction in the sum total of discretion in criminal sentencing—probably a greater net reduction than anywhere else. The central thrust of reform has been away from the principle of indeterminacy and toward determinacy. A variety of proposals designed to accomplish that end have been introduced, and some have been relatively more successful than others. But the dominant trend has been clear. Moreover, unlike the areas of police discretion and plea bargaining, there have been fewer credible voices raised in opposition to the control of discretion and in favor of retaining current practices.

At the same time, however, it must be said that the movement toward indeterminacy is incomplete at best. Some jurisdictions have moved boldly in the direction of greater determinacy, but most have not. While the changes in California, Minnesota, and the federal system are extremely important, most convicted offenders in the United States still confront the traditional indeterminate sentence.

In the movement toward indeterminacy, there has been a substantial reallocation of discretionary power. The central question in sentencing reform involves the locus of power and control. Without doubt, the great losers have been paroling authorities. Parole is the one area where the idea of abolition has succeeded and where it retains intellectual credibility. The major winners in the reallocation of power have been legislatures and, to a lesser extent, judges. In California, Minnesota, and the federal system, legislatures have succeeded in determining the general length of criminal sentences. In the process, this also includes their success in imposing their social policy goals onto criminal sentencing. One consequence of this change is what the United States Sentencing Commission described as greater "honesty" in sentencing.[84] Unlike the indeterminate sentencing practices, the new determinate systems result in actual prison terms that are relatively close to those advertised by the law.

The growth of "honest" sentencing deserves some comment. One of the central thrusts of the discretion control movement has been to attack covert decision making, where actual practices bear little relationship to written laws and procedures. This pattern of covert decision making, and the variety of goals it served, was one of the principal findings of the ABF survey.[85] In their respective areas, reformers have sought to bring decision making out of the closet, to make it visible and accountable. It may well be that the drive for honesty has made more progress in sentencing than in any other area.

The most important new institutional development of the sentencing reform movement is the sentencing commission. The concept of a sentencing commission is consistent with the principles of administrative law espoused by Kenneth C. Davis.[86] Under this approach, the legislature establishes some general principles and objectives and then delegates to a commission the task of developing the specific policies to achieve them. In theory, this approach has several advantages. First, it removes the development of specific sentences from the politically intense environment of the legislature. Not only can a commission do its work free from direct political pressure and without the distorting time constraints of the legislative process, but it can employ a professional staff to collect and weigh relevant evidence. In practice, the commission approach seems to have worked very well in Minnesota, whereas the federal sentencing commission has been embroiled in political controversy.

There is no reason why the sentencing commission approach could not be applied to other parts of the criminal justice system. A number of years ago, one expert recommended an analogous statewide body to establish administrative rules for the police.[87] Although nothing ever came of it, the idea deserves consideration.

Evidence on how the new determinate sentencing systems have affected sentencing outcomes is conflicting. Imprisonment rates increased in California, but that appears to have been the result of a general trend that began before the new law. At the same time, however, the Minnesota sentencing guidelines have successfully curbed the imprisonment rate. Perhaps most important, determinate sentencing appears to result in greater uniformity in sentencing. The evidence is still limited and this conclusion remains tentative, but the indications at this point are rather promising.

All in all, then, the sentencing reform movement can count some successes. The limitations on discretion, the increase in sentencing honesty, and the reduction in disparities are all significant accomplishments.

Nothing stands still, however. The future of sentencing reform is uncertain. The recent trend toward limiting discretion may or may not continue. The trend could easily reverse and lead to an increase in discretionary authority. It is worth noting, for example, that the most important new idea in sentencing reform is the call for intermediate sanctions, punishments that lie somewhere "between prison and probation."[88]

Finally, the experience of recent sentencing reform dramatizes how much remains to be done. The item that looms largest on the agenda is the problematic relationship between sentencing and plea bargaining. There is much wisdom in the observation Norval Morris made seventeen years ago, at the outset of the recent era of sentencing reform: "There can be no rational future for imprisonment unless present plea bargaining practices, which are the main dispositive technique for sentencing criminals, are rendered principled and orderly."[89]

The insight embodied in Morris's remark has been recognized by most criminal justice experts for nearly thirty years now. The idea that the criminal process is a "system," with various decisions interacting with each other in a complex fashion, has been the conventional wisdom for many years. Yet as we look back on the history of the attempt to control discretion, we find that reform efforts have generally ignored this insight. Efforts to control discretion have been undertaken piecemeal, as if each decision point existed in isolation from others. The agenda for the future clearly calls for a broader, more comprehensive approach to the control of discretion.

6

A System Tamed?
An Interim Report
on the Control of Discretion

An Interim Report

After thirty years of efforts to control discretion in criminal justice, what has been accomplished? Has the system been tamed? Is discretion under control, or at least more controlled than before? Or has the effort been a fool's errand? Are the cynics correct? Is discretion inherently beyond control? What are the prospects for the future?

A little more than twenty years ago, Kenneth C. Davis published a pathbreaking book on discretion in criminal justice. His subtitle, *A Preliminary Inquiry*, reflected the fact that recognition of the pervasiveness of discretion was new.[1] Experts in the field were just beginning to appreciate the full nature of discretion, the problems associated with it, and the possibilities for controlling it. Today, it is possible to assess the impact of reform efforts designed to control discretion. The control movement is far from over and it is still too early to say where it will lead. It has not even been a coordinated movement. The problems associated with particular decision points have been addressed largely in isolation from others. Nonetheless, some general conclusions are possible. If Davis offered a preliminary inquiry, the conclusions here represent an interim report on the control of discretion in criminal justice.

In brief, it is possible to say that the movement to control discretion has enjoyed some important although modest success. At a number of key decision points, there is far more control over discretion than ever before. This is not to say that it is completely controlled, but the new controls succeed in advancing important social goals. A good start, in other words, has been made. But it is only a start. The evidence of success is persuasive but limited to a short list of decision points. Many critical decisions remain as uncontrolled as before. Some historical perspective is important in this regard. If the accomplishments to date are limited, they still represent a major advance over the state of affairs twenty-five years ago.

The Achievements to Date

The single most important achievement for criminal justice in the last thirty years has been the recognition of the problem of discretion. The issue is out in the open, where it is freely discussed and studied. This represents an intellectual revolution. The discovery of discretion by the American Bar Foundation field surveys in the mid-1950s demolished the existing paradigm of criminal justice and replaced it with one where discretion was a central feature. Prior to the ABF survey, there was little appreciation for the fact that low-level officials routinely made critical decisions affecting the lives and liberties of individual citizens. With respect to the police, there was a concerted effort to deny that discretion even existed—a denial that persisted until the early 1970s.[2]

The new awareness of discretion introduced a refreshing and necessary element of realism to discussions of the administration of justice. It is no longer possible to deny that police officers make critical decisions on the street, or that prosecutors dispose of most cases through conscious decisions to dismiss charges or to accept a guilty plea. Sentencing reformers argue that determinate sentencing has led to greater "honesty" in sentencing.

The new realism has made it possible to focus reform efforts more clearly. The pursuit of a broader social policy goal—whether it is promoting greater justice or enhancing crime control effectiveness—requires the effective control of the relevant decisions. One of the great accomplishments of the ABF survey was the discovery of the gap between law and practice, between what the formal law (including both the substantive criminal law and the law of criminal procedure) stated and what officials actually did. Closing that gap is the way to make the justice system accomplish the things we want it to do.

Turning now to specific areas of criminal justice, it is possible to summarize the major achievements in the control of discretion.

It the area of policing, the control of deadly force is an achievement of enormous significance. The development of administrative rules limiting police shootings has substantially reduced the number of number of persons shot and killed, while simultaneously narrowing the disparity between numbers of blacks and whites shot and killed. This has been accomplished without posing any danger to police officers or to the community as a whole. New rules governing police handling of domestic violence and high-speed pursuits represent promising beginnings, but it is still too early to say that these controls have achieved their objectives.

The achievement in the control of deadly force, however, dramatizes the extent to which most critical police decisions remain free of effective controls. Whether administrative rulemaking, which appears to work with respect to deadly force and has been applied to domestic violence and high-speed pursuits, is a viable method for controlling other police decisions is a question of enormous importance.

The first bail reform movement helped to reduce the number of persons detained in jail pending trial. This represents a significant advance in social justice. The evidence is persuasive that the persons released under ROR programs pose no great danger, either in terms of committing another crime while out on bail or failing to appear in court. Like the reduction in police shootings, advancing social justice did not threaten community safety. It is true, of course, that the first bail reform movement did not fully achieve its goal of ending discrimination against the poor in the bail process. Nor did it achieve its goal of guaranteeing pretrial release to all criminal defendants. It is also true, as some observers have noted, that the major achievement of the first bail reform movement, the reduction in pretrial detention, might have occurred without the benefit of a formal reform movement at all.

The consequences of the second bail reform movement are more difficult to assess. Preventive detention provides official sanction for the denial of a historic right. The evidence, however, indicates that preventive detention laws have had little impact on actual bail practices. In the federal system, roughly the same percentage of defendants are being detained as before. This attempt to control discretionary bail decisions, in other words, has primarily provided legal justification for decisions that were being made anyway.

The efforts to control plea bargaining present an even more complex picture. The various attempts to abolish the practice, either generally or with respect to specific crimes, have not been successful. The total ban in Alaska had little significant effect. Other crime-specific bans had either no effect or effects that were contrary to the original crime control goals. The major reason for this general failure of total bans is the fact that plea bargaining is not as wild and uncontrolled a decision point as many critics believed. Detailed studies of criminal court systems at work repeatedly find that case outcomes are highly predictable given certain known facts about the seriousness of the crime and the defendant's criminal record. A related finding has been that dangerous offenders are not regularly beating the system and getting off easy.

At the same time, however, administrative controls over prosecutorial practices have been effective in improving the quality of justice in some jurisdictions. These improvements include a greater consistency in charging practices, which has some beneficial effect on police arrest and charging practices, and reduced case disposition time. The price of greater controls over prosecutorial discretion, however, appears to be some displacement of discretion in the direction of judges.

With respect to sentencing, the Minnesota sentencing guidelines have been very successful in furthering two important social policy goals. First, there has been selective use of imprisonment, with Minnesota enjoying the second lowest incarceration rate in the country. Second, sentencing disparities based on race and income have been reduced. A different form of determinate sentencing in California failed to limit the use of incarceration but may have had some success in curbing racial discrimination in sentencing. These are important accomplishments.

Discretion and Social Policy

The conclusion that controlling discretion can advance social policy goals is extremely important, with implications for the criminal justice system as a whole. The basic conclusion here is that it is possible to advance certain social policy goals through the control of discretion. It must be added quickly, however, that the same evidence clearly suggests that not all goals are equally attainable. The surprising point is that liberal goals appear to be more attainable than conservative goals.

This book opened with a discussion of two celebrated incidents involving young black men. The shooting of Edward Garner dramatized the demand for controls designed to reduce racial discrimination. The Willie Horton controversy dramatized the demand for controls designed to close alleged loopholes that allow dangerous offenders to escape punishment. The evidence reviewed here indicates that those controls designed to promote justice have been consistently more successful than those designed to get tough with crime. The new police deadly force rules have reduced shootings and reduced racial disparities in shootings. The Minnesota sentencing guidelines also appear to have promoted equity in sentencing. To a lesser extent, the first bail reform movement reduced some of the discrimination against the poor. These are particularly important achievements in a time of worsening race relations.

The reforms designed to get tough with crime appear to have been consistent failures. The attempts to abolish plea bargaining failed, primarily because research has found that plea bargaining is not the loophole that so many people thought it was. The various mandatory-sentencing schemes also appear to have failed to achieve their intended goals. In some cases the mandatory provisions attacked a nonexistent problem; in other cases they produced results that undermined the intent of the new provisions. The second bail reform movement—preventive detention—has neither made drastic changes in pretrial detention practices nor reduced crime by persons on bail.[3]

These findings are not only surprising, but they provide some unexpected comfort for liberals. The conventional wisdom has it that the last twenty years have been a very conservative period. A lot of surface evidence—on imprisonment, the death penalty, public attitudes toward crime—seems to support that. Under the surface, however, other forces have been at work and the last several years have actually seen some advances in liberal criminal justice goals.

Reflections on the Successful Control of Discretion

Although only four decision points have been examined here, the evidence permits some general conclusions about the successful control of discretion.

The basic conclusion, of course, is that discretion can be controlled. Carefully designed rules, with meaningful procedures for accountability, can achieve modest goals. The four reservations about discretion control cited in Chapter 1 represent an overly pessimistic view. First, it is not true that "nothing works." Reforms do not necessarily backfire and produce undesirable consequences. Nor are they always negated by covert resistance. Second, controls do not necessarily degenerate into empty formalism. The number of police shootings has been reduced, and the Minnesota sentencing guidelines did control the use of imprisonment—to cite only the two most prominent examples. Third, discretion is not always displaced upstream or downstream. There is evidence of some displacement, but these shifts appear to be relatively minor and do not necessarily subvert the intent of the controls. The major disruptions predicted by many observers did not occur. The abolition of plea bargaining did not cause the Alaska criminal justice system to collapse, for example. Fourth, controls do not necessarily induce lying or other forms of improper evasion. It appears that, given the proper controls, officials comply with rules restricting their discretion—witness police compliance with deadly force rules and judicial compliance with the Minnesota sentencing guidelines. In short, some things work.

The second important point is that the successful control of discretion is not a simple matter. Broadaxe controls, such as the attempt to "abolish" discretion, do not work. Recognition of this phenomenon is another part of the new realism about the administration of justice. The great accomplishment of the ABF survey in the 1950s was to illuminate the enormous complexity of the criminal process. The law-in-action bears little relationship to the law-on-the-books. The pervasive exercise of discretion is the central element of that complexity. The research that has accumulated over the intervening years has provided only more detail on the precise dimensions of that complexity.

Because discretion is highly complex, there is no single way of controlling it. A variety of legislative, judicial, and administrative tools are available. There was a point in the history of criminal justice, during the heyday of the Warren Court, when the Supreme Court was the primary instrument in the attack on uncontrolled discretion. The present Supreme Court has largely abandoned that role. The evidence from the discretion control movement, however, is that other remedies are available.

The cases reviewed here suggest that the most promising avenue for the control of discretion is administrative rulemaking. This is the means by which police use of deadly force has been limited. The same technique has been used in the promising initiatives in the control of police handling of domestic violence and police high-speed pursuits. Turning to the area of plea bargaining, there is some evidence that administrative rulemaking has helped to control prosecutorial discretion in New Orleans, King County, Washington, and California.

As Kenneth C. Davis argued more than twenty years ago, administrative rules have the advantage of being detailed and of being developed and administered close to the decision they seek to control. The existence of mechanisms of accountability close to the decision point are crucial to the success of any control effort. Rules are not self-implementing. Simply passing a law does not solve a problem. Criminal justice officials are no more likely to obey a general prohibition than are ordinary citizens. Creating a new rule of procedure does not remedy a problem in the abuse of discretion. There need to be detailed procedures requiring officials to account for their actions to their appropriate supervisors. Those supervisors, in turn, must have the commitment to enforce those rules.

A final point is that controls which limit the discretion of criminal justice officials in the interest of promoting justice do not endanger the community. This is an extremely important point given the political controversies of the last three decades. The public debate has been posed in terms of a choice between individual rights and public safety: By enhancing the rights of individual citizens, suspects, defendants, and prisoners, do we necessarily reduce the safety of law-abiding people? The evidence here clearly indicates that this is a false dichotomy. The reduction in police shootings has not resulted in greater danger to either police officers or the community at large. Pretrial release of poor defendants does not lead to more crime in the community. The highly restricted use of imprisonment in Minnesota has not produced a higher than normal crime rate in that state.

The Limits of Discretion Control

The successes to date, however promising, should not be overstated. The effort to control discretion faces a number of important obstacles.

The first is sheer inertia and the lack of commitment. Innumerable discretionary decisions remain outside the scope of effective control. In large part, this is due to the fact that the responsible officials have not made a commitment to impose any controls. Police departments are notorious for their "crisis management" approach to problems. Rules tend to be developed in response to a serious mistake and the accompanying controversy, which often includes litigation. Here, as in other areas of criminal justice, problems get attention only when there is a crisis. One of the important items on the agenda for the future is the development of a more systematic and proactive approach to the control of discretion.

A second major obstacle is the working environment of criminal justice agencies. Research on various agencies offers a compelling picture of the extent to which officials in various agencies develop their own group norms about how things should be done. These group-defined norms are highly resistant to externally imposed changes.

Actually, there is mixed evidence of the impact of rules on work group norms. The most disheartening evidence is found in the research on bail reform. There is strong evidence that two bail reform movements have had only marginal effect on the determination of judges not to release defendants they consider dangerous. The seriousness of the charge and the prior record of the defendant remain the two most important factors in bail decisions. Two bail reform movements appear to have had only modest impact on these considerations.[4]

At the same time, however, there is also evidence that work group norms are amenable to change. Police deadly force rules have reduced the number of shootings. Determinate sentencing laws have greatly curbed the discretion of judges. Some of the controls over plea bargaining appear to have had some effect on the processing of cases. In short, some kinds of rules can effectively penetrate the working environment and change the behavior of officials.

One of the great unanswered questions in American criminal justice is the extent to which the entire working environment of the system has been affected by the "rights revolution." To what extent have claims of rights, and the body of rules that have developed to protect those rights, affected the day-to-day operations of criminal justice agencies?

The future of discretion control requires more detailed exploration of the precise conditions of success. What exactly does it take to change the norms of a work group? How much change can we realistically expect? The evidence examined here leads to the conclusion that administrative rulemaking is the most viable approach. But because this inquiry is offered as an interim report on discretion control, this remains a tentative conclusion. Related questions demand further inquiry. What are the conditions of successful rule development? Of successful rule compliance?

Finally, the control of discretion is heavily influenced by the external political environment. Many of the successful efforts to date have been propelled by political forces—forces that reformers can neither create nor stop. Bail reform is an excellent example. The first bail reform movement was created by a new political climate and then stopped dead in its tracks by a sudden shift in that climate. There are some serious questions about how much a reform effort can accomplish in the face of an indifferent or hostile political atmosphere.

One of the most hopeful findings of this book is that the political mood of a period is not always what the pundits declare it to be. Two of the most important developments in policing—the control of deadly force and the control of police response to domestic violence—represent movements on behalf of justice for victimized groups in an allegedly conservative period. By the same token, sentencing reform in Minnesota and California appears to have reduced racial disparities in sentencing. This is an enormously significant development in a period of apparently rising racism and a time when, in the political arena, the issue of crime is heavily weighted with racial overtones. In other words, there may be opportunities for reducing racism in particular areas of criminal justice even though the larger climate suggests otherwise.

The question of sentencing introduces one final somber point. The justice system is at the mercy not just of political forces but of social and economic forces as well. The determinants of crime lie in these external forces and the best the justice system can do is try to cope with them. Improvements in prison conditions as a result of the prisoners' rights movement began to be offset by the enormous increase in the size of prison populations. Many of the improvements in policing since the 1960s—in personnel standards, supervision, and so on—have been overtaken by an increase in crime among the underclass and by the rise in racism throughout society. The weight of these forces can easily overwhelm the fragile efforts to control discretionary decision making.

The Future of the Discretion Control Movement

This interim report reaches a cautiously optimistic conclusion about the control of discretion: given the right conditions, it is possible to control discretion and improve the administration of justice. One scenario for the future would involve more of the same: continued piecemeal attacks on particular discretionary decision points. This would be a mistake, however. The evidence to date suggests that bolder, more comprehensive attacks on uncontrolled discretion are appropriate.

To date, reform efforts have been almost entirely discrete movements, focusing on particular problem areas with little reference to one another. The future of discretion control calls for a more comprehensive approach. This involves a number of different strategies.

In the case of the police, a comprehensive approach involves addressing "horizontal" discretion. It is necessary to begin thinking about controlling the full range of discretionary decisions police officers make, most of which are unrelated to one another (i.e., the shooting decision, the arrest decision, and undercover tactics decisions are made by different people at different times).

In theory, the research and planning departments of police departments have the task of devloping policies proactively to prevent crises from occurring. Every serious student of the police, however, knows that these research and planning departments fail in this regard. The new law enforcement accreditation standards require departments to have a process for developing written policies. Unfortunately, the standards do not indicate particular decision points that should be covered by policies.[5]

An alternative approach would be for state legislatures to compel rulemaking by law enforcement agencies in their state. That is, the legislature could identify a discrete number of critical decision points—deadly force, physical force, pursuits, arrest, intelligence gathering, and the like—and require every agency to have a written policy covering them. The substance of each policy would be left to the individual departments.[6] There is ample precedent for this approach. Legislatures have long had statutes governing deadly force; several have added laws governing domestic violence and high-speed pursuits. These developments are typical of the haphazard, crisis management approach to police policy-making. There is no reason why a more comprehensive approach cannot be taken.

The recent sentencing guidelines commissions, in fact, provide a model for a statewide approach to the control of discretion. The legislature could establish a criminal justice standards commission, with explicit authority to develop rules for all agencies over a specific list of legislatively defined areas. The commission could then conduct the necessary research, hold public hearings, and then promulgate appropriate rules. This could include rules governing all forms of police use of force. It could also include a rule requiring law enforcement agencies to have a civilian review process. Nor does the commission have to be limited to law enforcement. It could, with apropriate statutory authorization, promulgate rules governing plea bargaining.

A comprehensive approach to discretion control could also address the issue of vertical discretion and the problem of discretion being displaced either upstream or downstream. While this problem has not proved to be the major obstacle to discretion control that many anticipated, there is nonetheless some evidence of controls causing shifts in the locus of discretion (particularly from charge bargaining to sentence bargaining).

Several of the reforms examined here highlight the important role of decisions by related officials regarding information that is provided to a key decision maker. The decision of a judge to release a person on his or her own recognizance depends heavily on the information supplied by the pretrial services agency staff. The bail decision is influenced by the substance of the report, which in turn reflects decisions about the gathering and interpreting of information. Along the same lines, decisions under the Minnesota sentencing guidelines are dependent upon the computation of criminal history scores by probation officers. These problems highlight a general point. The effective controls over discretion to date represent the process of bureaucratization: the development and implementation of formal written rules. In some instances this process includes the creation of a new bureaucratic agency, or the expansion of an old one; implementation of a rule involves, to a great extent, the flow of information. Ultimately, the effective control of discretion will depend on controls over that information flow and, consequently, on the officials who gather, interpret, and supply that information.

This problem has not been addressed squarely to date because of the fragmented nature of the various reform movements. Plea-bargaining reforms have been attempted without a simultaneous attempt to control sentencing discretion. A comprehensive approach would begin to explore the possibility of simultaneously imposing controls over these interrelated decisions.

Conclusion

The administration of criminal justice in the United States has come a long way in the past thirty years. The most important change has been an intellectual revolution which has focused attention on the phenomenon of discretion. This has been accompanied by a legal and administrative revolution, which has imposed a number of controls over discretionary decision points. The basic conclusion of this interim report is that the control of discretion is possible. Some things work. The task that lies ahead involves assessing in great detail the conditions of successful discretion control and developing a more comprehensive approach to the problem. The system has not been fully tamed, but a start has been made. Much has been accomplished, but much remains to be done. The real difference between today and thirty years ago is that we now understand the nature of the problem, we have been disabused of our belief in simple solutions, and we have a sense of the general direction future reform should take.

NOTES

Chapter 1

1. The facts of the case are set forth in *Tennessee v. Garner*, 471 U.S. 1 (1985).

2. The basic framework of what is now the informal consensus among the experts was first set forth in Kenneth Culp Davis, *Discretionary Justice: A Preliminary Inquiry* (1969; Urbana: University of Illinois Press, 1971).

3. Kenneth Culp Davis, *Police Discretion* (St. Paul, Minn.: West, 1975), pp. 62–66

4. *McCleskey v. Kemp*, 481 U.S. 279 (1987).

5. Herbert Packer, *The Limits of the Criminal Sanction* (Stanford, Calif.: Stanford University Press, 1968), chap. 8.

6. Samuel Walker, *Popular Justice: A History of American Criminal Justice* (New York: Oxford University Press, 1980), chap. 9.

7. A more complete history is found in Samuel Walker, "Origins of the Contemporary Criminal Justice Paradigm: The American Bar Foundation Survey, 1953–1969," *Justice Quarterly* 9 (March 1992): 201–230. An earlier account, by a participant, is Donald J. Newman, "Sociologists and the Administration of Justice," in *Sociologists at Work*, ed. Arthur B. Shostak (Homewood, Ill.: Dorsey, 1966), pp. 177–187.

8. Frank Remington, Memo to Field Staff, September 24, 1956, ABF Papers. Unless otherwise noted, all survey documents cited here are located in the ABF Survey Papers, Criminal Justice Library, University of Wisconsin Law School, Madison, Wis.

9. Robert F. Jackson, "Criminal Justice: The Vital Problem of the Future," *ABA Journal* 39 (August 1953): 743–746.

10. The American Bar Foundation (ABF) has been an important center for empirical research on legal issues. ABF officials have long recognized that the Criminal Justice Survey was its first major project and played a major role in

establishing the foundation as a viable entity (Jack Heinz, former ABF director, interview with Samuel Walker, 1987).

11. Morris Ploscowe, *Organized Crime and Law Enforcement*, 2 vols. (New York: Grosby Press, 1952, 1953); William H. Moore, *The Kefauver Committee and the Politics of Crime, 1950–1952* (Columbia: University of Missouri Press, 1974).

12. American Bar Foundation, *A Plan for a Survey* (Chicago: ABF, 1955).

13. On how the survey fit into the larger agenda of the Ford Foundation, see Richard Magat, *The Ford Foundation at Work: Philanthropic Choices, Methods, and Styles* (New York: Plenum, 1979).

14. Discussed in ABF, *Plan for a Survey*, pp. 5–12.

15. Thomas S. Kuhn, *The Structure of Scientific Revolutions*, 2nd ed. (Chicago: University of Chicago Press, 1970). See the discussion in Walker, "Origins of the Contemporary Criminal Justice Paradigm."

16. On Progressive reform and criminal justice, see Walker, *Popular Justice*, chap. 6.

17. The three most important crime commissions were Cleveland Survey of Criminal Justice, *Criminal Justice in Cleveland* (Cleveland: Cleveland Foundation, 1922); Missouri Association for Criminal Justice, *The Missouri Crime Survey* (1926; Montclair, N.J.: Patterson Smith, 1968); Illinois Association for Criminal Justice, *Illinois Crime Survey* (1929; Montclair, N.J.: Patterson Smith, 1968).

18. Newman, "Sociologists and the Administration of Justice."

19. ABF Survey, Field Report 10027. ABF Papers.

20. ABF Survey, Field Reports 11037–11042, 11051, 11056, 11066, 11115. A general summary is found in 11105. ABF Papers. H. Goldstein, interview with Samuel Walker, 1987.

21. ABF Survey, Field Report 11084. ABF Papers.

22. ABF Survey, Field Report 11042. ABF Papers.

23. ABF Survey, Field Report 11051. ABF Papers.

24. H. Goldstein, interview with Samuel Walker, 1987.

25. Ibid.

26. Lloyd Ohlin, Memo to O. W. Wilson, March 15, 1956. ABF Papers.

27. Frank Remington, Memo to Herman Goldstein and Bruce Olson, May 11, 1956. ABF Papers.

28. Joseph Goldstein, "Police Discretion Not to Invoke the Criminal Process: Low-Visibilty Decisions in the Administration of Justice," *Yale Law Journal* 69, no. 4 (1960): 543–588; Wayne R. LaFave, *Arrest* (Boston: Little, Brown, 1965); Donald J. Newman, *Conviction: The Determination of Guilt or Innocence Without Trial* (Boston: Little, Brown, 1966); Sanford Kadish, "The Advocate and the Expert-Counsel in the Peno-Correctional Process," *Minnesota Law Review* 45 (1960–1961): 803–841; Sanford Kadish, "Legal Norm and Discre-

tion in the Police and Sentencing Processes," *Harvard Law Review* 75 (March 1962): 904–931.

29. LaFave, *Arrest.*

30. Ibid.

31. Newman, *Conviction.*

32. President's Commission on Law Enforcement and Administration of Justice, *The Challenge of Crime in a Free Society* (Washington, D.C.: Government Printing Office, 1967).

33. Walker, *Popular Justice,* chap. 9.

34. American Bar Association, *Standards for Criminal Justice,* 2nd ed. (Boston: Little, Brown, 1980).

35. American Law Institute, *Model Code of Pre-Arraignment Procedure* (Philadelphia: ALI, 1975).

36. *Mapp v. Ohio,* 367 U.S. 643 (1961); *Miranda v. Arizona,* 384 U.S. 436 (1966).

37. Anthony Amsterdam, "Perspectives on the Fourth Amendment," *Minnesota Law Review* 58 (1974): 349–477; Carl McGowan, "Rulemaking and the Police," *Michigan Law Review* 70 (March 1972): 659–694.

38. Walker, *Popular Justice.* That book, however, does not reflect my present views about the dominance of the issue of discretion.

39. Michael R. Gottfredson and Don M. Gottfredson, *Decision Making in Criminal Justice: Toward the Ratonal Exercise of Discretion,* 2nd ed. (New York: Plenum, 1988), is a comprehensive discussion of discretionary decision making, but it does not purport to evaluate reforms designed to control discretion.

40. This theme is developed at greater length in Samuel Walker, "Historical Roots of the Legal Control of Police Behavior," in *Police Innovation and the Rule of Law,* ed. David Weisburd and Craig Uchida (New York: Springer, 1993).

41. My view of the broader trends in twentieth-century American history are set forth in *In Defense of American Liberties: A History of the ACLU* (New York: Oxford University Press, 1990), which examines the growth and impact of the "rights revolution." For a recent treatment of this theme with respect to the medical profession, see David J. Rothman, *The Strangers at the Bedside* (New York: Basic Books, 1991).

42. Gottfredson and Gottfredson, *Decision Making in Criminal Justice,* p. 3.

43. Walker, *Popular Justice.*

44. See, for example, Eugene Doleschal, "The Dangers of Criminal Justice Reform," *Criminal Justice Abstracts* 14 (March 1982): 133–152. The most famous example of a report that was misinterpreted to read that "nothing works" is Robert Martinson, "What Works? Questions and Answers About Prison Reform," *Public Interest* 35 (Spring 1974): 22–54. The bulk of the literature

embodying this cynical view is based on correctional treatment programs, to the exclusion of other areas of the criminal justice system.

45. Malcolm Feeley, *Court Reform on Trial* (New York: Basic Books, 1983).

46. See, for example, an early study of the impact of *Miranda*: R. J. Medalie, L. Zeitz, and P. Alexander, "Custodial Police Interrogation in Our Nation's Capital: The Attempt to Implement Miranda," *Michigan Law Review* 66 (May 1968): 1347–1422.

47. Paul Sutton, "The Fourth Amendment in Action: An Empirical View of the Search Warrant Process," *Criminal Law Bulletin* 22 (September–October 1986): 405–429.

48. Dallin H. Oaks, "Studying the Exclusionary Rule in Search and Seizure," *University of Chicago Law Review* 37 (1970): 665–757.

49. Michael Tonry, "Structuring Sentencing," in *Crime and Justice: A Review of Research*, vol. 10, ed. Michael Tonry and Norval Morris (Chicago: University of Chicago Press, 1988), p. 331.

50. Goldstein, "Police Discretion Not to Invoke the Criminal Process."

51. U.S. National Advisory Commission on Criminal Justice Standards and Goals, *Courts* (Washington, D.C.: Government Printing Office, 1973), p. 46.

52. American Friends Service Committee (AFSC), *Struggle for Justice* (New York: Hill and Wang, 1971), pp. 124, 135.

53. See the excellent review of the literature in Norval Morris and Michael H. Tonry, *Between Prison and Probation: Intermediate Punishments in a Rational Sentencing System* (New York: Oxford University Press, 1990), p. 243.

54. AFSC, *Struggle for Justice*, pp. 143–144.

55. Davis, *Discretionary Justice*.

56. Kenneth Culp Davis, *Cases, Text and Problems on Administrative Law*, 5th ed. (St. Paul, Minn.: West, 1973).

57. Davis, *Discretionary Justice*, p. 65.

58. Mortimer R. Kadish and Sanford H. Kadish, *Discretion to Disobey: A Study of Lawful Departures from Legal Rules* (Stanford, Calif.: Stanford University Press, 1973), pp. 40–45.

59. Perhaps the best general discussion is in Kadish and Kadish, *Discretion to Disobey*. See also Samuel Walker, *The Rule Revolution: Reflections on the Transformation of American Criminal Justice, 1950–1988* (Madison, Wis.: Institute for Legal Studies, 1988), pp. 4–5.

60. Samuel Walker, *The Police in America: An Introduction*, 2nd ed. (New York: McGraw-Hill, 1992).

61. James B. Jacobs, *New Perspectives on Prisons and Imprisonment* (Ithaca, N.Y.: Cornell University Press, 1983).

62. Davis, *Discretionary Justice*, p. 3.

Chapter 2

1. *Report of the Independent Commission on the Los Angeles Police Department* (Los Angeles: The City of Los Angeles, 1991).

2. Samuel Walker, "Historical Roots of Legal Control of Police Behavior," in *Police Innovation and the Rule of Law*, ed. David Weisburd and Craig Uchida (New York: Springer, 1992).

3. There is no discussion of the full range of police discretionary decisions. For two attempts at a comprehensive approach, see Kenneth Culp Davis, *Police Discretion* (St. Paul, Minn.: West, 1975); Samuel Walker, *The Police in America: An Introduction*, 2nd ed. (New York: McGraw-Hill, 1992), pp. 200–201.

4. Donald Black, *The Manners and Customs of the Police* (New York: Academic Press, 1980), pp. 85–108.

5. See the data in David H. Bayley and James Garofalo, "The Management of Violence by Police Patrol Officers," *Criminology* 27 (February 1989): 1–25.

6. Geoffrey P. Alpert and Roger G. Dunham, *Police Pursuit Driving: Controlling Responses to Emergency Situations* (Westport, Conn.: Greenwood Press, 1990).

7. For detailed descriptions of police behavior, see Black, *Manners and Customs of the Police*, pp. 46, 109–192; Bayley and Garofalo, "Managment of Violence by Police Patrol Officers."

8. Black, *Manners and Customs of the Police*, pp. 65–84.

9. Peter Greenwood, Jan M. Chaiken, and Joan Peresilia, *The Criminal Investigation Process* (Lexington, Mass.: Lexington Books, 1977); John E. Eck, *Solving Crimes: The Investigation of Burglary and Robbery* (Washington, D.C.: Police Executive Research Forum, 1983).

10. Gary LaFree, *Rape and Criminal Justice* (Belmont, Calif.: Wadsworth, 1989), pp. 73, 76.

11. Lawrence P. Tiffany, Donald M. McIntyre, and Daniel Rotenberg, *Detection of Crime: Stopping and Questioning, Search and Seizure, Encouragement and Entrapment* (Boston: Little, Brown, 1967).

12. Gary T. Marx, *Undercover: Police Surveillance in America* (Berkeley: University of California Press, 1988).

13. Frank J. Donner, *Protectors of Privilege* (Berkeley: University of California Press, 1991).

14. See Chapter 4; William F. McDonald, *Plea Bargaining: Critical Issues and Current Practices* (Washington, D.C.: Government Printing Office, 1985).

15. Peter Scharf and Arnold Binder, *The Badge and the Bullet* (New York: Praeger, 1983), pp. 111–116.

16. William A. Geller, "Officer Restraint in the Use of Deadly Force: The

Next Frontier in Police Shooting Research," *Journal of Police Science and Administration* 13, no. 2 (1985): 153–171.

17. Lawrence W. Sherman and Ellen G. Cohn, *Citizens Killed by Big City Police, 1970–1984* (Washington, D.C.: Crime Control Institute, 1986); Kenneth J. Matulia, *A Balance of Forces: Model Deadly Force Policy and Procedure*, 2nd ed. (Gaithersburg, Md.: International Association of Chiefs of Police, 1985).

18. U.S. President's Commission on Law Enforcement and Administration of Justice, *Task Force Report: The Police* (Washington, D.C.: Government Printing Office, 1967), pp. 189–190. For a general review of the subject, see James J. Fyfe, "Police Use of Deadly Force: Research and Reform," *Justice Quarterly* 5 (June 1988): 165–205.

19. President's Commission, *Task Force Report*, p. 189; Fyfe, "Police Use of Deadly Force," pp. 168–169.

20. Paul Jacobs, *Prelude to Riot: A View of Urban America from the Bottom* (New York: Vintage Books, 1968), pp. 31, 39.

21. *Report of the National Advisory Commission on Civil Disorders* (New York: Bantam Books, 1968), p. 36. This is generally called the Kerner Commission report.

22. The two best summaries of the many studies on police use of deadly force are William A. Geller and Michael Scott, *Deadly Force: What We Know* (Washington, D.C.: PERF, 1992), and Fyfe, "Police Use of Deadly Force."

23. American Law Institute, *Model Penal Code*, 3.07 (1962).

24. William B. Waegel, "The Use of Lethal Force by Police: The Effect of Statutory Change," *Crime and Delinquency* 30 (January 1984): 121–140. See the discussion by Fyfe, "Police Use of Deadly Force," p. 184, esp. n. 23.

25. Anthony M. Amsterdam, "Perspectives on the Fourth Amendment," *Minnesota Law Review* 58 (1973–1974): 349–477; Carl McGowan, "Rulemaking and the Police," *Michigan Law Review* 70 (March 1972): 659–694.

26. James J. Fyfe, "Administrative Interventions on Police Shooting Discretion: An Empirical Examination," *Journal of Criminal Justice* 7 (Winter 1979): 309–324. The article is adapted from James J. Fyfe, "Shots Fired: An Analysis of New York City Police Firearms Discharge" (Ph.D. diss., State University of New York at Albany, 1978).

27. Lawrence W. Sherman, "Restricting the License to Kill—Recent Developments in Police Use of Deadly Force," *Criminal Law Bulletin* 14 (November–December 1978): 577–583.

28. Commission on Accreditation for Law Enforcement Agencies, *Standards for Law Enforcement Agencies*, 2nd ed. (Fairfax, Va.: CALEA, 1988).

29. A useful collection of the various standards is found in Matulia, *Balance of Forces*, pp. 57–62.

30. *Tennessee v. Garner*, 471 U.S. 1 (1985).

31. Kenneth Culp Davis, *Discretionary Justice: A Preliminary Inquiry* (Urbana: University of Illinois Press, 1971), pp. 52–96.

32. Ibid.

33. Fyfe, "Administrative Interventions."

34. Ibid. "Accidents" accounted for 10 percent of the shootings by Chicago officers from 1974 to 1978 (William A. Geller and Kevin J. Karales, *Split-Second Decisions* [Chicago: Chicago Law Enforcement Study Group, 1981], p. 103).

35. Sherman and Cohn, *Citizens Killed by Big City Police*.

36. Matulia, *Balance of Forces*, p. A.1.

37. James J. Fyfe, "Blind Justice: Police Shootings in Memphis," *Journal of Criminal Law and Criminology* 73, no. 2 (1982): 707–722.

38. Federal Bureau of Investigation, *Officers Killed in the Line of Duty* (annual); FBI, *Law Enforcement Bulletin in the United States*, July 1991, p. 24.

39. Bureau of Justice Statistics, *Criminal Victimization in the United States, 1989* (Washington, D.C.: Government Printing Office, 1991), Table 4.

40. There is no detailed study of the trends in officers killed. The reduction could also be the result of greater use of bulletproof vests, together with better training of officers.

41. *Report of the Independent Commission on the Los Angeles Police Department*, pp. 151–179.

42. James J. Fyfe, comments (Academy of Criminal Justice Sciences, Washington, D.C., 1989). Annual Meeting,

43. The best summary of this rapidly changing subject is Eve S. Buzawa and Carl G. Buzawa, *Domestic Violence: The Criminal Justice Response* (Beverly Hills, Calif.: Sage, 1990).

44. Morton Bard, *Training Police as Specialists in Family Crisis Intervention* (Washington, D.C.: Government Printing Office, 1970).

45. This philosophy pervades most of the President's Crime Commission report: President's Commission on Law Enforcement and Administration of Justice. *The Challenge of Crime in a Free Society* (Washington, D.C.: Government Printing Office, 1967).

46. Wayne R. LaFave, *Arrest* (Boston: Little, Brown, 1965).

47. Black, *Manners and Customs of the Police*, pp. 109–192. A most comprehensive review of the literature is Delbert S. Elliott, "Criminal Justice Procedures in Family Violence Crimes," in *Crime and Justice: A Review of Research*, vol. 11, *Family Violence*, ed. Lloyd Ohlin and Michael Tonry (Chicago: University of Chicago Press, 1989), pp. 427–480.

48. Nancy Loving, *Responding to Spouse Abuse and Wife Beating: A Guide for Police* (Washington, D.C.: Police Executive Research Forum, 1980).

49. Ibid., pp. 163–168.

50. Lawrence W. Sherman and Richard A. Berk, "The Specific Deterrent Effects of Arrest for Domestic Assault," *American Sociological Review* 49 (1984): 261–272.

51. Ellen G. Cohn and Lawrence W. Sherman, *Police Policy on Domestic Violence, 1986: A National Survey* (Washington, D.C.: Crime Control Institute, 1987).

52. Richard E. Lempert, "From the Editor," *Law and Society Review* 18, no. 4 (1984): 505–513; Lawrence W. Sherman and Ellen G. Cohn, "The Impact of Research on Legal Policy: The Minneapolis Domestic Violence Experiment," *Law and Society Review* 23, no. 1 (1989): 117–144; Richard Lempert, "Humility as a Virtue: On the Publicization of Policy-Relevant Research," *Law and Society Review* 23, no. 1 (1989): 145–161.

53. Franklyn W. Dunford, David Huizinga and, Delbert S. Elliott, "The Role of Arrest in Domestic Assault: The Omaha Police Experiment," *Criminology* 28 (May 1990): 183–206; Lawrence W. Sherman, *Policing Domestic Violence: Experiments and Dilemmas* (New York: Free Press, 1992).

54. Buzawa and Buzawa, *Domestic Violence*, chap. 11.

55. Along the same lines, rape law reform in the 1970s enjoyed the support of feminists, who thought it would improve the treatment of rape victims, and prosecutors, who thought it would yield more prosecutions and convictions (Cassie Spohn and Julie Horney, *Rape Law Reform in Six Jurisdictions: A Study of Legal Change* [New York: Plenum, 1993]). Also, the concept of "determinate sentencing" briefly enjoyed the support of both liberals and conservatives in the mid–1970s, even though the groups had very different objectives. See Chapter 5.

56. Susan L. Miller, "Unintended Side Effects of Pro-Arrest Policies and Their Race and Class Implications for Battered Women: A Cautionary Note," *Criminal Justice Policy Review* 3, no. 3 (1989): 299–317.

57. In Omaha, officers telephoned police headquarters and described the nature of the incident; if it met the terms of the experiment, they were instructed on the course of action to take.

58. There was, however, some suggestion that officers in Minneapolis may have subverted the experiment on occasion, substituting their judgment about how best to handle the incident.

59. See, for example, Eric J. Scott, *Calls for Police Service: Citizen Demand and Initial Police Response* (Washington, D.C.: Government Printing Office, 1981), pp. 28–30.

60. See the discussion in Walker, *Police in America*, pp. 113–114.

61. Black, *Manners and Customs of the Police*, pp. 85–108.

62. Dennis J. Kenney, interview with Samuel Walker, 1991. I spoke with officers in one police department where new policies are distributed to officers by mail. Officers reported leaving the manila envelopes in a pile, unopened.

63. I am indebted to my colleagues Cassie Spohn and Dennis J. Kenney for this point.

64. Federal Bureau of Investigation, *Uniform Crime Reports* (annual).

65. Lawrence W. Sherman and Barry D. Glick, *The Quality of Police Arrest Statistics* (Washington, D.C.: The Police Foundation, 1984).

66. LaFave, *Arrest*, p. 349; on the general problem of "unrecorded detention," see pp. 347–351.

67. Robert Tillman, "The Size of the "Criminal Population': The Prevalence and Incidence of Adult Arrest," *Criminology* 25 (August 1987): 561–579.

68. See the discussion of the problems with official data in Barbara Boland, Catherine H. Conly, Lynn Warner, Ronald Jones, and William Martin, *The Prosecution of Felony Arrests, 1986* (Washington, D.C.: Government Printing Office, 1989), p. 12.

69. As this book was being completed, the International Association of Chiefs of Police opened the first tentative discussion of what departments should do in the event of "unarrests" and recommended the development of appropriate policy (although it did not offer a model policy) (IACP, *Policy Review* 3 [June 1991]: 3).

70. Author's survey of standard operating procedure manuals from selected police departments (Omaha, Detroit, Minneapolis, etc.).

71. Joan Petersilia, *Racial Disparities in the Criminal Justice System* (Santa Monica, Calif.: Rand Corporation, 1983), p. 21.

72. Mortimer R. Kadish and Sanford H. Kadish, *Discretion to Disobey: A Study of Lawful Departures from Legal Rules* (Stanford, Calif.: Stanford University Press, 1973), p. 76.

73. The most comprehensive treatment is Alpert and Dunham, *Police Pursuit Driving*. See also a valuable comparative analysis in Geoffrey P. Alpert and Lorie A. Fridell, *Police Vehicles and Firearms: Instruments of Deadly Force* (Prospect Heights, Ill.: Waveland Press, 1992).

74. Alpert and Dunham, *Police Pursuit Driving*, pp. 35–38.

75. "In Hot Pursuit," *Chicago Sun-Times*, 30 June 1991, p. 1.

76. For a discussion of communicating values to police officers that I consider utterly wrongheaded, see Robert Wasserman and Mark H. Moore, "Values in Policing," in *Perspectives on Policing*, no. 8 (Washington, D.C.: Government Printing Office, 1988). Their approach opts for global statements rather than policies directed toward specific decisions.

77. Nebraska Revised Statutes, sec. 29–211 (1989).

78. Samuel Walker, "Controlling the Cops: A Legislative Approach to Police Rulemaking," *University of Detroit Law Review* 63 (Spring 1986): 364–370.

79. *Mapp v. Ohio*, 367 U.S. 643 (1961).

80. *Miranda v. Arizona*, 384 U.S. 436 (1966).

81. See the discussion in Samuel Walker, *Sense and Nonsense About Crime: A Policy Guide*, 2nd ed. (Pacific Grove, Calif.: Brooks/Cole, 1989).

82. The literature on the exclusionary rule is enormous. The best summary is Thomas Y. Davies, "A Hard Look at What We Know (and Still Need to Learn) About the "Costs' of the Exclusionary Rule: The NIJ Study and Other Studies of 'Lost' Arrests," *American Bar Foundation Research Journal*, Summer 1983, pp. 611–690.

83. Brian Forst, Judith Lucianovic, and Sarah J. Cox, *What Happens After Arrest?* (Washington, D.C.: INSLAW, 1977).

84. National Institute of Justice, *The Effects of the Exclusionary Rule: A Study in California* (Washington, D.C.: Government Printing Office, 1982). But see the devastating criticism of the report in Davies, "A Hard Look."

85. Sheldon Krantz, Bernard Gilman, Charles G. Benda, Carol Rogoff Hallstrom, and Eric J. Nadworny, *Police Policymaking* (Lexington, Mass.: Lexington Books, 1979).

86. Dallin H. Oaks, "Studying the Exclusionary Rule in Search and Seizure," *University of Chicago Law Review* 37 (Summer 1970): 665–757.

87. McGowan, "Rulemaking and the Police"; Amsterdam, "Perspectives on the Fourth Amendment."

88. Scott, *Calls for Police Service*; Albert Reiss, *The Police and the Public* (New Haven, Conn.: Yale University Press, 1971).

89. Note, "Interrogations in New Haven: The Impact of Miranda," *Yale Law Journal* 76 (July 1967): 1519–1648; R. J. Medalie, L. Zeitz, and P. Alexander, "Custodial Police Interrogation in Our Nation's Capital: The Attempt to Implement Miranda," *Michigan Law Review* 66 (May 1968): 1347–1422.

90. Neal Milner, *The Court and Local Law Enforcement: The Impact of "Miranda"* (Beverly Hills, Calif.: Sage, 1971).

91. Marx, *Undercover*, passim.

92. Narcotics officers in New York City began supplying drugs to their informants in the belief that this was necessary to maintain their relationship and the supply of information (Robert Daley, *Prince of the City* [Boston: Houghton Mifflin, 1978]). During the Cold War, anti-Communist witnesses and advisers for the House Un-American Activities Committee were widely suspected of inventing charges of Communist activity about certain people simply to satisfy official investigators.

93. Paul Sutton, "The Fourth Amendment in Action: An Empirical View

of the Search Warrant Process,'' *Criminal Law Bulletin* 22 (September–October 1986): 405–429; Richard van Duizen, L. Paul Sutton, and Charlotte A. Carter, *The Search Warrant Process* (Williamburg, Va.: National Center for State Courts, 1985).

94. Note [Myron Orfield], ''The Exclusionary Rule and Deterrence: An Empirical Study of Chicago Narcotics Officers,'' *University of Chicago Law Review* 54 (Summer 1987): 1016–1055.

95. Ibid.

96. Ibid.

97. Walker, *Sense and Nonsense About Crime.*

98. Note, ''Exclusionary Rule and Deterrence.''

99. Joan Petersilia, Allan Abrahamse, and James Q. Wilson, *Police Performance and Case Attrition* (Santa Monica, Calif.: Rand Corporation, 1987).

100. ''Poll Finds Only 33% Can Identify Bill of Rights,'' *New York Times*, 15 December 1991, p. 33.

101. Summarized in Walker, *Police in America.*

102. The classic statement of this issue, circa the early 1960s, is Jerome Skolnick, *Justice Without Trial* (New York: Wiley, 1967).

103. This argument that the working environment, as defined by Skolnick, has been significantly altered is developed at greater length in Walker, ''Historical Roots of Legal Control of the Police.''

Chapter 3

1. Wayne Thomas, *Bail Reform in America* (Berkeley: University of California Press, 1976).

2. John S. Goldkamp, ''Danger and Detention: A Second Generation of Bail Reform,'' *Journal of Criminal Law and Criminology* 76, no. 1 (Spring 1985): 1–74.

3. *United States v. Salerno*, 481 U.S. 739 (1987).

4. Caleb Foote, ''The Coming Constitutional Crisis in Bail: I,'' *University of Pennsylvania Law Review* 113 (May 1965): 959–999; Caleb Foote, ''The Coming Constitutional Crisis in Bail: II,'' *University of Pennsylvania Law Review* 113 (June 1965): 1125–1185.

5. Caleb Foote, ''Compelling Appearance in Court: Administration of Bail in Philadelphia,'' *University of Pennsylvania Law Review* 102 (1954): 1031–1079.

6. A later study using more sophisticated controls did not find pretrial status to be a factor in these decisions (John Goldkamp, *Two Classes of Accused* [Cambridge, Mass.: Ballinger, 1979]).

7. Foote, ''Compelling Appearance in Court.''

8. The first important critique along these lines was Francis A. Allen, "Legal Values and the Rehabilitative Ideal," *Journal of Criminal Law, Criminology, and Police Science* 50 (1959): 226–232, reprinted in Francis A. Allen, *The Borderland of Criminal Justice* (Chicago: University of Chicago Press, 1964), pp. 25–41. The attack was deepened in American Friends Service Committee (AFSC), *Struggle for Justice* (New York: Hill and Wang, 1971), to which Caleb Foote was a major contributor.

9. A prominent example would be Ronald Goldfarb, *Ransom: A Critique of the American Bail System* (New York: McGraw-Hill, 1965), who delivered a stinging criticism of prevailing bail practices but also endorsed a system of preventive detention (pp. 127–149). The only "absolutists," arguing for an absolute right to bail in all noncapital cases, would be Foote and the American Friends Service Committee (*Struggle for Justice*).

10. James Eisenstein and Herbert Jacob, *Felony Justice* (Boston: Little, Brown, 1977), p. 200.

11. Wayne R. LaFave, *Arrest* (Boston: Little, Brown, 1965); Donald J. Newman, *Conviction: The Determination of Guilt or Innocence Without Trial* (Boston: Little, Brown, 1966).

12. Paul B. Wice, *Freedom for Sale: A National Study of Pretrial Release* (Lexington, Mass.: Lexington Books, 1974), pp. 43–63.

13. Michael R. Gottfredson and Don M. Gottfredson, *Decision Making in Criminal Justice*, 2nd ed. (New York: Plenum, 1988).

14. This aspect of police discretion was not discussed in the classic study, LaFave, *Arrest*.

15. The best discussion is in Wice, *Freedom for Sale*, p. 45. This was also not discussed in LaFave, *Arrest*.

16. Wice, *Freedom for Sale*, p. 47.

17. Frederick Suffett, "Bail Setting: A Study of Courtroom Interaction," *Crime and Delinquency* 12 (October 1966): 318–331.

18. Wice, *Freedom for Sale*, pp. 48–50; Suffett, "Bail Setting."

19. Newman, *Conviction*. See also the discussion in Chapter 4.

20. Wice, *Freedom for Sale*, p. 48.

21. On the variations in criminal defense systems, see Peter F. Nardulli, James Eisenstein, and Roy B. Flemming, *The Tenor of Justice: Criminal Courts and the Guilty Plea Process* (Urbana: University of Illinois Press, 1988).

22. Wice, *Freedom for Sale*, p. 50.

23. Suffett, "Bail Setting."

24. Roy B. Flemming, *Punishment Before Trial: An Organizational Perspective of Felony Bail Processes* (New York: Longman, 1982).

25. The most comprehensive review of the subject is Don M. Gottfredson and Michael Tonry, eds., *Crime and Justice: A Review of Research*, vol. 9,

Prediction and Classification: Criminal Justice Decision Making (Chicago: University of Chicago Press, 1987).

26. Robert Martinson, "California Research at the Crossroads," *Crime and Delinquency* 24 (April 1976): 180–191.

27. On the pervasiveness of these two factors throughout the criminal justice system, see Gottfredson and Gottfredson, *Decision Making in Criminal Justice*.

28. Thomas, *Bail Reform in America*, chap. 20.

29. Bureau of Justice Statistics, *Pretrial Release of Felony Defendants, 1988* (Washington, D.C.: Government Printing Office, 1991), Table 11.

30. "Preventive Detention: An Empirical Analysis," *Harvard Civil Rights–Civil Liberties Review* 6 (March 1971): 289–396.

31. Thomas E. Scott, "Pretrial Detention Under the Bail Reform Act of 1984: An Empirical Analysis," *American Criminal Law Review* 27, no. 1 (1989): 1–51.

32. Flemming, *Punishment Before Trial*, p. 151.

33. Suffett, "Bail Setting."

34. Arthur Beeley's pioneering 1927 study of bail had stimulated no interest in reform, despite the fact that it documented many serious problems, including the pretrial detention of many poor defendants (*The Bail System in Chicago* [1927; Chicago: University of Chicago Press, 1966]). The various crime commission studies of the 1920s and 1930s gave little attention to bail.

35. Foote, "Compelling Appearance."

36. Caleb Foote, interview with Samuel Walker, 1900; Caleb Foote, Address, in National Conference on Bail and Criminal Justice, *Proceedings and Interim Report* [1965] (New York: Arno Press, 1974), p. 223.

37. The early history of the bail reform movement is told in Patricia M. Wald, "The Right to Bail Revisited: A Decade of Promise Without Fulfillment," in *The Rights of the Accused*, ed. Stuart S. Nagel (Beverly Hills, Calif.: Sage, 1972), pp. 175–205; and Thomas, *Bail Reform in America*.

38. National Conference on Bail and Criminal Justice, *Proceedings and Interim Report*, pp. 5, 9; Attorney General's Committee on Poverty and the Administration of Federal Criminal Justice, *Poverty and the Administration of Federal Criminal Justice* (Washington, D.C.: Government Printing Office, 1963).

39. Thomas, *Bail Reform in America*, p. 24.

40. On the ideological links between the "war on poverty" and the report of the President's Crime Commission, see Samuel Walker, *Popular Justice: A History of American Criminal Justice* (New York: Oxford University Press, 1980), pp. 234–235.

41. On the impact of the civil rights movement on judicial thinking about

criminal procedure, see Archibald Cox, *The Warren Court* (Cambridge, Mass.: Harvard University Press, 1968), chap. 4.

42. Goldfarb, *Ransom*.

43. Goldkamp, *Two Classes of Accused*, Table 4-1.

44. Ibid., pp. 120–121.

45. Thomas, *Bail Reform in America*, pp. 211–213.

46. Wald, "Right to Bail Revisited"; Daniel Freed and Patricia M. Wald, *Bail in the United States: 1964* (Washington, D.C.: National Conference on Bail and Criminal Justice, 1964).

47. John S. Goldkamp, "Philadelphia Revisited: An Examination of Bail and Detention Two Decades After Foote," *Crime and Delinquency* 26 (April 1980): 179–192.

48. Thomas, *Bail Reform in America*, pp. 37–38.

49. Bureau of Justice Statistics, *Pretrial Release of Felony Defendants, 1988*, Table 1.

50. Thomas, *Bail Reform in America*, pp. 37–38, esp. Table 1.

51. Bureau of Justice Statistics, *Pretrial Release of Felony Defendants, 1988*, Table 1; Bureau of Justice Statistics, *Felony Defendants in Large Urban Countries, 1988* (Washington, D.C.: Government Printing Office, 1990), p. 8.

52. Kathleen B. Brosi, *A Cross-City Comparison of Felony Case Processing* (Washington, D.C.: INSLAW, 1979), p. 29.

53. Goldkamp, "Philadelphia Revisited."

54. Wald, "Right to Bail Revisited."

55. Ibid., p. 188.

56. Thomas, *Bail Reform in America*, p. 67.

57. Ibid., p. 252.

58. Malcolm M. Feeley, *Court Reform on Trial: Why Simple Solutions Fail* (New York: Basic Books, 1983), p. 70.

59. Ibid., p. 71.

60. Bureau of Justice Statistics, *Pretrial Release of Felony Defendants, 1988*.

61. Chris W. Eskridge, *Pretrial Release Programming: Issues and Trends* (New York: Clark Boardman, 1983), pp. 82–84.

62. Goldkamp, *Two Classes of Accused*, p. 222.

63. Ibid., p. 224.

64. Ibid., p. 225.

65. Feeley, *Court Reform on Trial*, p. 69.

66. Bureau of Justice Statistics, *Felony Defendants in Large Urban Counties, 1988*, p. 8; Bureau of Justice Statistics, *Pretrial Release of Felony Defendants, 1988*.

67. Bureau of Justice Statistics, *Felony Defendants in Large Urban Counties, 1988*, p. 9.

68. This is one of the major conclusions of Gottfredson and Gottfredson, *Decision Making in Criminal Justice*.

69. Bureau of Justice Statistics, *Pretrial Release of Felony Defendants, 1988*, Tables 1, 2.

70. Goldkamp, *Two Classes of Accused*, p. 223.

71. On parole, see Don M. Gottfredson, Colleen A. Cosgrove, Leslie T. Wilkins, Jane Wallerstein, and Carol Rauh, *Classification for Parole Decision Policy* (Washington, D.C.: Government Printing Office, 1978). On sentencing, see the various contributions in Gottfredson and Tonry, *Crime and Justice*, vol. 9.

72. See the discussion in John S. Goldkamp and Michael R. Gottfredson, *Policy Guidelines for Bail: An Experiment in Court Reform* (Philadelphia: Temple University Press, 1985), pp. 39–40.

73. Ibid.

74. Ibid.

75. On "crime control theology," a failing common to both conservatives and liberals, see Samuel Walker, *Sense and Nonsense About Crime: A Policy Guide*, 2nd ed. (Pacific Grove, Calif.: Brooks/Cole, 1989), pp. 10–17.

76. Suffett, "Bail Setting"; Gottfredson and Gottfredson, *Decision Making in Criminal Justice*.

77. Feeley, *Court Reform on Trial*, p. 49.

78. Nan C. Bases and William F. McDonald, *Preventive Detention in the District of Columbia: The First Ten Months* (Washington, D.C.: Georgetown Institute of Criminal Law and Procedure, 1972).

79. Brosi, *Cross-City Comparison of Felony Case Processing*, p. 29.

80. *United States v. Salerno*, 481 U.S. 739 (1987).

81. "2,500 Suspects Held as Threats Under Bail Law," *New York Times*, 27 May 1987, p. 1.

82. The total number of criminal cases filed in federal courts increased 22.8 percent between 1984 and 1988, from 35,911 to 43,116 (Administrative Office of the United States Courts, *Annual Report of the Director* [Washington, D.C.: Government Printing Office, annual]).

83. Scott, "Pretrial Detention Under the Bail Reform Act of 1984."

84. Bureau of Justice Statistics, *Pretrial Release and Detention: The Bail Reform Act of 1984* (Washington, D.C.: Government Printing Office, 1988).

85. General Accounting Office, *Criminal Bail: How Bail Reform Is Working in Selected District Courts* (Washington, D.C.: Government Printing Office,

October 1987); Scott, "Pretrial Detention Under the Bail Reform Act of 1984," pp. 19–25.

86. *Preventive Detention: The Impact of the 1984 Bail Reform Act in the Eastern District of California* (1987); Scott, "Pretrial Detention Under the Bail Reform Act of 1984," pp. 17–19.

87. Bureau of Justice Statistics, *Pretrial Release and Detention*, p. 1.

88. Scott, "Pretrial Detention Under the Bail Reform Act of 1984."

89. Ibid., pp. 23–24. See also Bureau of Justice Statistics, *Pretrial Release and Detention*, Table 9.

Chapter 4

1. The classic work on plea bargaining is Donald J. Newman, *Conviction: The Determination of Guilt or Innocence Without Trial* (Boston: Little, Brown, 1966). The most thorough analysis of current practices is William F. McDonald, *Plea Bargaining: Critical Issues and Current Practices* (Washington, D.C.: Government Printing Office, 1985).

2. The classic statement of this view is in President's Commission on Law Enforcement and Administration of Justice, *Task Force Report: Science and Technology* (Washington, D.C.: Government Printing Office, 1967), p. 61. But see the criticisms in Charles Silberman, *Criminal Violence/Criminal Justice* (New York: Random House, 1978), pp. 257–264; Samuel Walker, *Sense and Nonsense About Crime: A Policy Guide*, 2nd ed. (Pacific Grove, Calif.: Brooks/Cole, 1989), chap. 3.

3. Bureau of Justice Statistics, *The Prosecution of Felony Arrests, 1986* (Washington, D.C.: Government Printing Office, 1989).

4. Walker, *Sense and Nonsense About Crime*, chap. 3.

5. Newman, *Conviction*.

6. Michael R. Gottfredson and Don M. Gottfredson, *Decision Making in Criminal Justice*, 2nd ed. (New York: Plenum, 1988), p. 114.

7. Abraham S. Blumberg, *Criminal Justice: Issues and Ironies*, 2nd ed. (New York: New Viewpoints, 1979), chaps. 8–11. On the "horrors" of plea bargaining, see Albert W. Alschuler, "The Prosecutor's Role in Plea Bargaining," *University of Chicago Law Review* 36, no. 1 (1968): 50–112; Albert W. Alschuler, "The Defense Attorney's Role in Plea Bargaining," *Yale Law Journal* 84 (May 1975): 1179–1314.

8. On the ambiguity of the evidence, see James Eisenstein, Roy B. Flemming, and Peter F. Nardulli, *The Contours of Justice: Communities and Their Courts* (Boston: Little, Brown, 1988), pp. 131–132, 252–253; Peter F. Nardulli, James Eisenstein, and Roy B. Flemming, *The Tenor of Justice: Criminal Courts*

and the Guilty Plea Process (Urbana: University of Illinois Press, 1988), pp. 243–245.

9. Jonathan Casper, *American Criminal Justice: The Defendant's Perspective* (Englewood Cliffs, N.J.: Prentice-Hall, 1972), p. 101.

10. Nearly all the defendants interviewed by McDonald expressed this view (*Plea Bargaining*, pp. 131–134).

11. Cassie Spohn, John Gruhl, and Susan Welch, "The Impact of the Ethnicity and Gender of Defendants on the Decision to Reject or Dismiss Felony Charges," *Criminology* 25 (February 1987): 175–191.

12. Joan Petersilia, *Racial Disparities in the Criminal Justice System* (Santa Monica, Calif.: Rand Corporation, 1983).

13. Cleveland Survey of Criminal Justice, *Criminal Justice in Cleveland* (Cleveland: Cleveland Foundation, 1922), pp. 89–96; Missouri Association for Criminal Justice, *The Missouri Crime Survey* (1926; Montclair, N.J.: Patterson Smith, 1968); Raymond Moley, *Our Criminal Courts* (New York: Minton, Balch, 1930), pp. 109–129.

14. The classic study is Frank W. Miller, *Prosecution: The Decision to Charge a Suspect with a Crime* (Boston: Little, Brown, 1969). See also the discussion in McDonald, *Plea Bargaining*, p. 11.

15. On the problem of defining plea bargaining, see the discussion in McDonald, *Plea Bargaining*, p. 6.

16. See the recommendation in President's Task Force on Victims of Crime, *Final Report* (Washington, D.C.: Government Printing Office, 1982), p. 65.

17. Wayne Kerstetter, "Police Participation in Structured Plea Negotiations," *Law and Policy Quarterly* 3, no. 1 (1981): 95–119.

18. McDonald, *Plea Bargaining*, pp. 11–13.

19. On the courtroom work group, see James Eisenstein and Herbert Jacob, *Felony Justice: An Organizational Analysis of Criminal Courts* (Boston: Little, Brown, 1977); Eisenstein, Flemming, and Nardulli, *Contours of Justice*, pp. 123–162; Walker, *Sense and Nonsense About Crime*.

20. See the discussion in Malcolm Feeley, *Court Reform on Trial: Why Simple Solutions Fail* (New York: Basic Books, 1983), pp. 156–180.

21. A caveat is in order here. The solitary character of police decision making can be overdrawn. In fact, there is good evidence that individual police officers are constrained by group or bureaucratic norms; the expectations of fellow officers; the review, for example, of arrest decisions by sergeants (which does result in frequent dismissals of arrests); and so on.

22. Cleveland Survey of Criminal Justice, *Criminal Justice in Cleveland*; Moley, *Our Criminal Courts*.

23. See the discussion in McDonald, *Plea Bargaining*, p. 6; on the problems with language, see Stephen J. Schulhofer, "No Job Too Small: Justice

Without Bargaining in the Lower Criminal Courts," *American Bar Foundation Research Journal* 1985 (Summer 1985): 519–598; on the practice of "slow pleas," see Lynn Mather, *Plea Bargaining or Trial?* (Lexington, Mass.: Lexington Books, 1979), and Nardulli, Eisenstein, and Flemming, *Tenor of Justice*, p. 205.

24. Robert Jackson, "The Federal Prosecutor," *Journal of the American Judiciary Society* 24 (1940): 18–19, quoted in Kenneth Culp Davis, *Discretionary Justice: A Preliminary Inquiry* (Urbana: University of Illinois Press, 1971), p. 190.

25. Mortimer R. Kadish and Sanford H. Kadish, *Discretion to Disobey: A Study of Lawful Departures from Legal Rules* (Stanford, Calif.: Stanford University Press, 1973), pp. 80–82.

26. Kathleen B. Brosi, *A Cross-City Comparison of Felony Case Processing* (Washington, D.C.: Government Printing Office, 1979), p. 14.

27. Brian Forst, Judith Lucianovic, and Sarah J. Cox, *What Happens After Arrest?* (Washington, D.C.: INSLAW, 1977), pp. 67, 69.

28. Petersilia, *Racial Disparities in the Criminal Justice System*, p. 21.

29. See the cautionary comments in Bureau of Justice Statistics, *Prosecution of Felony Arrests, 1986*, p. 12.

30. McDonald, *Plea Bargaining*, p. 34.

31. Ibid., pp. 43–44.

32. The best discussion of the issue is in ibid., pp. 19–26.

33. American Law Institute, *Model Code of Pre-Arraignment Procedure* (Philadelphia: ALI, 1975), 350.3(3)(b)(c); National Advisory Commission on Criminal Justice Standards and Goals, *Courts* (Washington, D.C.: Government Printing Office, 1973), pp. 57–58.

34. American Bar Association, *Standards for Criminal Justice*, 2nd ed. (Boston: Little, Brown, 1980), Standard 3-3.9.

35. Newman, *Conviction*, chaps. 8, 13.

36. Boyd Littrell, *Bureaucratic Justice: Police, Prosecutors, and Plea Bargaining* (Beverly Hills, Calif.: Sage, 1979), chap. 5.

37. I am indebted to Cassie Spohn for suggesting this point.

38. Police officers, interviews with Samuel Walker.

39. Richard M. Cohen and Jules Witcover, *A Heartbeat Away: The Investigation and Resignation of Vice President Spiro T. Agnew* (New York: Viking, 1974).

40. The initial call for abolition is in Alschuler, "Prosecutor's Role," p. 52; the quote is from Alschuler, "Defense Attorney's Role," p. 1313.

41. National Advisory Commission on Criminal Justice Standards and Goals, *Courts*, pp. 46–49.

42. See the discussion and refutation of the case pressure argument in Milton

Heumann, *Plea Bargaining: The Experience of Prosecutors, Judges, and Defense Attorneys* (Chicago: University of Chicago Press, 1978); Milton Heumann, "A Note on Plea Bargaining and Case Pressure," *Law and Society Review* 9 (Spring 1975): 515–528.

43. Joseph Goldstein, "Police Discretion Not to Invoke the Criminal Process: Low-Visibility Decisions in the Administration of Justice," *Yale Law Journal* 69, no. 4 (1960): 543–588.

44. Twentieth Century Fund Task Force on Criminal Sentencing, *Fair and Certain Punishment* (New York: McGraw-Hill, 1976); Andrew von Hirsch, *Doing Justice: The Choice of Punishments* (New York: Hill and Wang, 1976).

45. With respect to the police, see Chapter 2.

46. See Michael L. Rubinstein, Stevens H. Clarke, and Teresa J. White, *Alaska Bans Plea Bargaining* (Washington, D.C.: Government Printing Office, 1980).

47. Heumann, *Plea Bargaining*, pp. 27–30. See also the contributions on the history of plea bargaining in *Law and Society Review* [special issue on plea bargaining] 13 (Winter 1979).

48. U.S. Department of Justice, *The Prosecution of Felony Arrests, 1986* (Washington, D.C.: Government Printing Office, 1989).

49. McDonald, *Plea Bargaining*, pp. 37–40, 103.

50. Feeley, *Court Reform on Trial*, pp. 156–188.

51. McDonald, *Plea Bargaining*, pp. 103–104; Rubinstein, Clarke, and White, *Alaska Bans Plea Bargaining*, p. 266.

52. McDonald, *Plea Bargaining*, pp. 104–105.

53. Malcolm M. Feeley, "Perspectives on Plea Bargaining," *Law and Society Review* 13 (Winter 1979): 199; Nardulli, Eisenstein, and Flemming, *Tenor of Justice*, pp. 207–208.

54. "Dead-bang" cases were defined as those where there was (1) a confession, (2) physical evidence of guilt, (3) two or more witnesses (one was generally not considered sufficient), and (4) a positive identification through one means or another (Nardulli, Eisenstein, and Flemming, *Tenor of Justice*, p. 226).

55. One of the best descriptions of plea bargaining as a highly routinized process is Mather, *Plea Bargaining or Trial?*

56. Nardulli, Eisenstein, and Flemming, *Tenor of Justice*, pp. 233, 372–375.

57. Colin Loftin and David McDowall, " 'One with a Gun Gets You Two': Mandatory Sentencing and Firearms Violence in Detroit," *The Annals* 455 (May 1981): 150–167.

58. Walker, *Sense and Nonsense About Crime*, p. 43.

59. Ibid.

60. U.S. Department of Justice, *The Nation's Toughest Drug Law: Evaluating the New York Experience* (Washington, D.C.: Government Printing Office, 1978).

61. Thomas W. Church, "Plea Bargains, Concessions, and the Courts: Analysis of a Quasi-Experiment," *Law and Society Review* 10 (Spring 1976): 377–401.

62. McDonald, *Plea Bargaining*, pp. 37–40.

63. Mather, *Plea Bargaining or Trial?*

64. McDonald, *Plea Bargaining*, pp. 34–37.

65. Ibid., pp. 44–46.

66. Ibid.

67. J. Jacoby, *The Prosecutor's Charging Decision: A Policy Perspective* (Washington, D.C.: Government Printing Office, 1977), discussed in Gottfredson and Gottfredson, *Decision Making in Criminal Justice*, pp. 132–137.

68. Newman, *Conviction*, pp. 10–22.

69. McDonald, *Plea Bargaining*, pp. 124–134.

70. Ibid., p. 129.

71. Newman, *Conviction*, pp. 47–52.

72. McDonald, *Plea Bargaining*, p. 114.

73. Ibid., p. 120.

74. On the existence of a "trial penalty," see Nardulli, Eisenstein, and Flemming, *Tenor of Justice*, pp. 243–245.

75. McDonald, *Plea Bargaining*, p. 132.

76. Ibid.

77. Casper, *American Criminal Justice*, pp. 100–125.

78. Anne M. Heinz and Wayne A. Kerstetter, *Pretrial Settlement Conference: An Evaluation* (Washington, D.C.: Government Printing Office, 1979); Anne M. Heinz and Wayne A. Kerstetter, "Pretrial Settlement Conference," *Law and Society Review* 13 (Winter 1979): 349–366.

79. Raymond T. Nimmer and Patricia Ann Krauthals, "Plea Bargaining: Reform in Two Cities," *Justice System Journal* 3, no. 1 (1977): 6–21.

80. Institute for Law and Social Research, *Evaluation of the Structured Plea Negotiation Project: Executive Summary* (Washington, D.C.: INSLAW, 1984).

81. McDonald, *Plea Bargaining*, p. 123.

82. *Gideon v. Wainwright*, 372 U.S. 335 (1963). See also the classic book on the case: Anthony Lewis, *Gideon's Trumpet* (New York: Vintage Books, 1966).

83. *Escobedo v. Illinois*, 378 U.S. 478 (1964).

84. *Miranda v. Arizona*, 384 U.S. 436 (1966).

85. *Argersinger v. Hamlin*, 407 U.S. 25 (1972).

86. Samuel Walker, *Popular Justice: A History of American Criminal Justice* (New York: Oxford University Press, 1980); Samuel Walker, *In Defense of*

American Liberties: A History of the ACLU (New York: Oxford University Press, 1990).

87. Newman, *Conviction*, p. 204.

88. Donald J. Newman, "Pleading Guilty for Considerations: A Study of Bargain Justice," *Journal of Criminal Law, Criminology, and Police Science* 46 (1956): 746; Newman, *Conviction*, p. 203, and see pp. 46–47, "Lack of Representation by Counsel."

89. Nardulli, Eisenstein, and Flemming, *Tenor of Justice*, pp. 190–196.

90. Lisa J. McIntyre, *The Public Defender: The Practice of Law in the Shadows of Repute* (Chicago: University of Chicago Press, 1987), p. 105.

91. Casper, *American Criminal Justice*, p. 101.

92. Paul Wice, *Chaos in the Courthouse: The Inner Workings of the Urban Criminal Courts* (New York: Praeger, 1985).

Chapter 5

1. The best survey of recent events is Michael Tonry, "Structuring Sentencing," in *Crime and Justice: A Review of Research*, vol. 10, ed. Michael Tonry and Norval Morris (Chicago: University of Chicago Press, 1988), pp. 267–268.

2. Two of the most important documents in this debate, both published in 1976, are Andrew von Hirsch, *Doing Justice: The Choice of Punishments* (New York: Hill and Wang, 1976), and Twentieth Century Fund Task Force on Criminal Sentencing, *Fair and Certain Punishment* (New York: McGraw-Hill, 1976).

3. David Rothman, *The Discovery of the Asylum* (Boston: Little, Brown, 1971); Samuel Walker, *Popular Justice: A History of American Criminal Justice* (New York: Oxford University Press, 1980).

4. The most comprehensive analysis is Robert O. Dawson, *Sentencing: The Decision as to Type, Length, and Conditions of Sentence* (Boston: Little, Brown, 1969).

5. The reports of the President's Crime Commission in 1967 represented the triumph of the rehabilitation concept, which had been growing over the previous thirty years (President's Commission on Law Enforcement and Administration of Justice, *The Challenge of Crime in a Free Society* [Washington, D.C.: Government Printing Office, 1967]).

6. Francis A. Allen, "Legal Values and the Rehabilitative Ideal," *Journal of Criminal Law, Criminology, and Police Science* 50 (1959): 226–232, reprinted in Francis A. Allen, *The Borderland of Criminal Justice* (Chicago: University of Chicago Press, 1964), pp. 25–41. Allen was heavily influenced

by the American Bar Foundation Survey, even though he was not directly involved in it.

7. American Correctional Association, *Standards for Adult Correctional Institutions*, 3rd ed. (College Park, Md.: ACA, 1990); James B. Jacobs, *New Perspectives on Prisons and Imprisonment* (Ithaca, N.Y.: Cornell University Press, 1983), pp. 33–60.

8. American Friends Service Committee (AFSC), *Struggle for Justice* (New York: Hill and Wang, 1971).

9. Ibid., p. 124.

10. Ibid., p. 135.

11. Marvin E. Fraenkel, *Criminal Sentences: Law Without Order* (New York: Hill and Wang, 1972).

12. Norval Morris, *The Future of Imprisonment* (Chicago: University of Chicago Press, 1974).

13. Andrew von Hirsch, *Past or Future Crimes* (New Brunswick, N.J.: Rutgers University Press, 1985).

14. John P. Conrad, *Justice and Its Consequences* (Lexington, Mass.: Lexington Books, 1981), chap. 9.

15. The most influential piece addressed to a popular audience was James Q. Wilson, *Thinking About Crime* (New York: Basic Books, 1975).

16. Robert Martinson, "What Works? Questions and Answers About Prison Reform," *Public Interest*, No. 35 (Spring 1974): 22–54.

17. Wilson, *Thinking About Crime*, p. 209.

18. Von Hirsch, *Doing Justice*.

19. Twentieth Century Fund Task Force, *Fair and Certain Punishment*.

20. Milton Heumann, *Plea Bargaining* (Chicago: University of Chicago Press, 1977), pp. 27–33. See also the discussion in Chapter 4.

21. Barry Alkin, "The Pardoning Power in Ante-Bellum Pennsylvania," *Pennsylvania Magazine of History and Biography* 100 (October 1976): 507–520.

22. This point will receive more attention in the revised second edition of Walker, *Popular Justice* (1994).

23. Lawrence M. Friedman, *A History of American Law* (New York: Simon and Schuster, 1973), p. 252.

24. Robert H. Gault, "The Parole System—A Means of Protection," *Journal of Criminal Law and Criminology* 5 (March 1915): 799–806.

25. See the discussion in Andrew von Hirsch and Kathleen J. Hanrahan, *Abolish Parole?* (Washington, D.C.: Government Printing Office, 1978), pp. 29–38.

26. Concentrating discretionary authority on the judge was the point argued by Morris in 1974 (*Future of Imprisonment*), and the general trend of reform has been in that direction.

27. Robert M. Carter and Leslie T. Wilkins, "Some Factors in Sentencing Policy," *Journal of Criminal Law, Criminology, and Police Science* 58 (1967): 503–514.

28. Dawson, *Sentencing*, chaps. 1, 2.

29. Ibid., chap. 5. See the pathbreaking article by Sanford H. Kadish, "The Advocate and the Expert in the Peno-Correctional Process," *Minnesota Law Review* 45 (April 1961): 803–841, and the discussion of the product of the ABF survey in Chapter 1.

30. *Mempa v. Rhay*, 389 U.S. 128 (1967)

31. The more precise formulation would be the choice between some form of incarceration and no incarceration. Judges make fairly heavy use of sentences to jail. In 1988, for example, state court judges sentenced 44 percent of all convicted felons to prison, 25 percent to jail, and 31 percent to some form of nonincarceration (Bureau of Justice Statistics, *Felony Sentences in State Courts, 1988* [Washington, D.C.: Government Printing Office, 1990], Table 2).

32. Norval Morris and Michael H. Tonry, *Between Prison and Probation: Intermediate Punishments in a Rational Sentencing System* (New York: Oxford University Press, 1990).

33. AFSC, *Struggle for Justice*.

34. *Morrissey v. Brewer*, 408 U.S. 471 (1971).

35. Morris, *Future of Imprisonment*, p. 46.

36. Bureau of Justice Statistics, *Sourcebook of Criminal Justice Statistics, 1990* (Washington, D.C.: Government Printing Office, 1991), Table 1.89.

37. J. S. Carroll, R. L. Wiener, D. Coates, J. Galegher, and J. J. Alibrio, "Evaluation, Diagnosis, and Prediction in Parole Decision Making," *Law and Society Review* 17 (1982): 199–227.

38. Official data on prisoner misconduct is found in Bureau of Justice Statistics, *Prison Rule Violators* (Washington, D.C.: Government Printing Office, 1989).

39. *Wolff v. McDonnell*, 418 U.S. 539 (1974).

40. James B. Jacobs, *New Perspectives on Prisons and Imprisonment* (Ithaca, N.Y.: Cornell University Press, 1983).

41. American Correctional Association, *Standards for Adult Correctional Institutions*, 2nd ed. (College Park, Md.: ACA, 1981).

42. Ibid., 2–4346.

43. Ben M. Crouch and James W. Marquart, "*Ruiz*: Intervention and Emergent Order in Texas Prisons," in *Courts, Corrections, and the Constitution*, ed. John J. DiIulio (New York: Oxford University Press, 1990), pp. 94–114.

44. David Rothman makes a persuasive argument that parole survived in the 1920s in the face of widespread criticism precisely because it served these latent functions (*Conscience and Convenience: The Asylum and Its Alternatives in Progressive America* [Boston: Little, Brown, 1980]).

45. Michael R. Gottfredson and Don M. Gottfredson, *Decision Making in Criminal Justice*, 2nd ed. (New York: Plenum, 1988), pp. 214–215. On the full context of "front door" and "back door" methods of controlling prison populations, see Alfred Blumstein, "Prison Populations: A System Out of Control?" in *Crime and Justice*, vol. 10, ed. Tonry and Morris, pp. 231–266. A study of 21,000 early releases in Illinois found that inmates released early were slightly less likely to be rearrested than those who served their full prison term (42 vs. 49%). This suggests that considerable savings could be made by shortening prison terms; the fact that nearly half of both groups were rearrested, however, is not cause for much optimism (James Austin, "Using Early Release to Relieve Prison Crowding: A Dilemma in Public Policy," *Crime and Delinquency* 32 [October 1986]: 404–502).

46. The best summary is Tonry, "Structuring Sentencing." The guidelines approach was initially developed for parole release (Donald M. Gottfredson, Colleen A. Cosgrove, Leslie T. Wilkins, Jane Wallerstein, and Carol Raul, *Classification for Parole Decision Policy* [Washington, D.C.: Government Printing Office, 1978]). It was then applied to sentencing (Leslie T. Wilkins, Jack M. Kress, and Don M. Gottfredson, *Sentencing Guidelines: Structuring Judicial Discretion* [Washington, D.C.: Government Printing Office, 1978]).

47. Kenneth Culp Davis, *Discretionary Justice: A Preliminary Inquiry* (Urbana: University of Illinois Press, 1971).

48. Von Hirsch and Hanrahan, *Abolish Parole?* is the most thoughtful reconsideration of the functions, latent and manifest, of parole; it concludes by arguing that many of these functions need to be retained.

49. United States Sentencing Commission, *Sentencing Guidelines and Policy Statements* (Washington, D.C.: Government Printing Office, 1987).

50. The primary focus of the constitutional challenge to the federal sentencing guidelines has been on the separation of powers issue. The Supreme Court rejected that challenge in *Mistretta v. United States*, 488 U.S. 361 (1989). Susan Herman of Brooklyn Law School pointed out in a review of this manuscript that other potential constitutional challenges have been neglected.

51. Twentieth Century Fund Task Force, *Fair and Certain Punishment*, p. 16.

52. On the political context of the 1976 California determinate sentencing law, see Sheldon L. Messinger and Phillip E. Johnson, "California's Determinate Sentencing Statute: History and Issues," in Law Enforcement Assistance Administration (LEAA), *Determinate Sentencing: Reform or Regression?* (Washington, D.C.: Government Printing Office, 1978), pp. 13–58.

53. Twentieth Century Fund Task Force, *Fair and Certain Punishment*, pp. 16–17.

54. Frederick A. Hussey and John H. Kramer, "Issues in the Study of

Criminal Code Revision: An Analysis of Reform in Maine and California,'' in LEAA, *Determinate Sentencing*, pp. 111–131.

55. Tonry, "Structuring Sentencing," pp. 316–317, 322–323. It should be noted that one of the few remaining defenses of parole involves its role in mitigating long sentences (Morris, *Future of Imprisonment*; von Hirsch and Hanrahan, *Abolish Parole?*).

56. Norval Morris, "Conceptual Overview and Commentary on the Movement Toward Determinacy," in LEAA, *Determinate Sentencing*, pp. 8–9. The story, along with others, comes from the ABF survey; see Robert O. Dawson, *Sentencing* (Boston: Little, Brown, 1969), pp. 173–192.

57. Donald J. Newman, *Conviction: The Determination of Guilt or Innocence Without Trial* (Boston: Little, Brown, 1966), pp. 112–125.

58. U.S. Department of Justice, *The Nation's Toughest Drug Law: Evaluating the New York Experience* (Washington, D.C.: Government Printing Office, 1978).

59. Ibid.

60. Colin Loftin and David McDowall, " 'One with a Gun Gets You Two': Mandatory Sentencing and Firearms Violence in Detroit," *The Annals* 455 (May 1981): 150–167. On the going rate and the impact of "tough" anticrime meaasures, see Samuel Walker, *Sense and Nonsense About Crime: A Policy Guide*, 2nd ed. (Pacific Grove, Calif.: Brooks/Cole, 1989).

61. Peter F. Nardulli, James Eisenstein, and Roy B. Flemming, *The Tenor of Justice: Criminal Courts and the Guilty Plea Process* (Urbana: University of Illinois Press, 1988), pp. 233, 372–375.

62. Walker, *Popular Justice*, pp. 208–220; Messinger and Johnson, "California's Determinate Sentencing Statute," pp. 13–17.

63. Jonathan D. Casper, David Brereton, and David Neal, *The Implementation of the California Determinate Sentencing Law: Executive Summary* (Washington, D.C.: Government Printing Office, 1982), pp. 15–16.

64. Ibid., pp. 16–18.

65. Ibid., pp. 28–29.

66. Stephen P. Klein, Susan Turner, and Joan Petersilia, *Racial Equity in Sentencing* (Santa Monica, Calif.: Rand Corporation, 1988). Another Rand study using the same data did find some evidence of racial discrimination in sentencing, but it used less sophisticated controls in examining sentencing decisions (Joan Petersilia, *Racial Disparities in the Criminal Justice System* [Santa Monica, Calif.: Rand Corporation, 1983]). The Klein study should be taken as the more exhaustive study.

67. Klein, Turner, and Petersilia, *Racial Equity in Sentencing*, pp. 42–43.

68. James Austin, *Parole Outcome in California* (Madison, Wis.: National Conference on Crime and Delinquency, 1989).

69. Tonry, "Structuring Sentencing," p. 287; Terance D. Miethe and Charles A. Moore, *Sentencing Guidelines: Their Effect in Minnesota* (Washington, D.C.: Government Printing Office, 1989); Terance D. Miethe and Charles A. Moore, "Socioeconomic Disparities Under Determinate Sentencing Systems: A Comparison of Preguideline and Postguideline Practices in Minnesota," *Criminology* 23 (May 1985): 337–363.

70. Tonry, "Structuring Sentencing," pp. 276–282. On the context of the Minnesota guidelines, see also von Hirsch, *Past or Future Crimes*, pp. 19–28, 179–181.

71. Minnesota Sentencing Guidelines Commission, *Guidelines and Commentary* (St. Paul: Minnesota Sentencing Guidelines Commission, August 1981), p. 1.

72. Ibid., I.4.

73. Miethe and Moore, "Socioeconomic Disparities Under Determinate Sentencing Systems." One troubling aspect of Minnesota sentencing practices needs to be noted, however. As of the mid-1980s, the state had the highest ratio of black to white incarceration rates of any state. Thus the generally low incarceration rate primarily benefited white men. The incarceration rate for black men was lower than many states but substantially higher than for white men in Minnesota (see Blumstein, "Prison Populations," Table 5). The original data are in Bureau of Justice Statistics, *Prisoners in State and Federal Institutions on December 31, 1982* (Washington, D.C.: Government Printing Office, 1984).

74. Tonry, "Structuring Sentencing," pp. 291–294; David Boerner, *Sentencing in Washington* (Seattle: Butterworth, 1985); Bureau of Justice Statistics, *Sourcebook of Criminal Justice Statistics, 1990* (Washington, D.C.: Government Printing Office, 1991), Table 6.56.

75. Edwin Zedlewski, *Making Confinement Decisions* (Washington, D.C.: Government Printing Office, 1987).

76. Miethe and Moore, *Sentencing Guidelines*, Table 3.

77. A study of the impact of the guidelines on probation officers found great disagreement among the officers regarding their role and indicated the need for more administrative and judicial controls over probation officers' roles in computing criminal history scores and in plea negotiations (Richard Lawrence and Shelva Lee Johson, "Effects of the Minnesota Sentencing Guidelines on Probation Agents," *Journal of Crime and Justice* 12, no. 2 [1990]: 77–104).

78. The best survey of the subject is A. Keith Bottomley, "Parole in Transition: A Comparative Study of Origins, Developments, and Prospects for the 1990's," in *Crime and Justice: A Review of Research*, vol. 12, ed. Michael Tonry and Norval Morris (Chicago: University of Chicago Press, 1990), pp. 319–374. On the question of abolition, see von Hirsch and Hanrahan, *Abolish Parole?*

79. Bureau of Justice Statistics, *Probation and Parole, 1987* (Washington, D.C.: Government Printing Office, 1988); Bottomley, "Parole in Transition," p. 342.

80. Donald M. Gottfredson, Colleen A. Cosgrove, Leslie T. Wilkins, Jane Wallerstein, and Carol Raul, *Classification for Parole Decision Policy* (Washington, D.C.: Government Printing Office, 1978).

81. Bottomley, "Parole in Transition."

82. von Hirsch and Hanrahan, *Abolish Parole?*

83. Ibid., p. 35.

84. U.S. Sentencing Commission, *Sentencing Guidelines and Policy Statements* (Washington, D.C.: Government Printing Office, 1987), p. 1.2.

85. Samuel Walker, "Origins of the Contemporary Criminal Justice Paradigm: The American Bar Foundation Survey, 1953–1969," *Justice Quarterly* 9 (March 1992): 201–230.

86. Davis, *Discretionary Justice*.

87. Wayne W. Schmidt, "A Proposal for a Statewide Law Enforcement Administrative Law Council," *Journal of Police Science and Administration* 2 (September 1974): 330–338.

88. Morris and Tonry, *Between Prison and Probation*. It is somewhat disturbing to find that in this otherwise fine book Norval Morris and Michael Tonry do not address the fact that their proposal would increase the range of discretionary options and, consequently, create potential problems requiring meaningful controls. Unfortunately, the authors, who are both experts on sentencing and discretion in general, fail to address this matter.

89. Morris, *Future of Imprisonment*, p. 57.

Chapter 6

1. Kenneth Culp Davis, *Discretionary Justice: A Preliminary Inquiry* (Urbana: University of Illinois Press, 1971).

2. Kenneth Culp Davis, *Police Discretion* (St. Paul, Minn.: West, 1975), chap. 3.

3. There is considerable evidence that more police, or more police patrol, or removing the procedural restraints on the police—issues not examined in this book—will also not reduce crime (Samuel Walker, *Sense and Nonsense About Crime: A Policy Guide*, 2nd ed. [Pacific Palisades, Calif.: Brooks/Cole, 1989]).

4. There is very persuasive evidence that these two factors are the most important considerations in all criminal justice decisions. See the evidence and conclusions in Michael R. Gottfredson and Don M. Gottfredson, *Decision Making in Criminal Justice* (New York: Plenum, 1988).

5. Commission on Accreditation for Law Enforcement Agencies, *Standards for Law Enforcement Agencies* (Fairfax, Va.: CALEA, 1988).

6. Wayne A. Schmidt, "A Proposal for a Statewide Law Enforcement Administrative Law Council," *Journal of Police Science and Administration* 2 (September 1974): 330–338; Samuel Walker, "Controlling the Cops: A Legislative Approach to Police Rulemaking," *University of Detroit Law Review* 63 (Spring 1986): 361–391.

Index